TREVOR APPLESON
FREE GROUND

FREE GROUND
TABLE OF CONTENTS

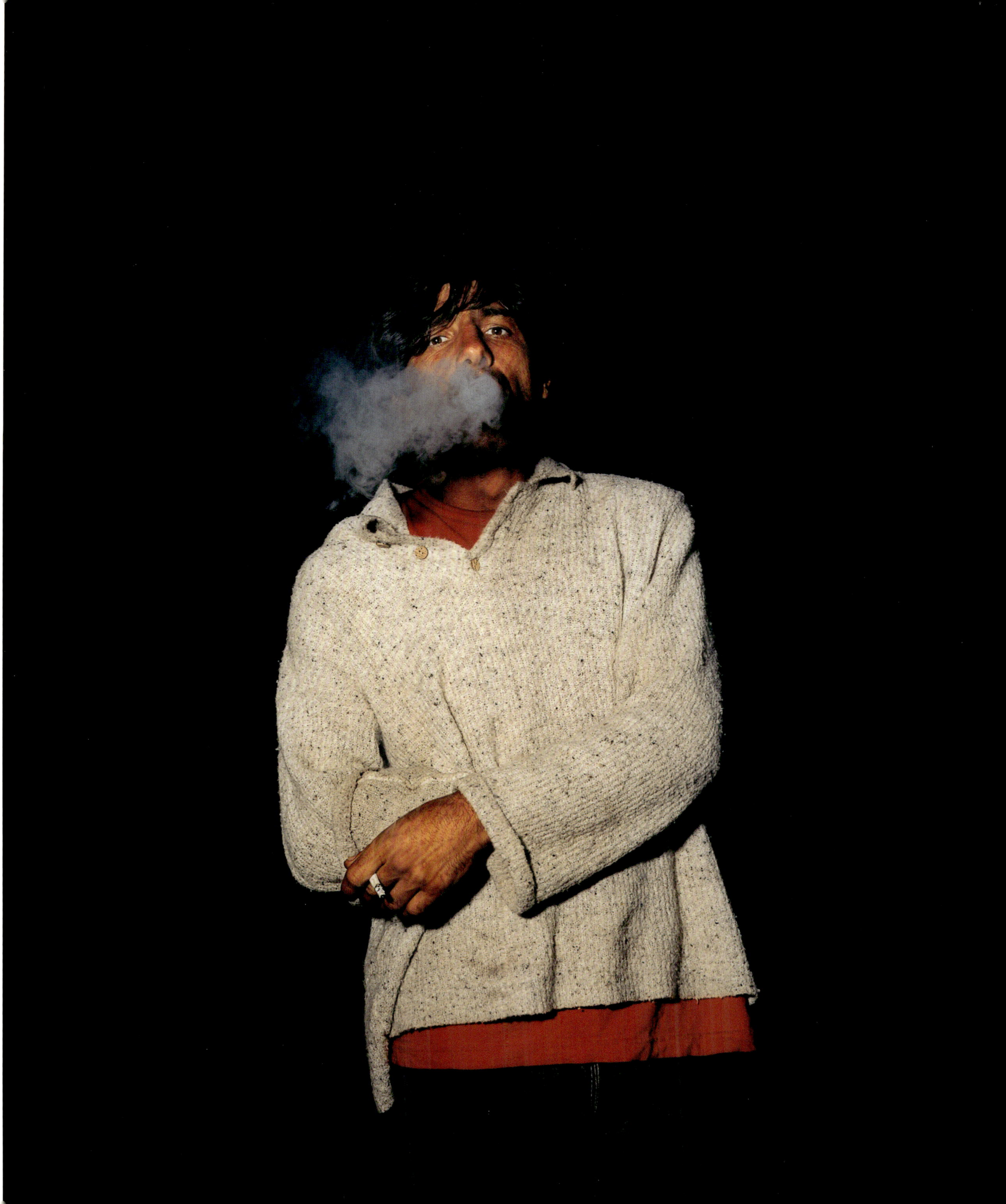

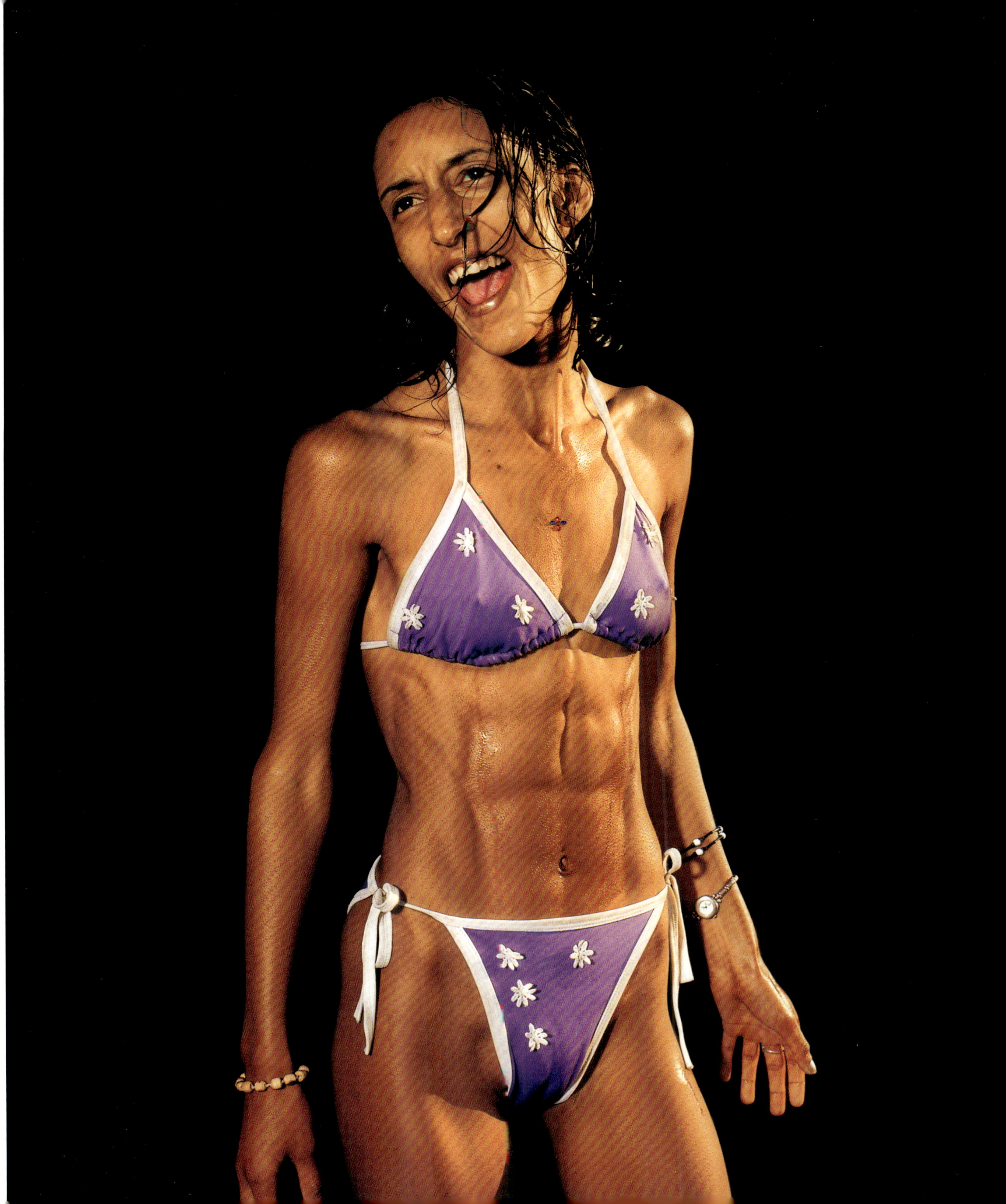

7

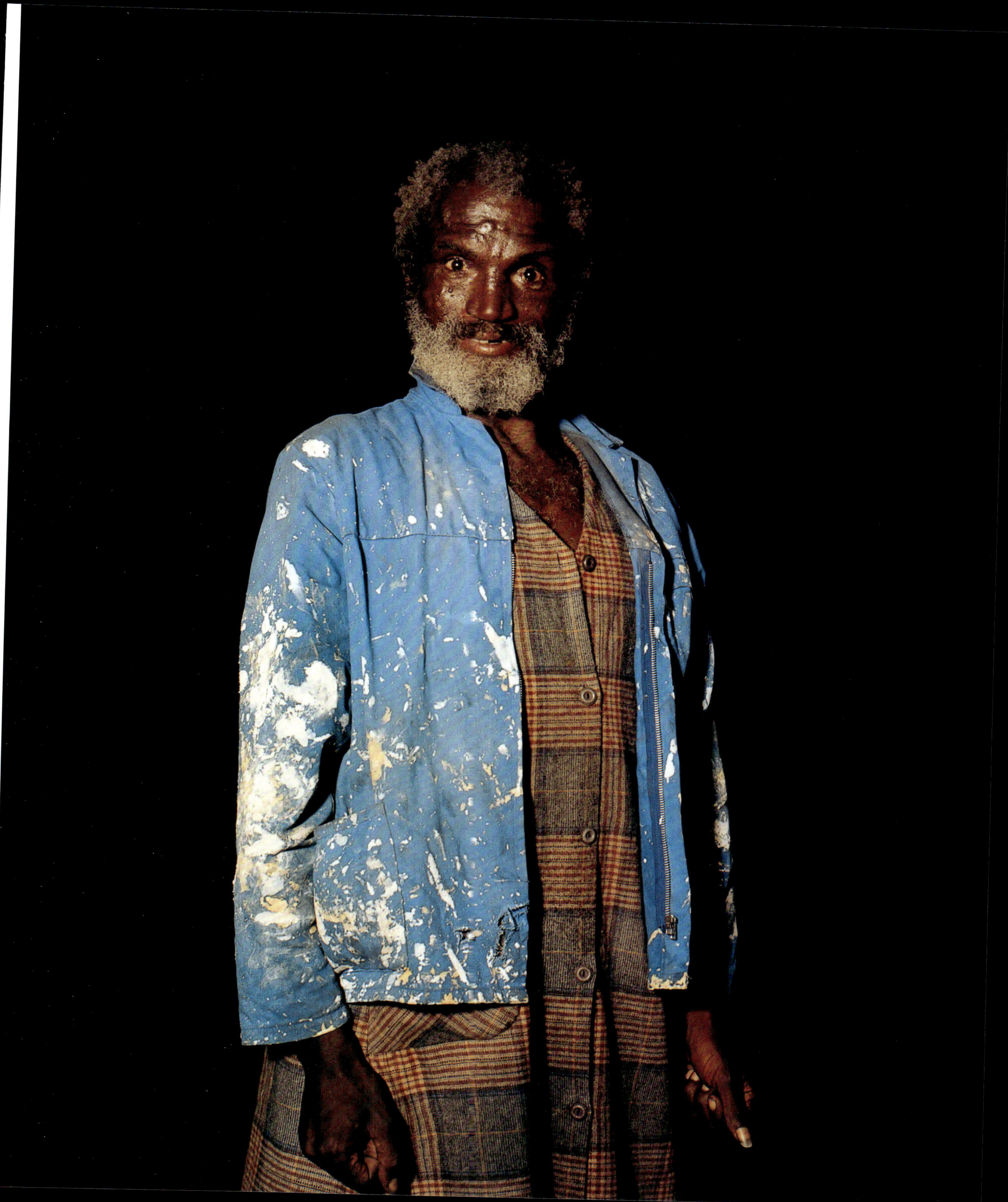

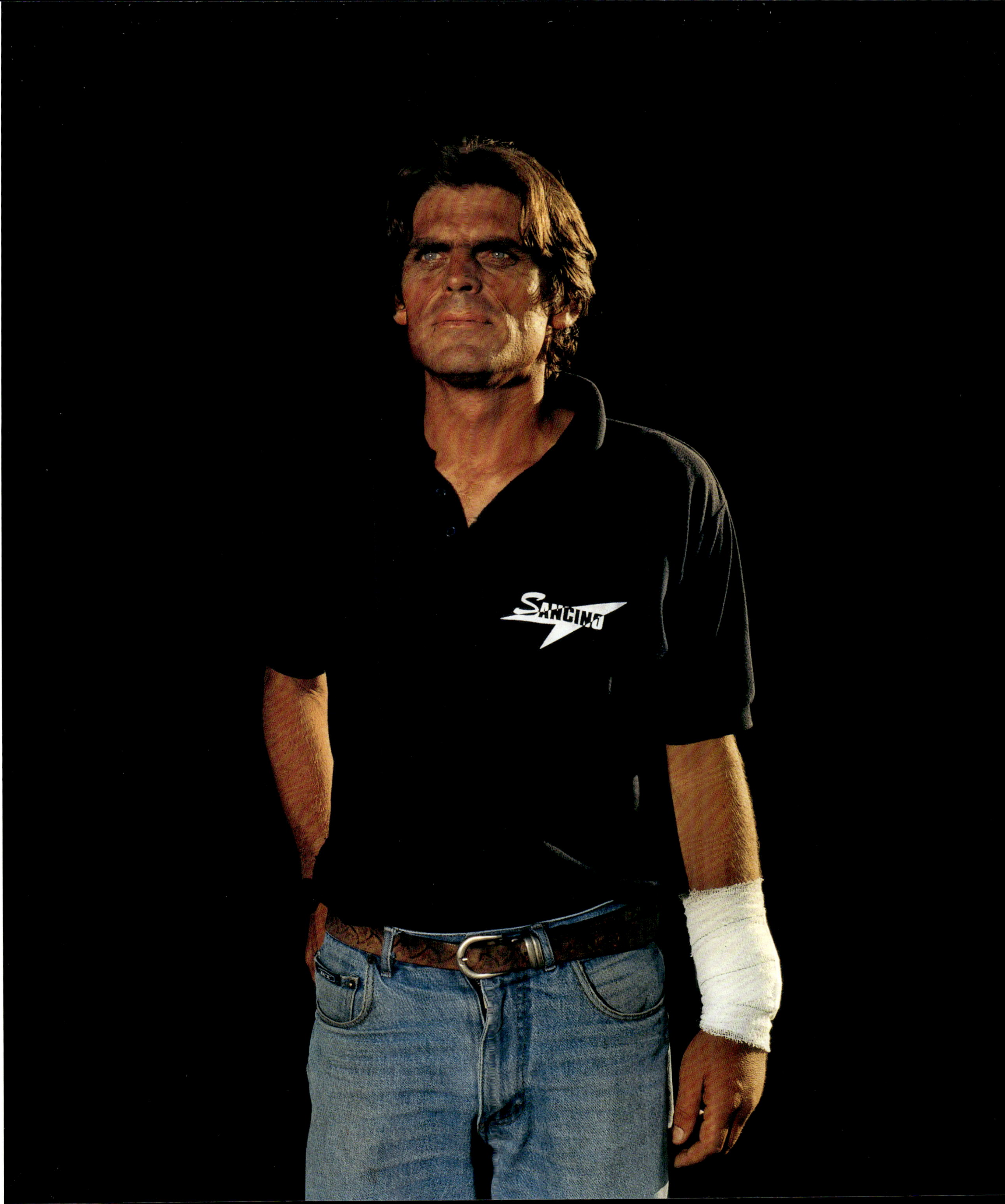
SANCINO

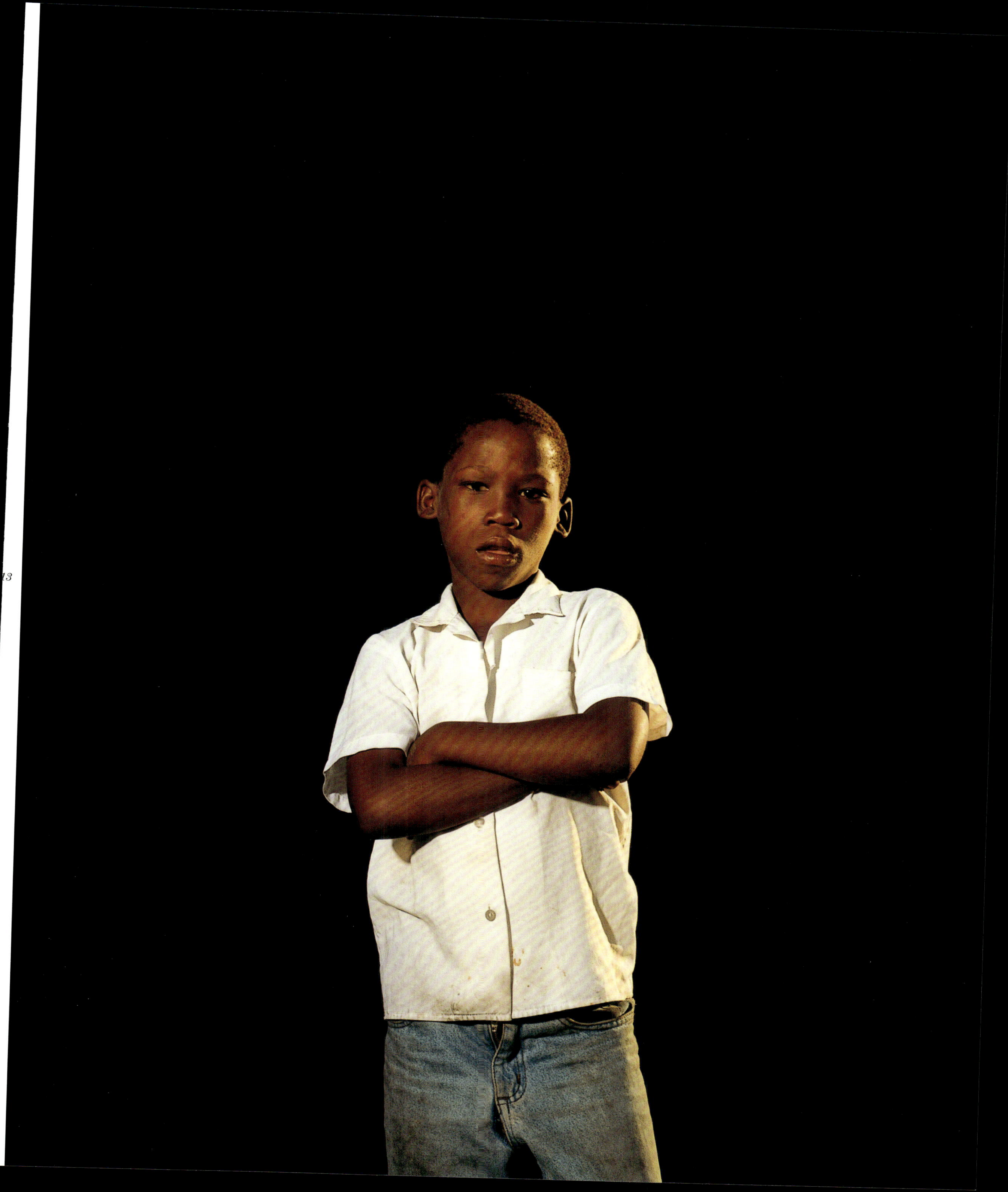

0

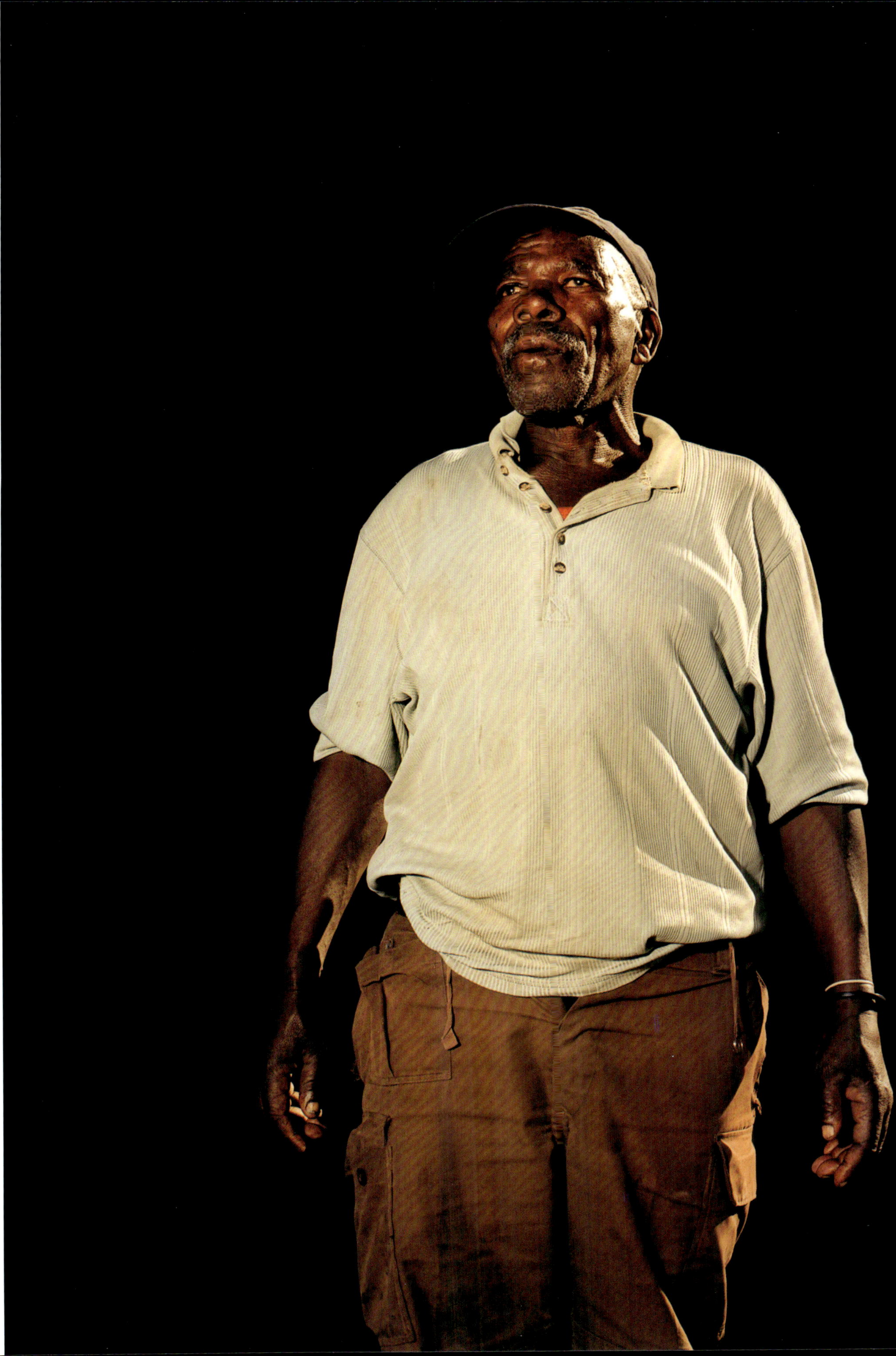

7

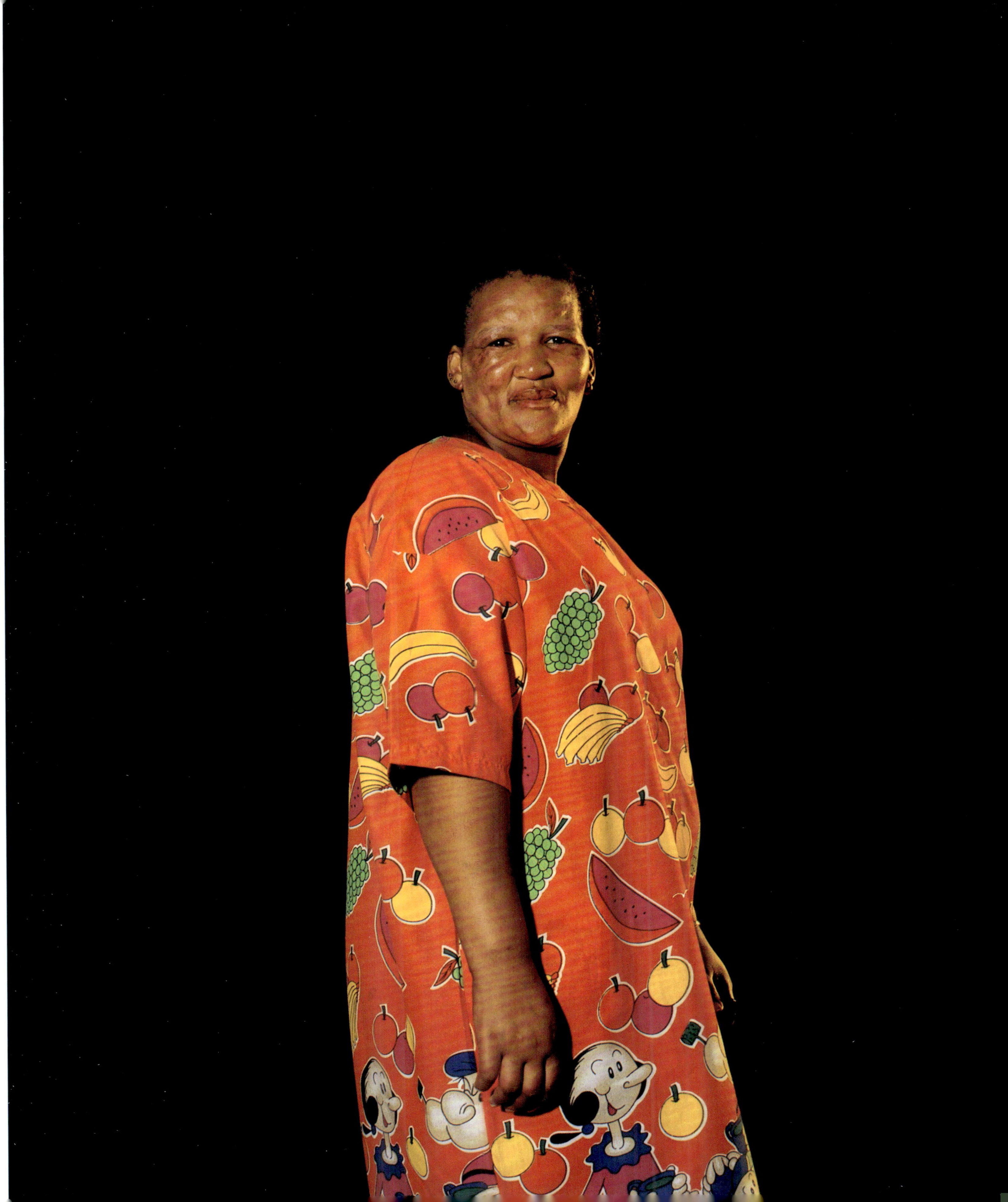

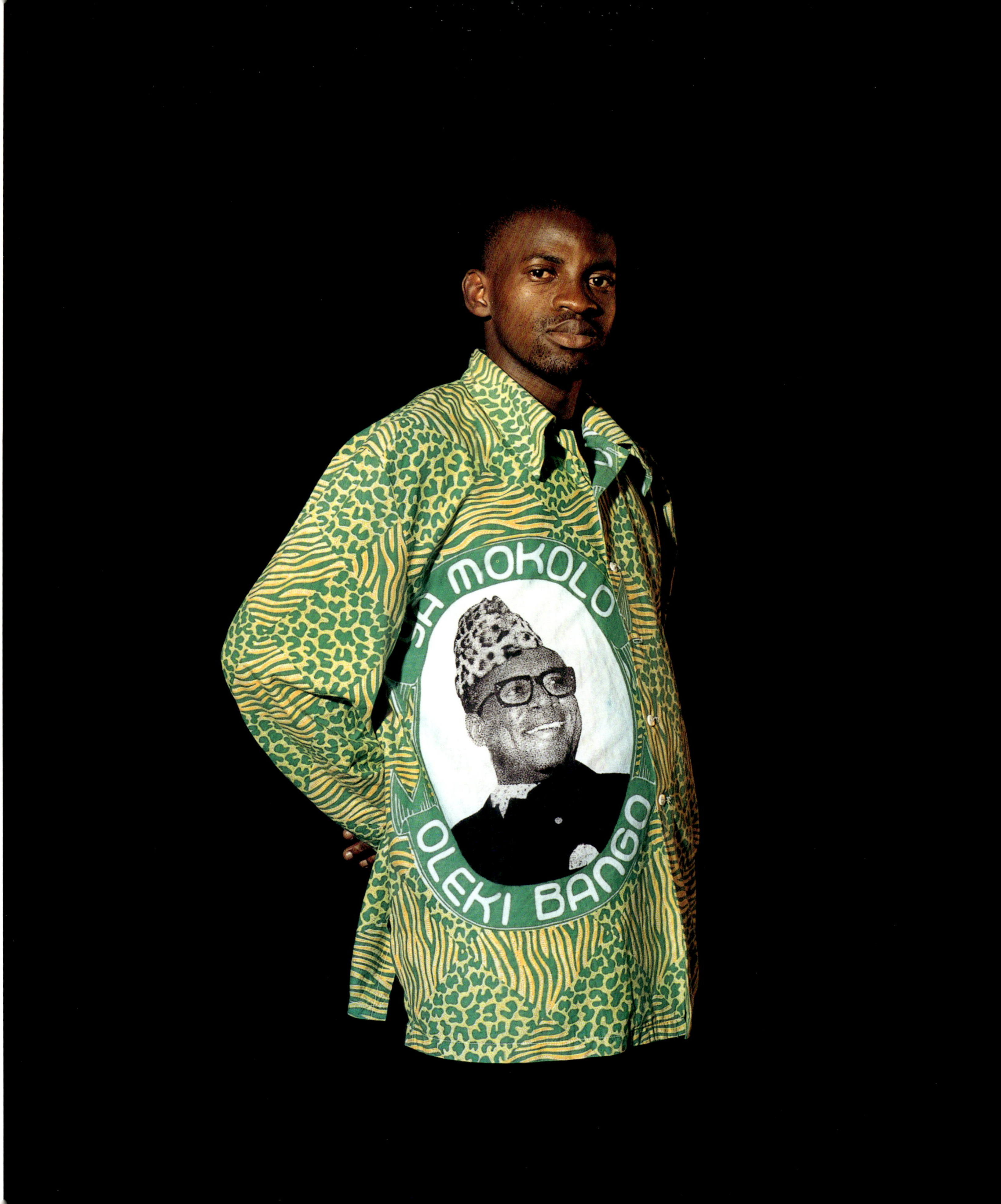
SA MOKOLO
OLEKI BANGO

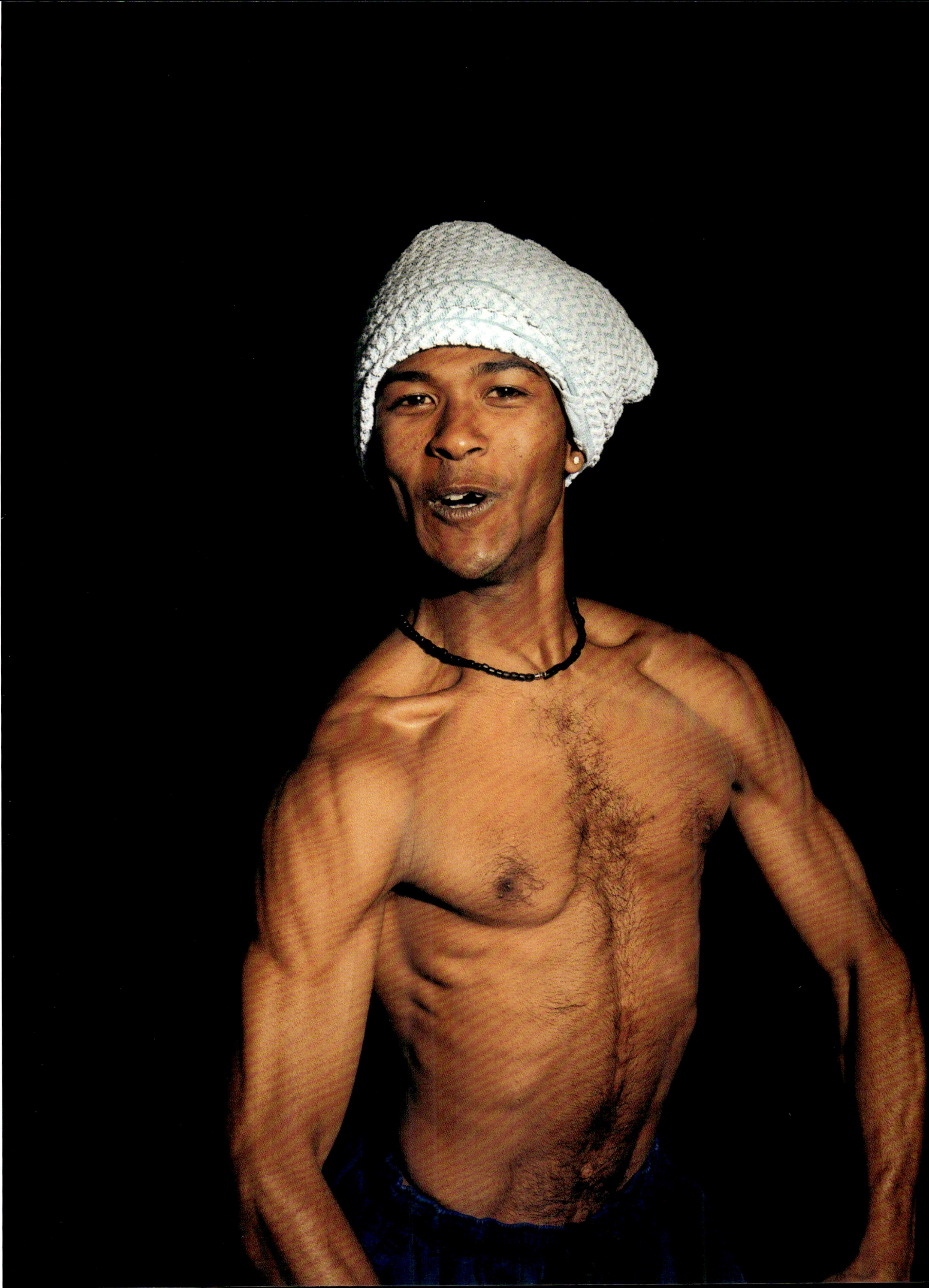

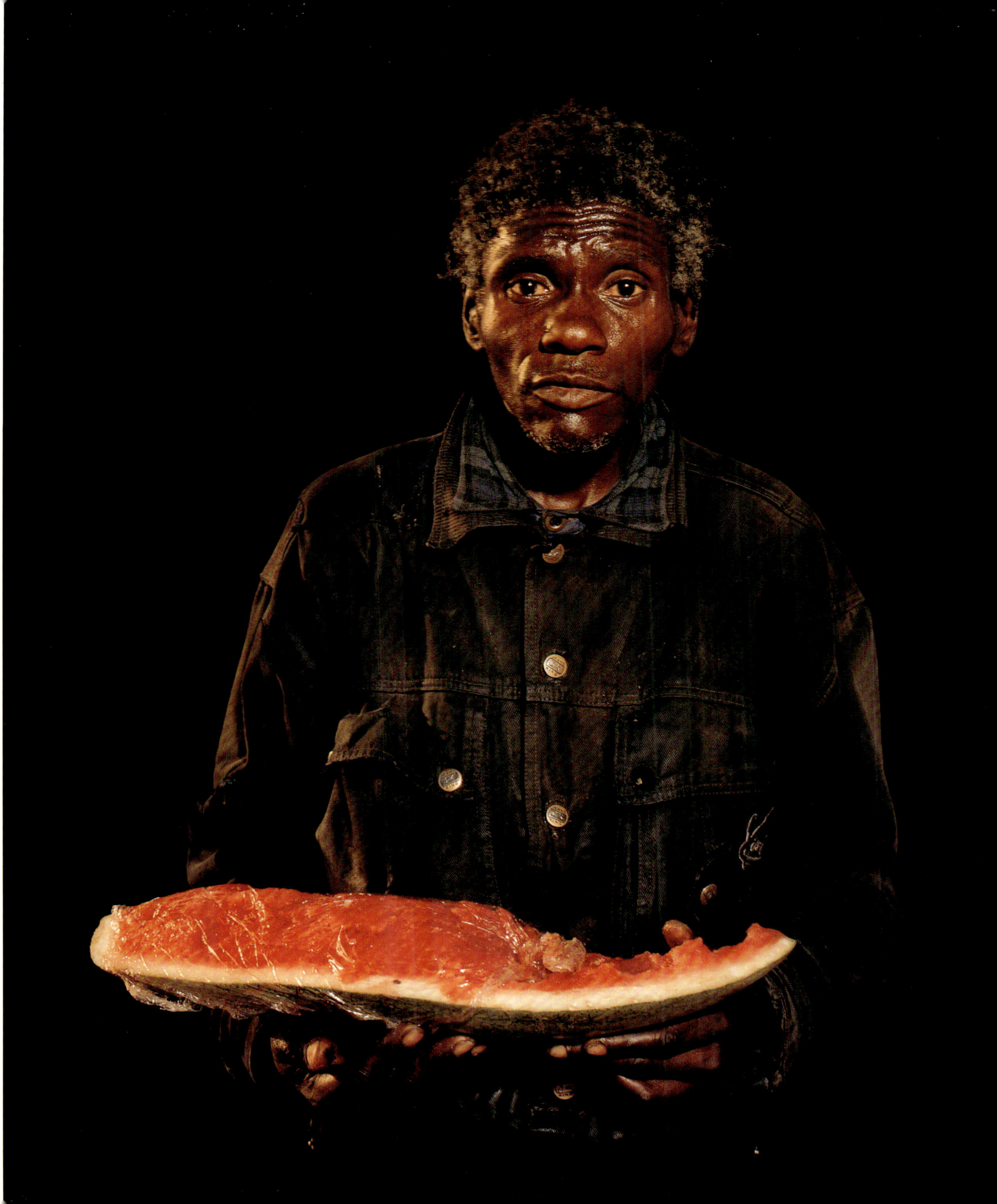

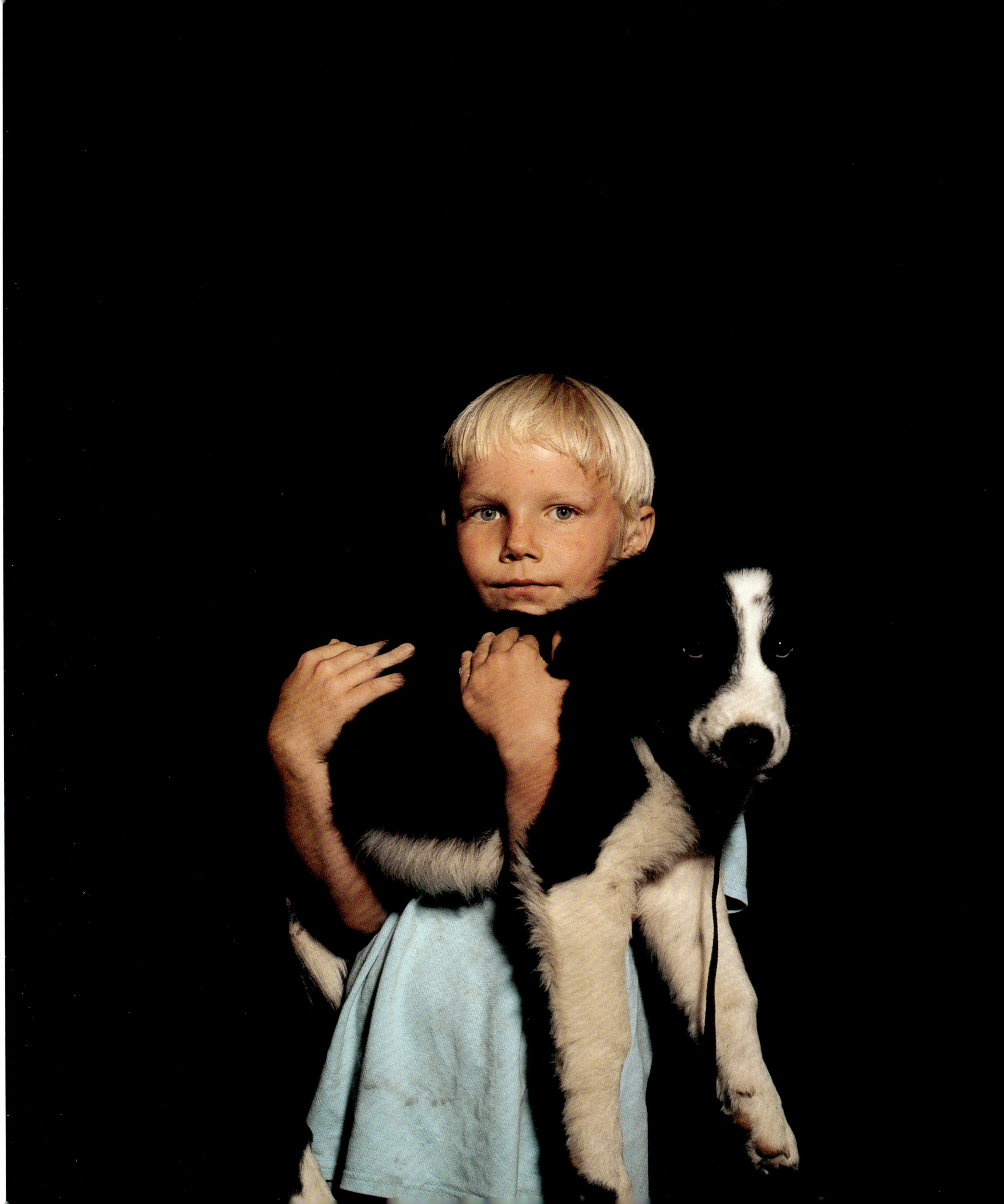

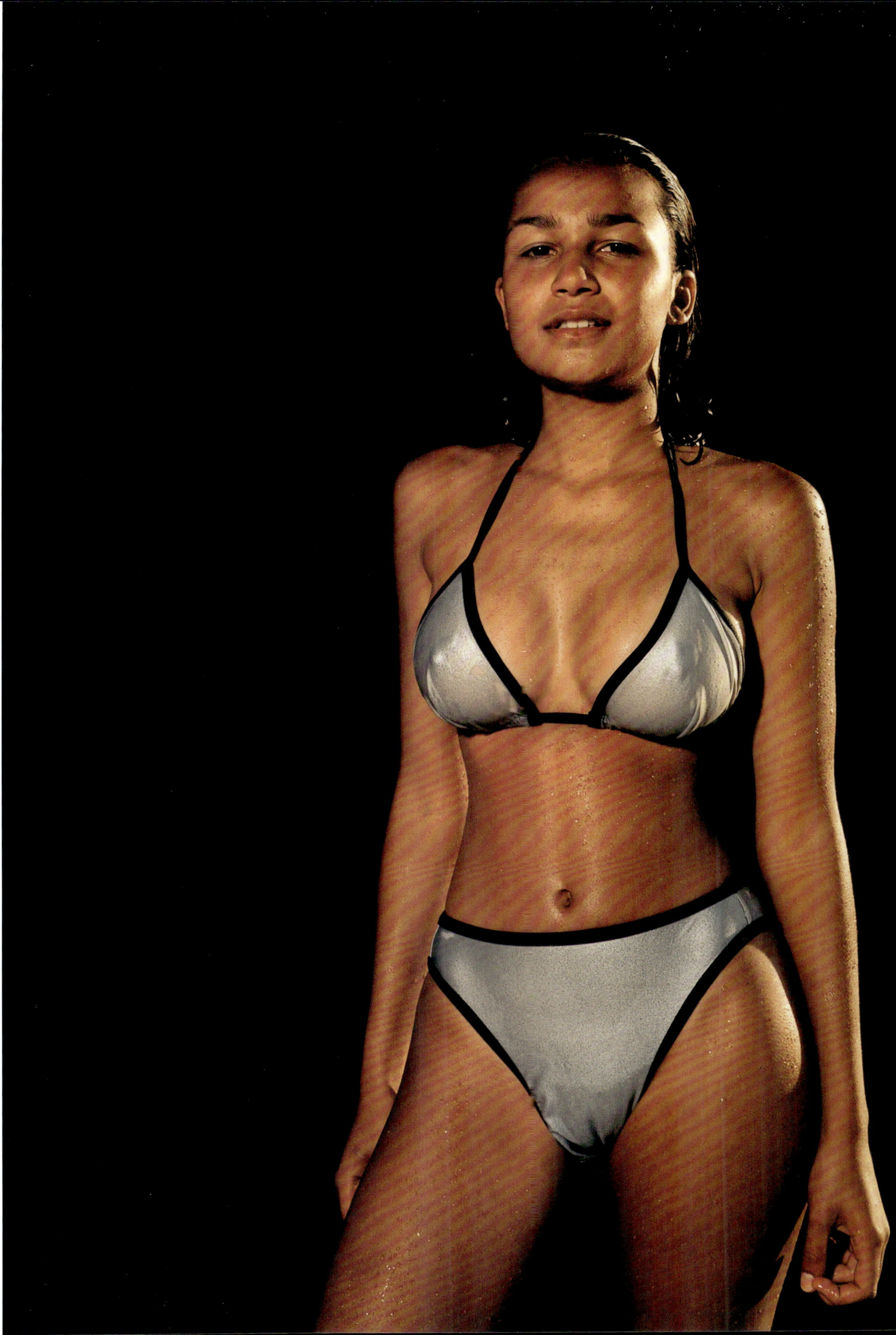

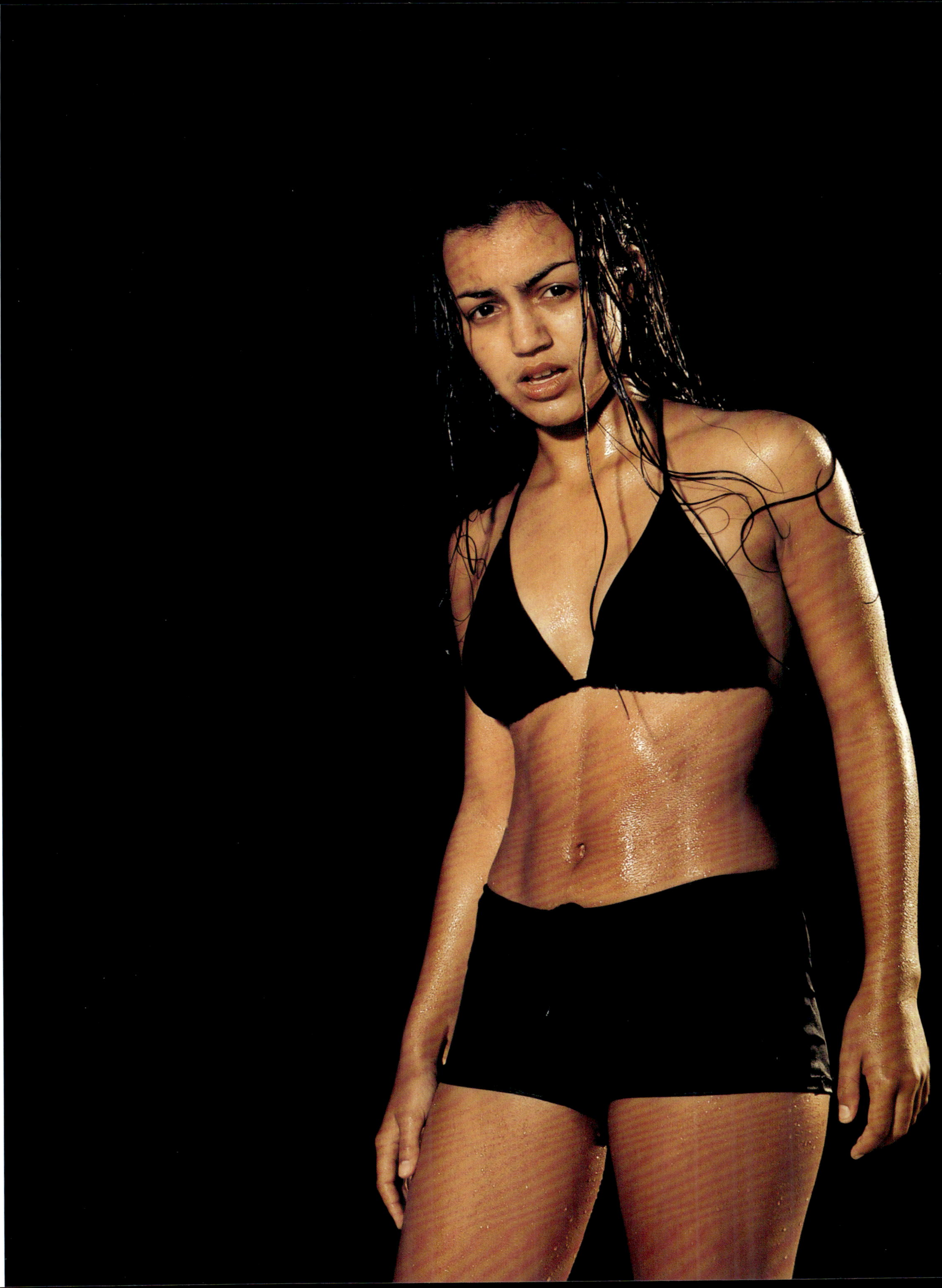

29

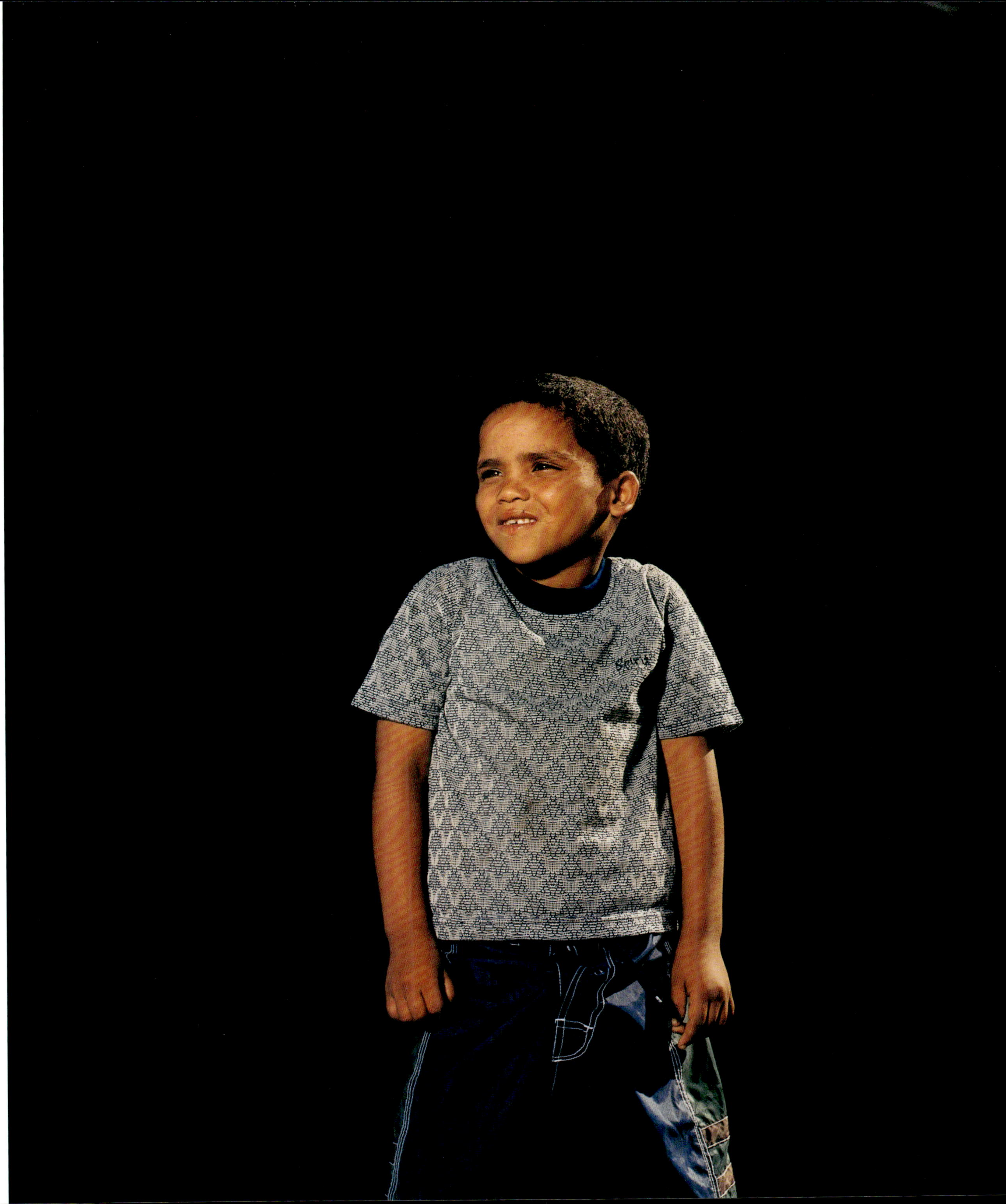

PLEASE
AFFIX
POSTAGE
HERE

BOOTH-CLIBBORN EDITIONS

1ST FLOOR DOMINICAN HOUSE

4 PRIORY COURT

PILGRIM STREET

LONDON

EC4V6DR *United Kingdom*

WE HOPE THAT YOU ENJOYED THIS BOOK. *We would be most grateful if you would fill out and return this card to us.* [PLEASE NOTE THAT POSTAGE MUST BE APPLIED]

I *found this book*
- OF GREAT INTEREST ☐
- OF MODERATE INTEREST ☐
- OF NO INTEREST ☐

YOUR BUSINESS OR OCCUPATION ____________________

AGE ____

YOUR COMMENTS ____________________

please send me more information on your books ☐

NAME ____________________

ADDRESS ____________________

CITY ________ STATE ________ COUNTRY ________

E-MAIL

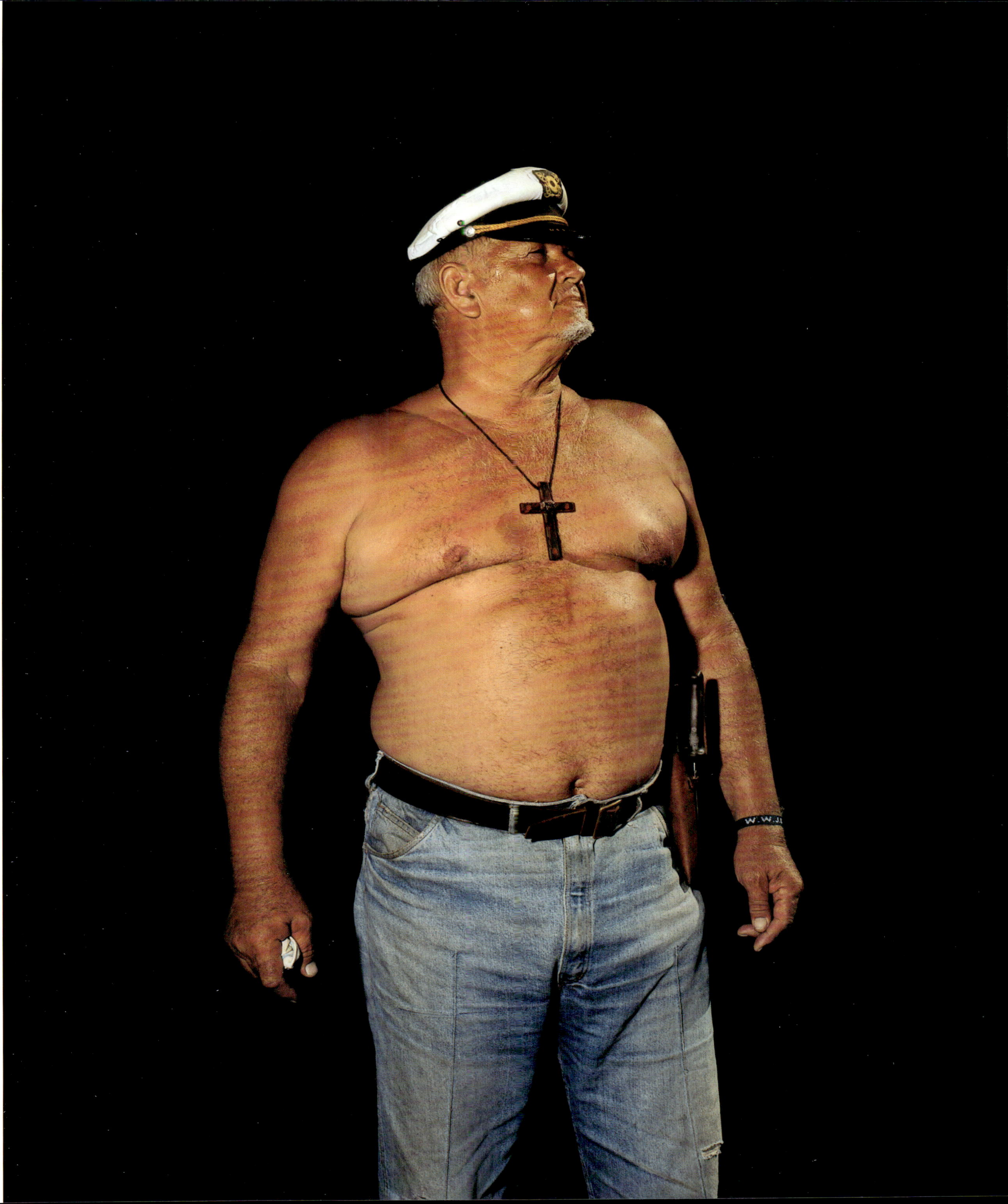

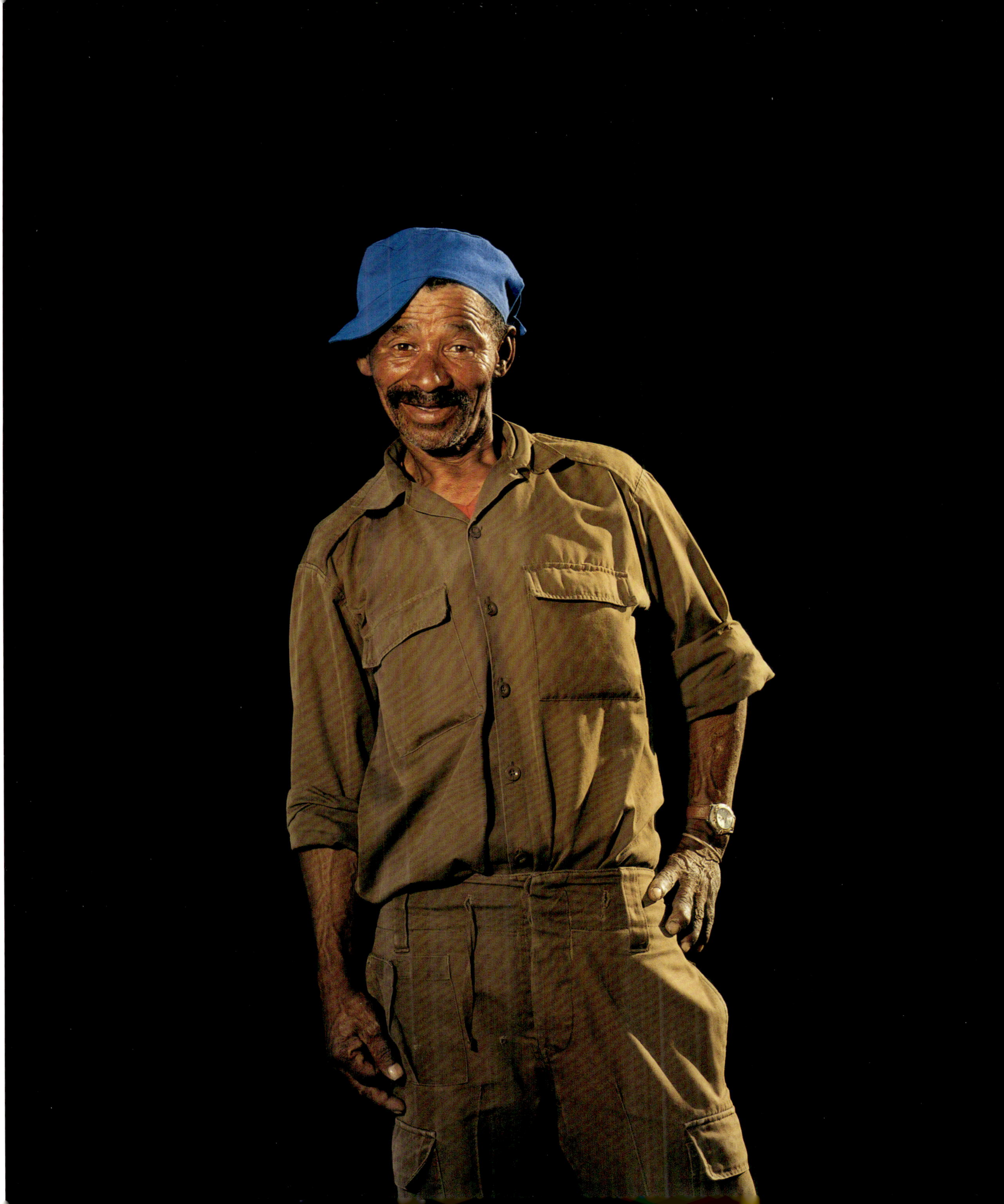

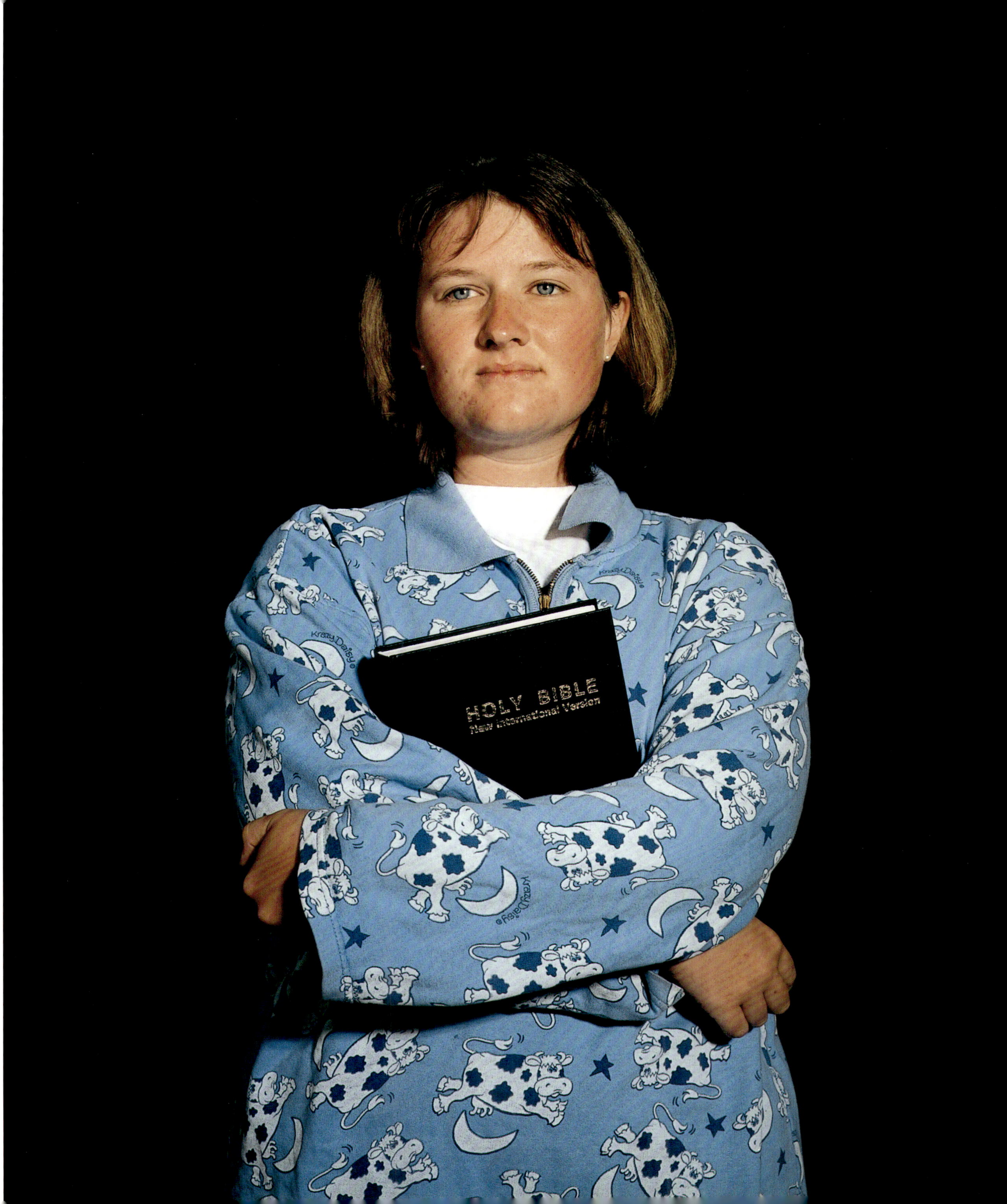
HOLY BIBLE
New International Version

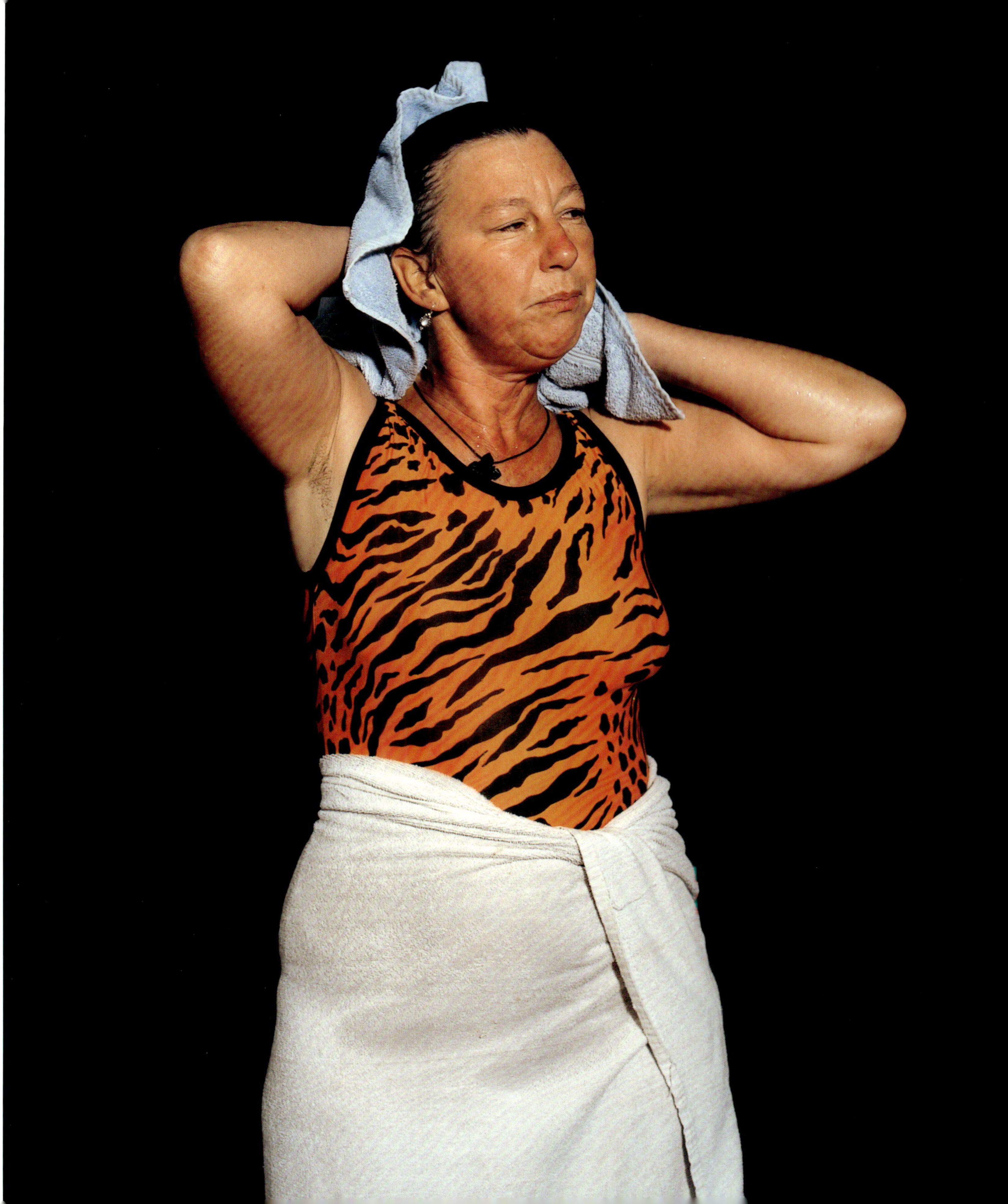

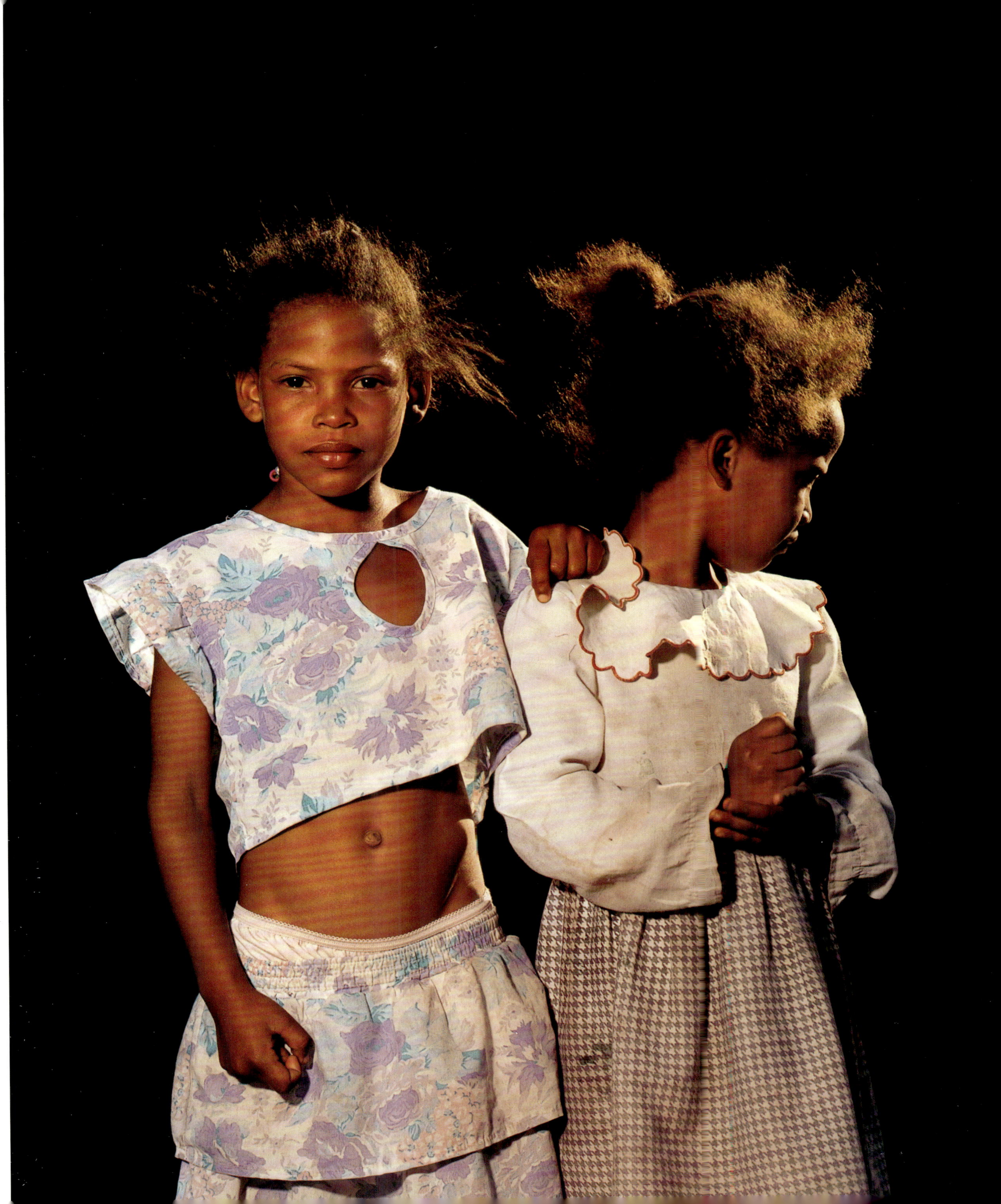

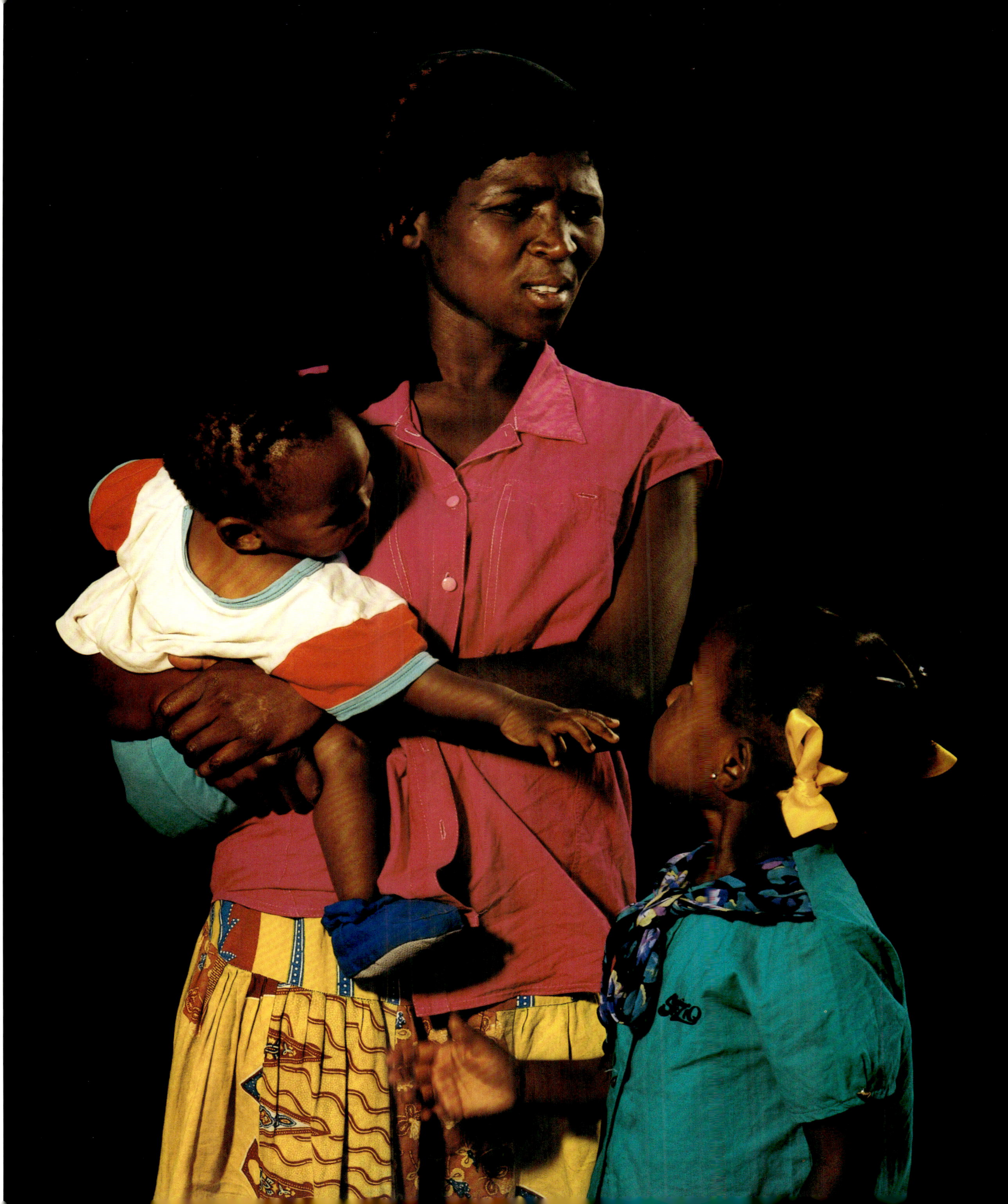

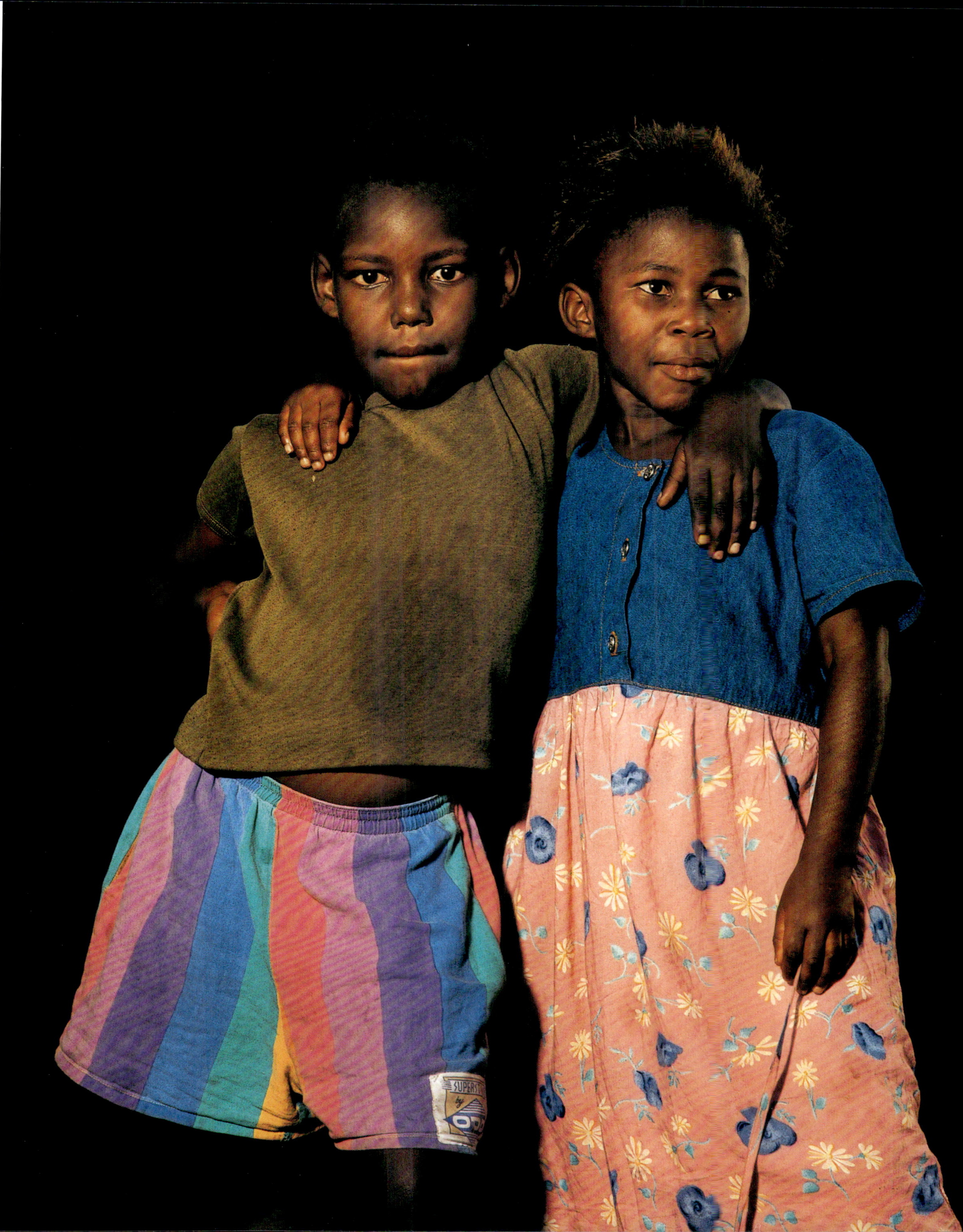

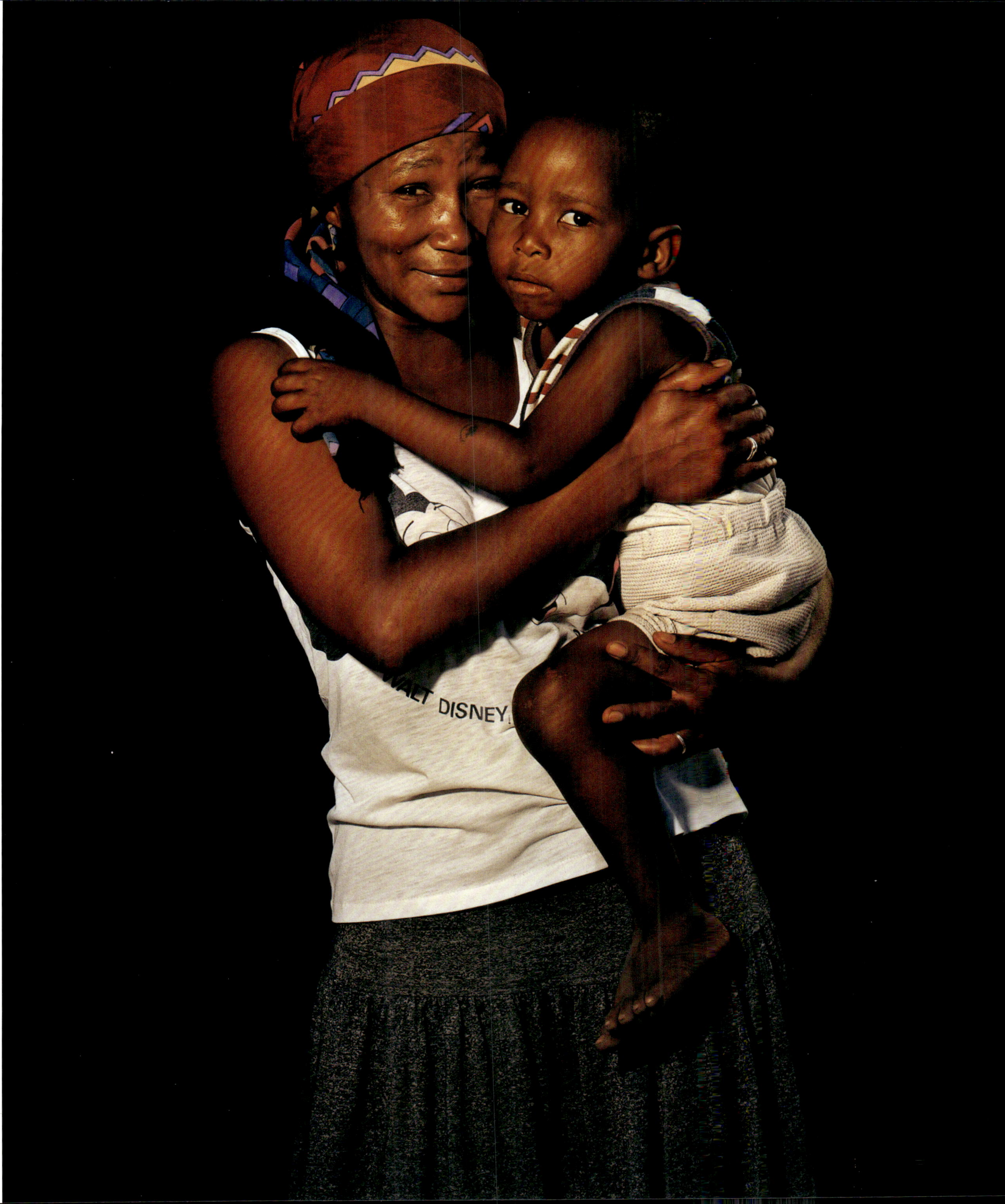
DISNEY

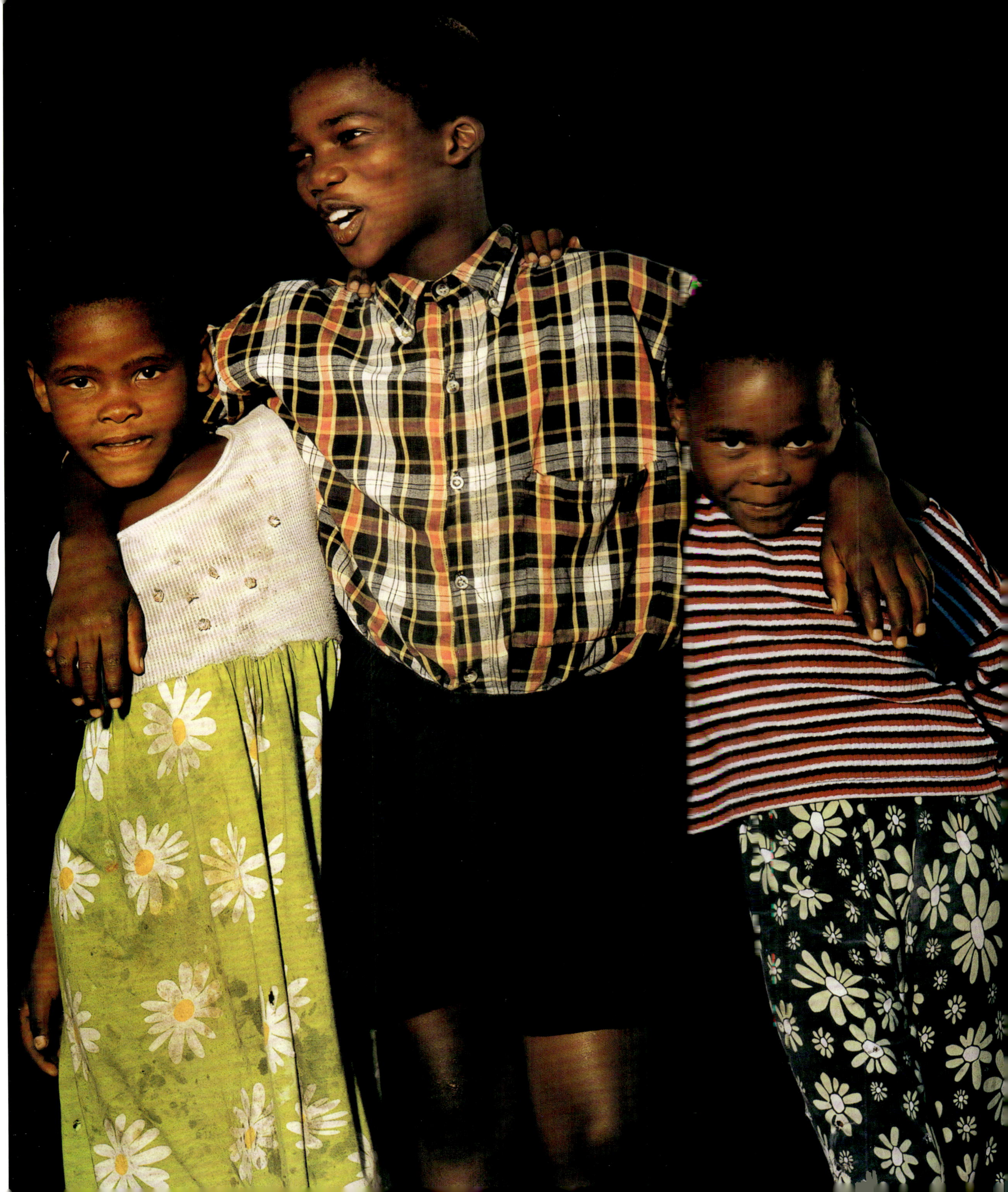

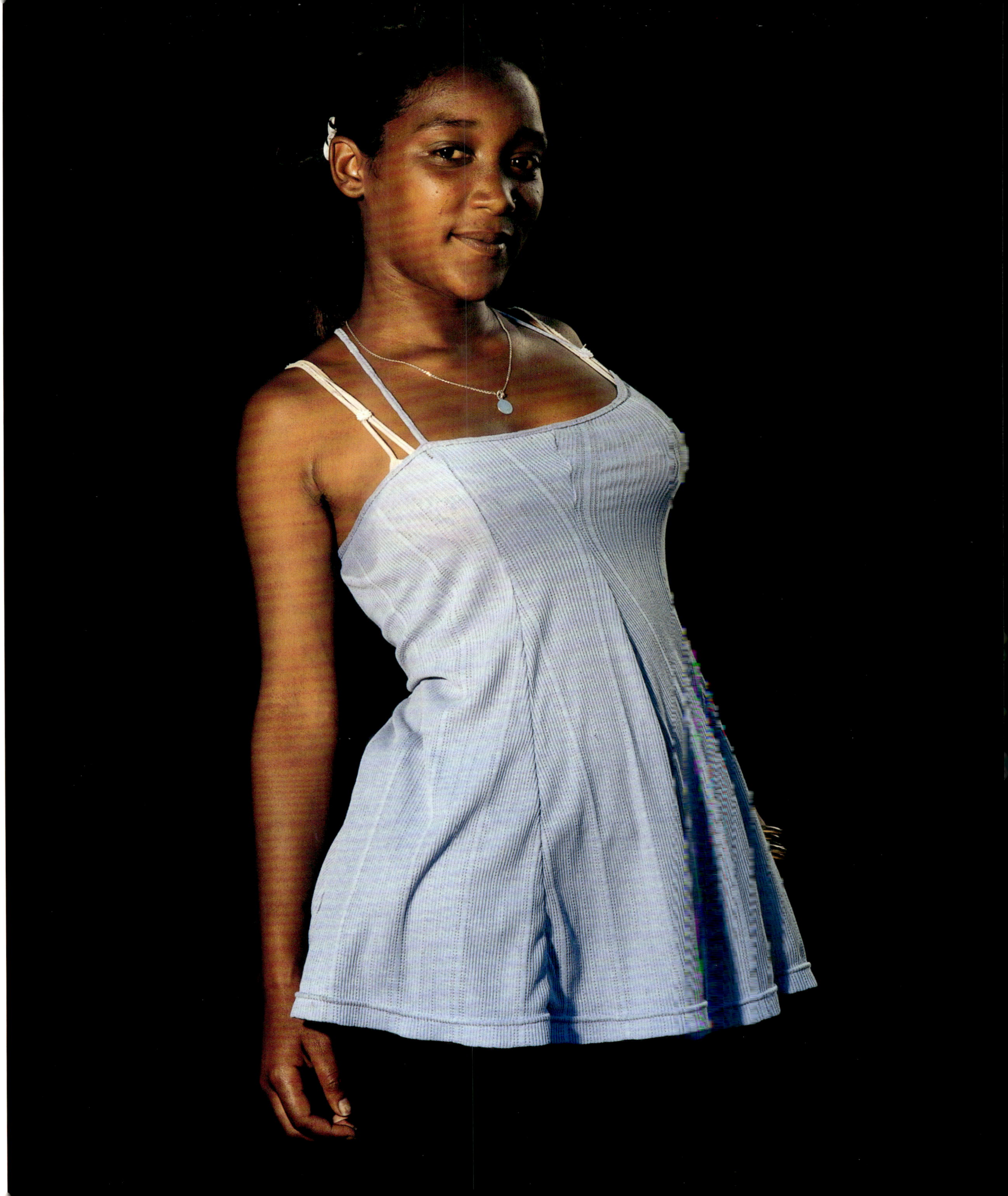

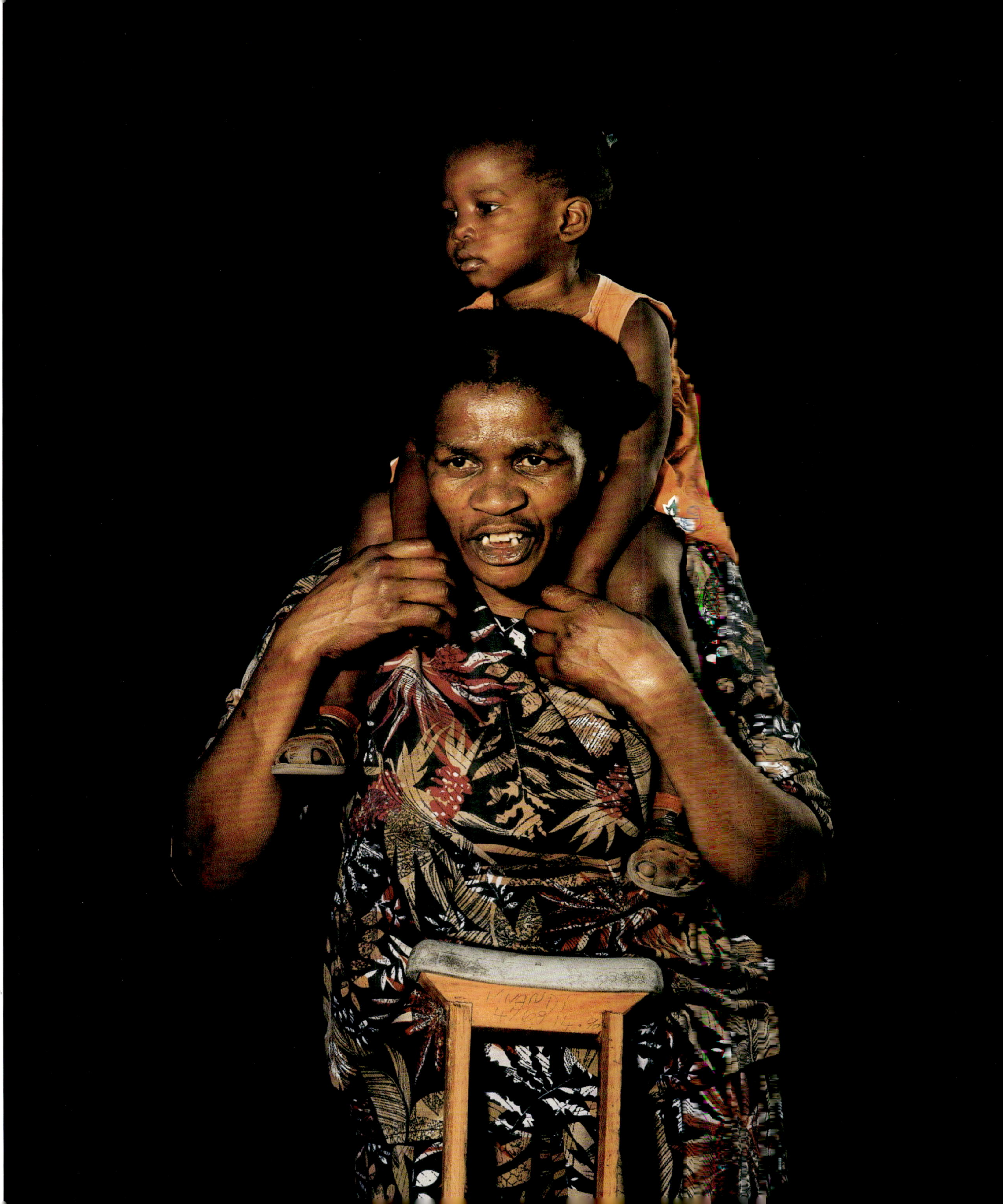

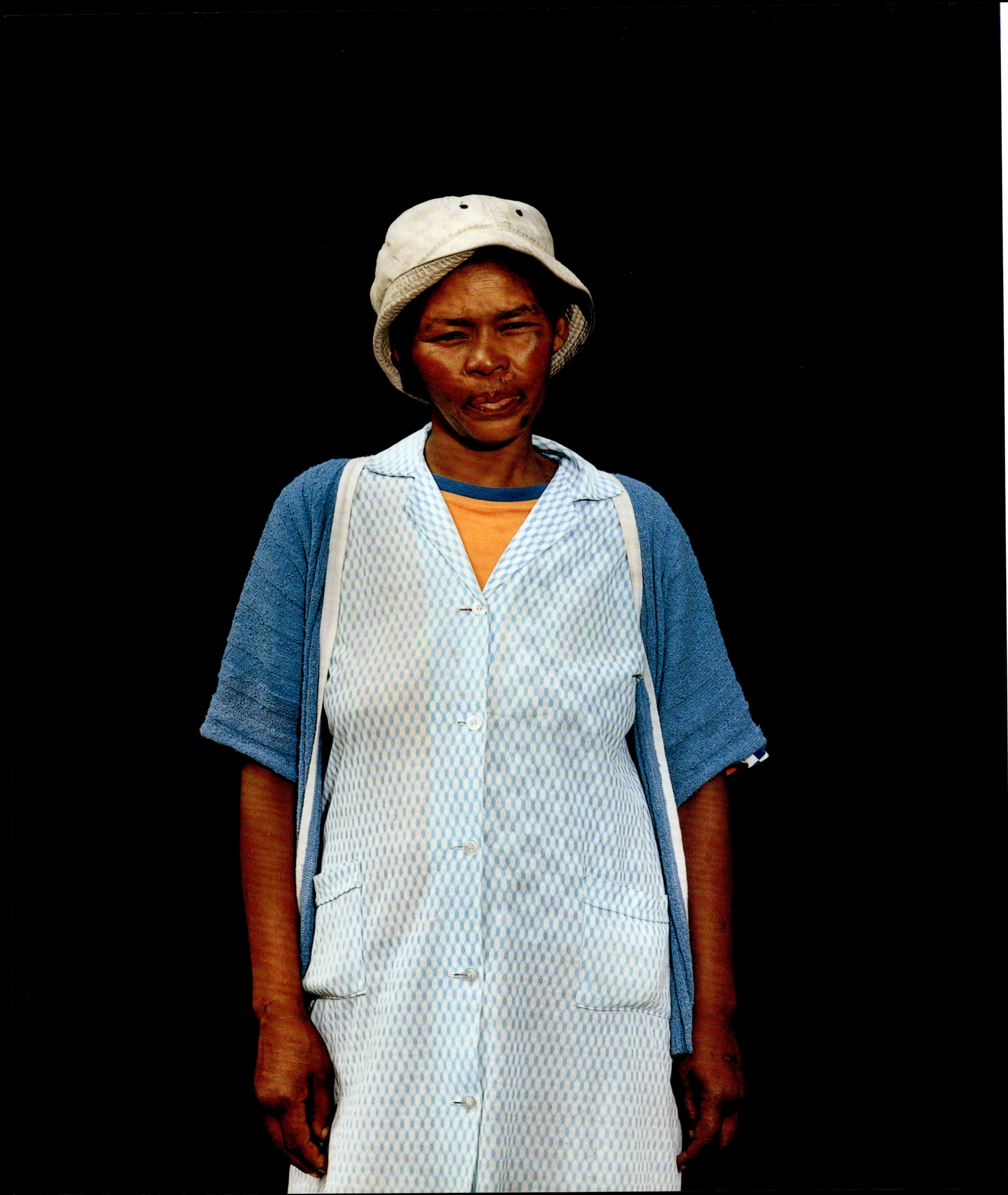

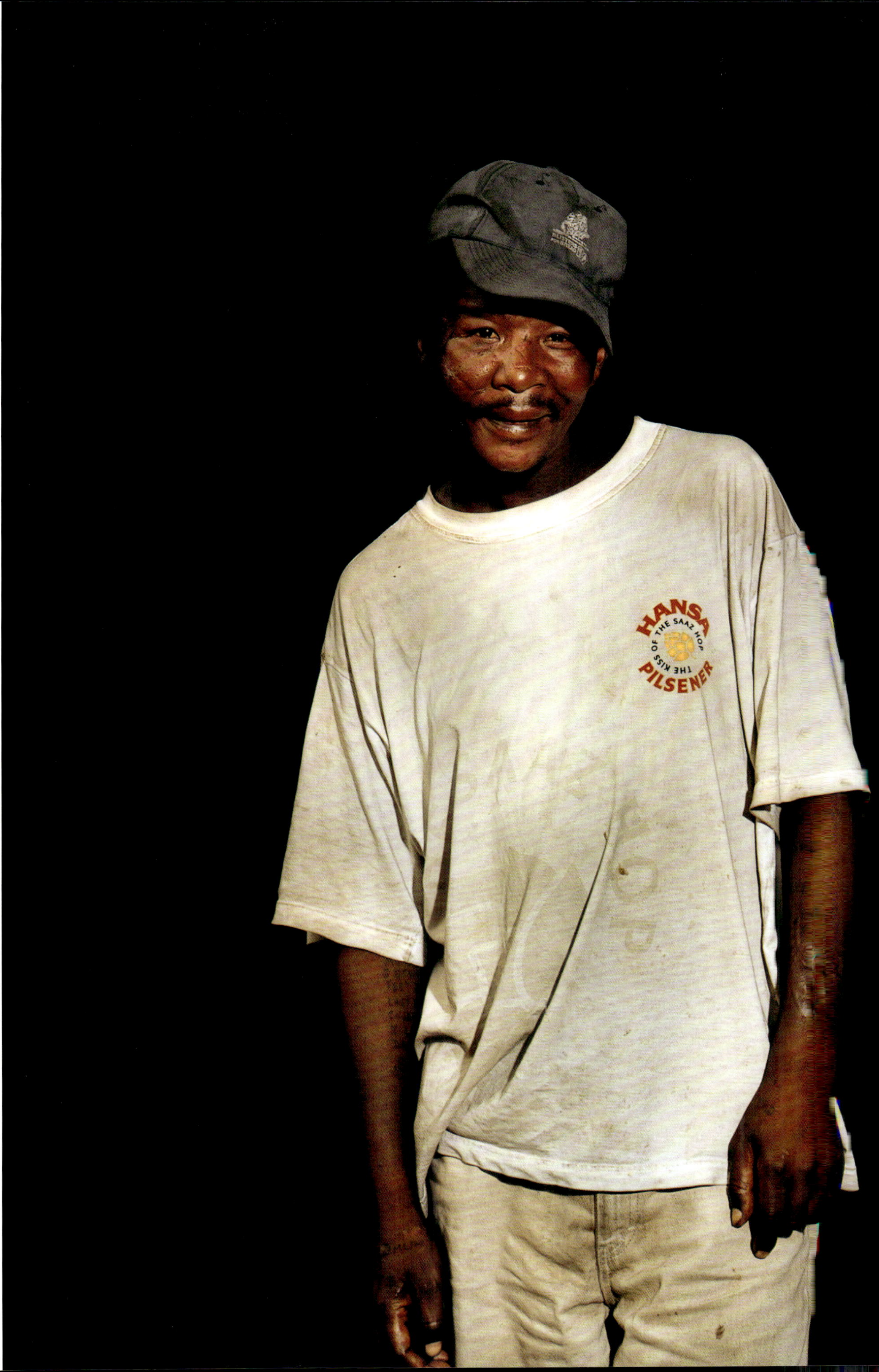
HANSA
THE KISS OF THE SAAZ HOP
PILSENER

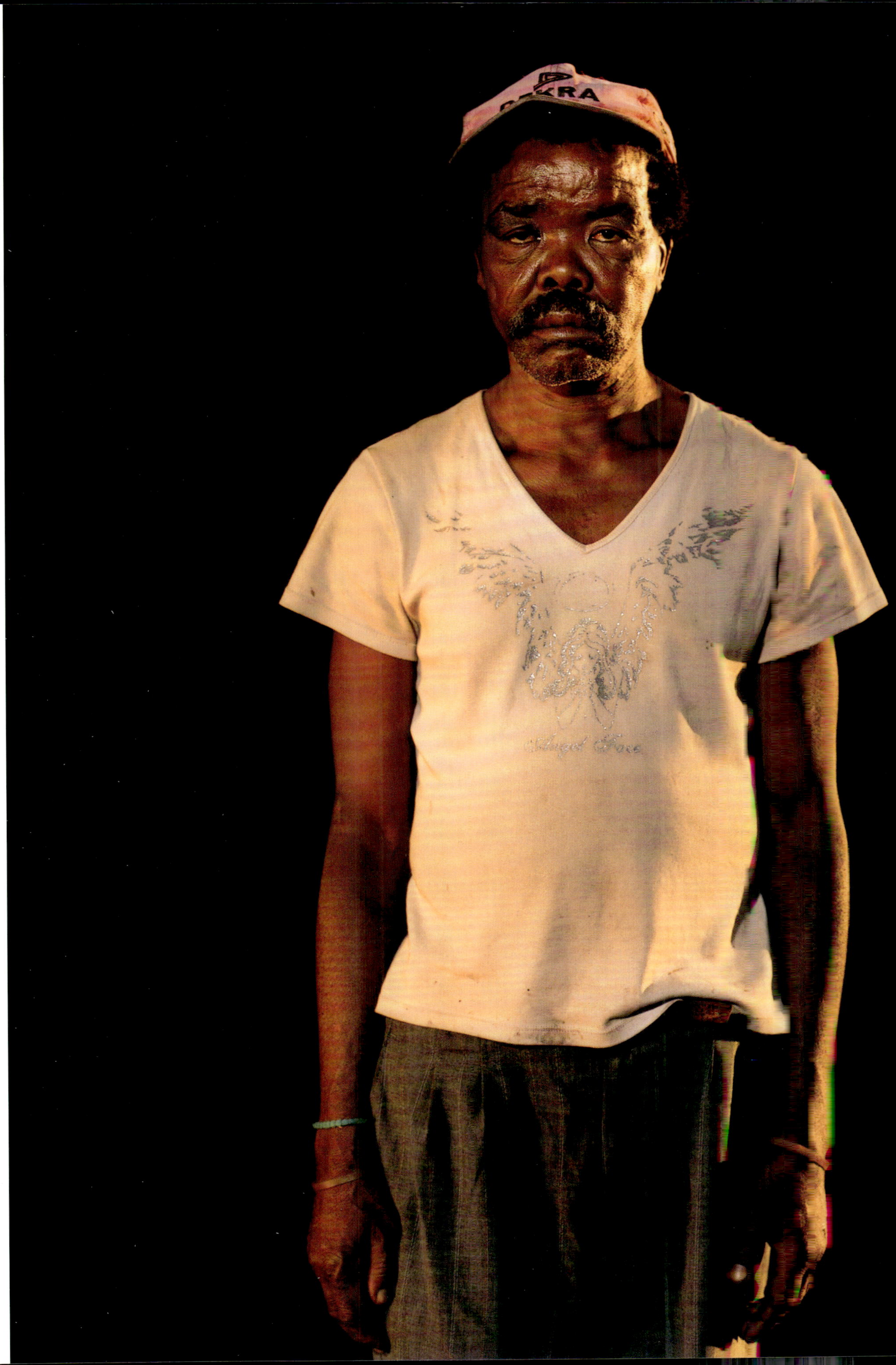

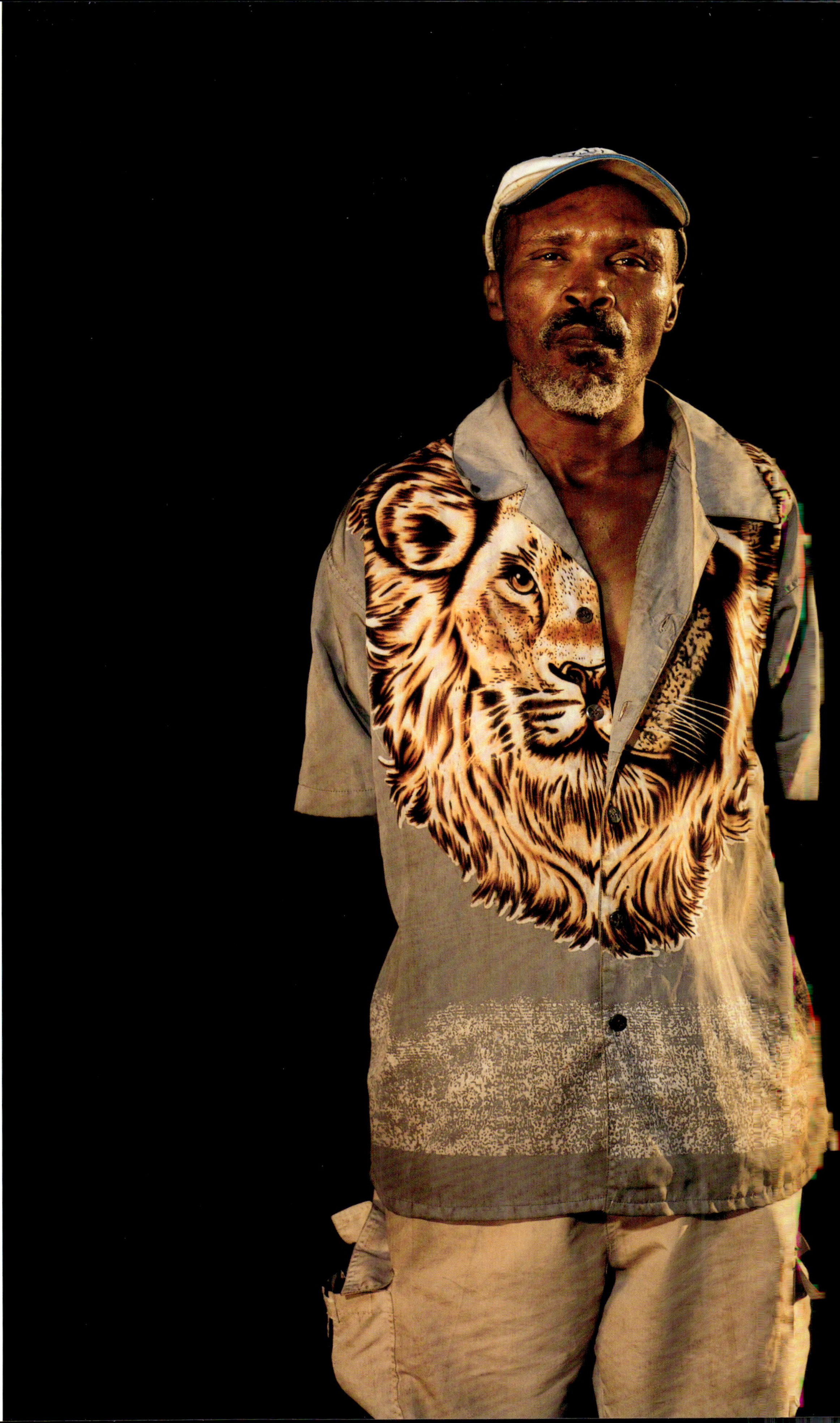

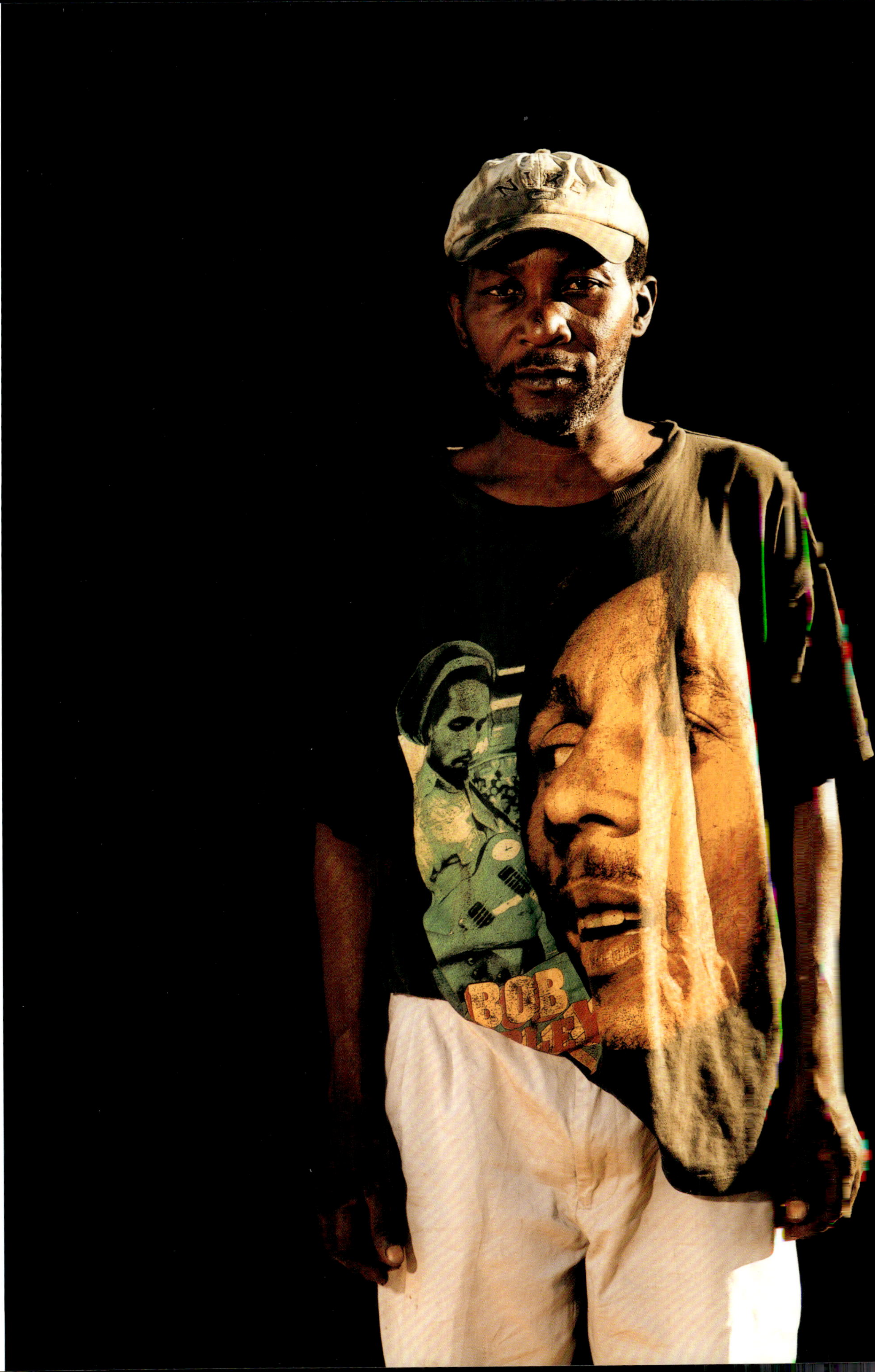
BOB

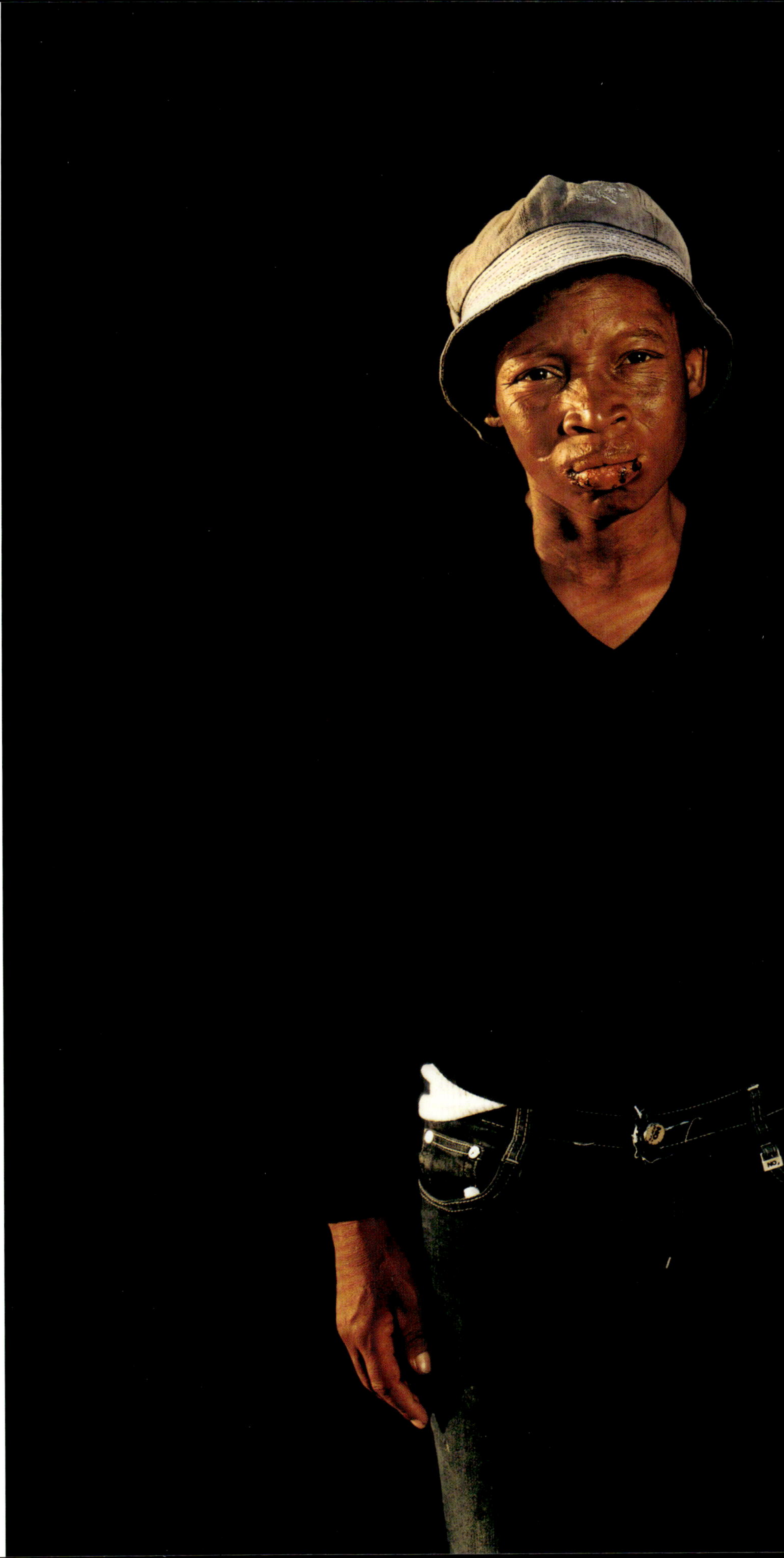

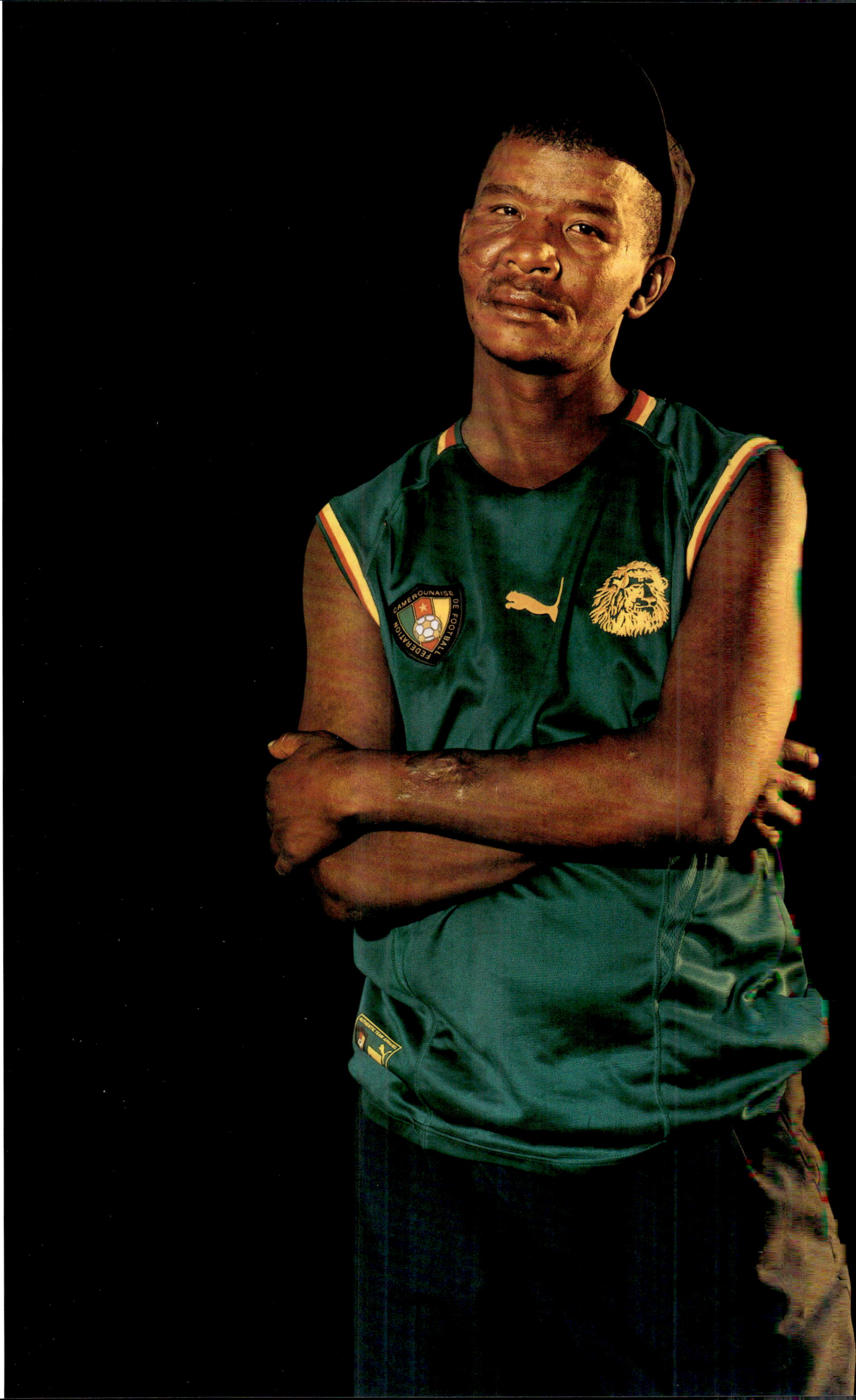
CAMEROUNAISE DE FOOTBALL
FEDERATION

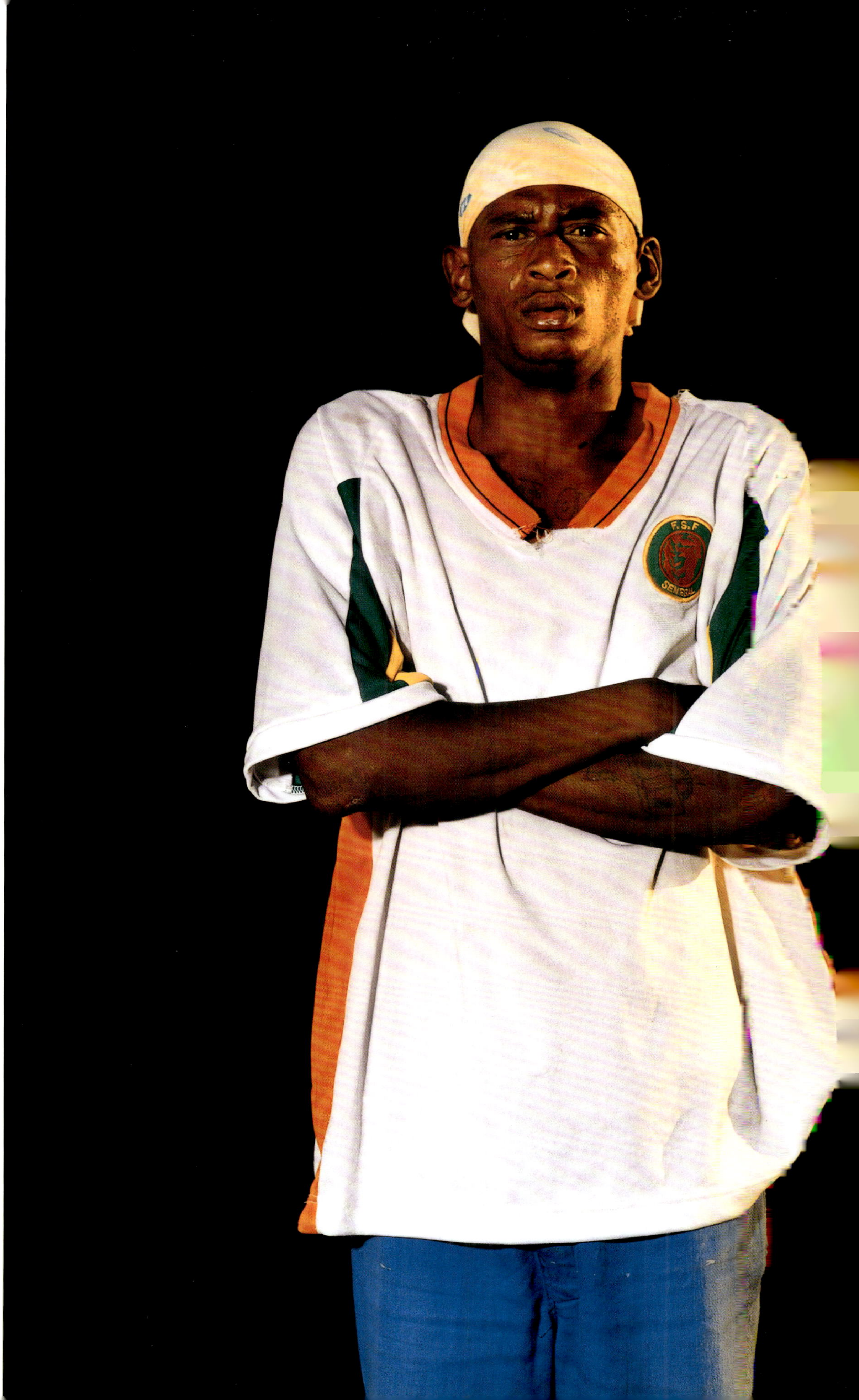
F.S.F
SENEGAL

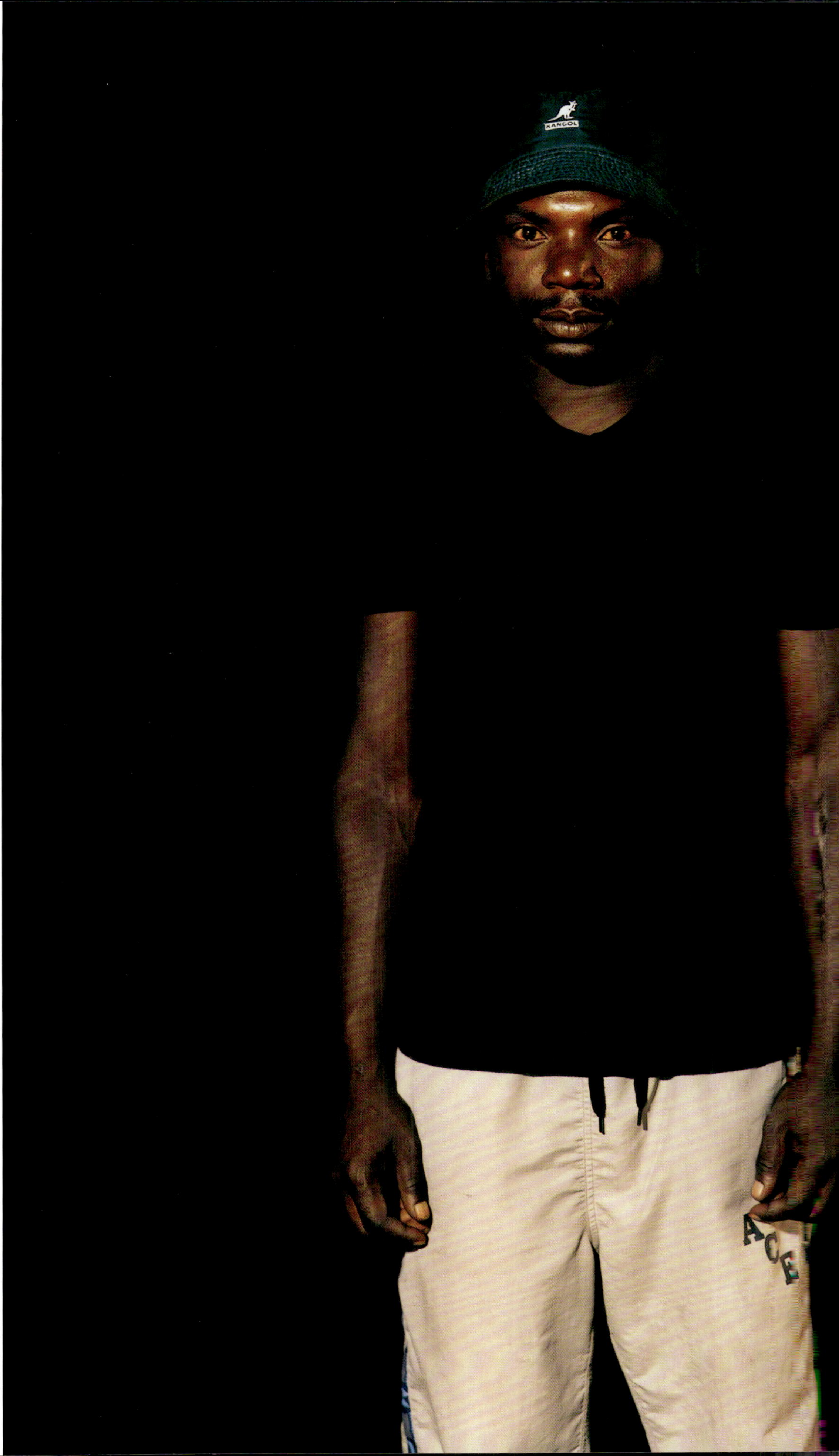
KANGOL
ACE

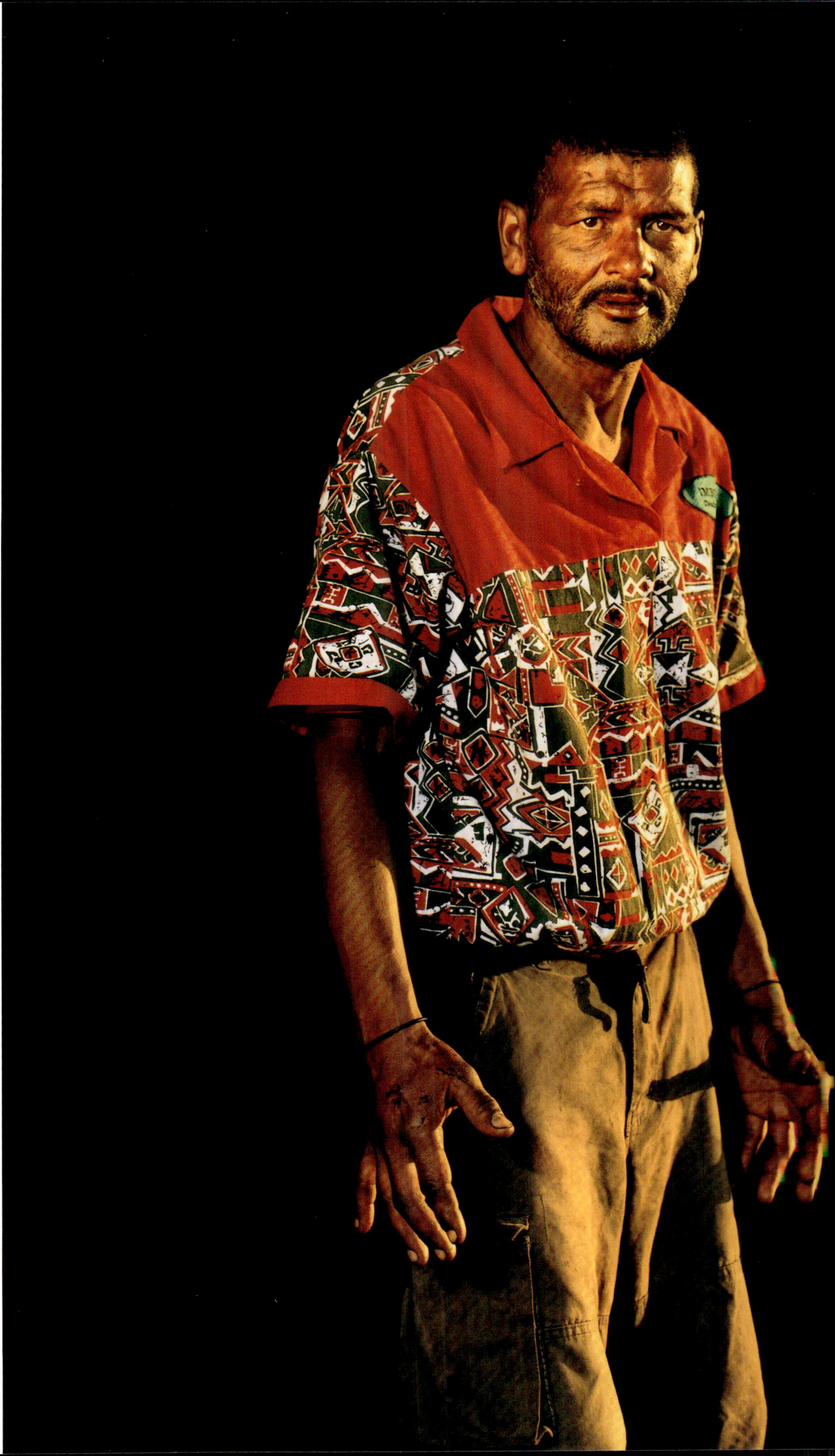

0

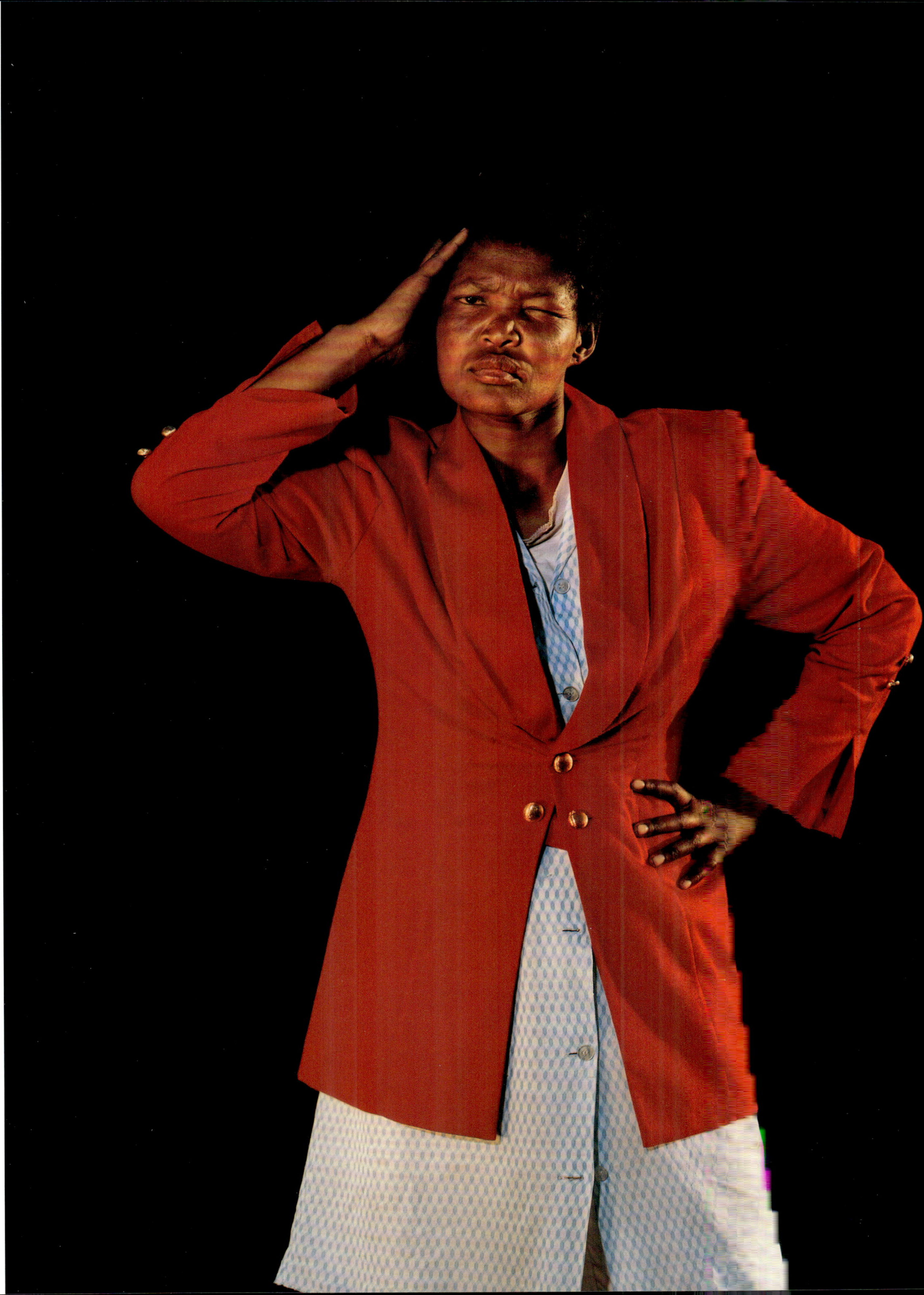

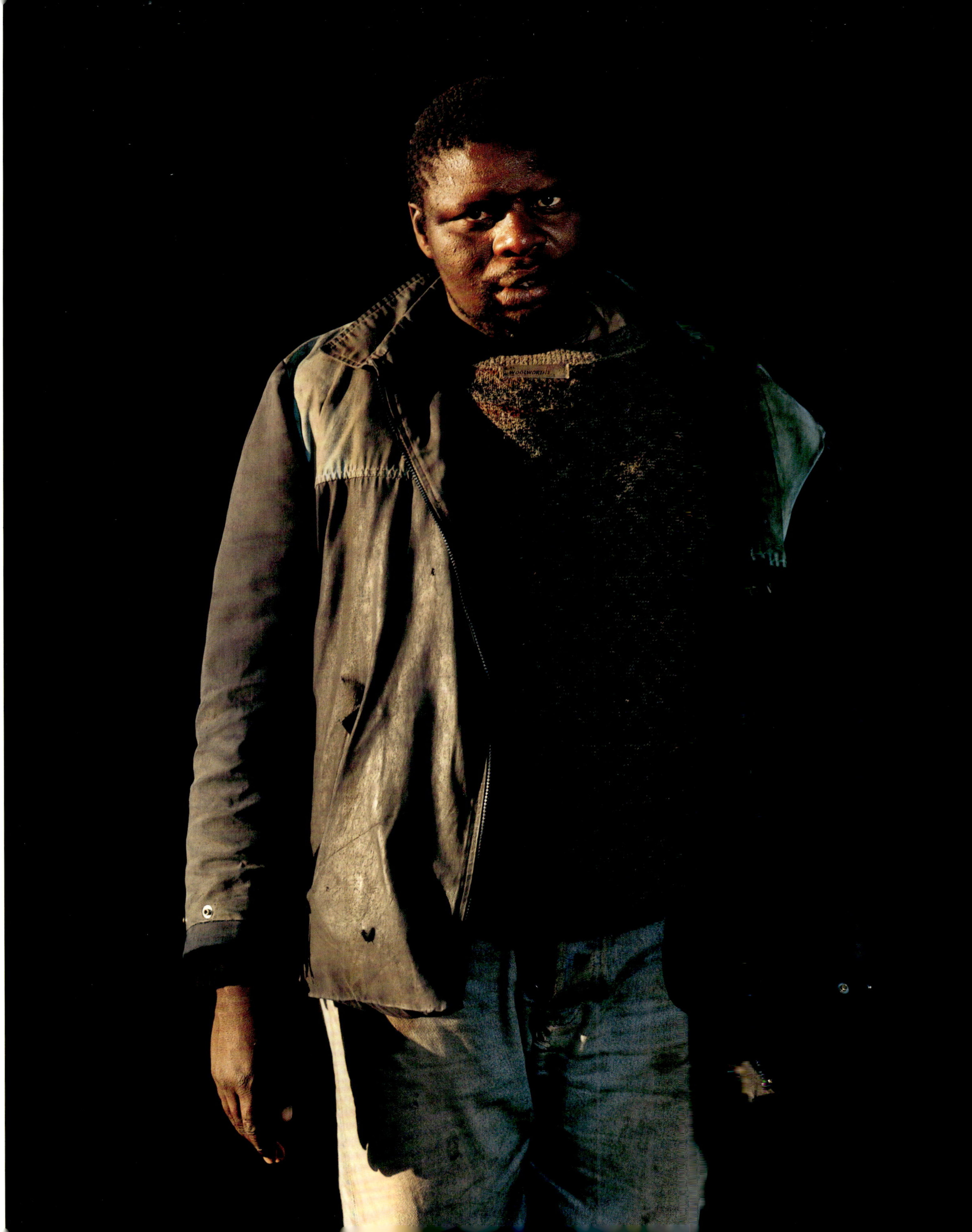

77

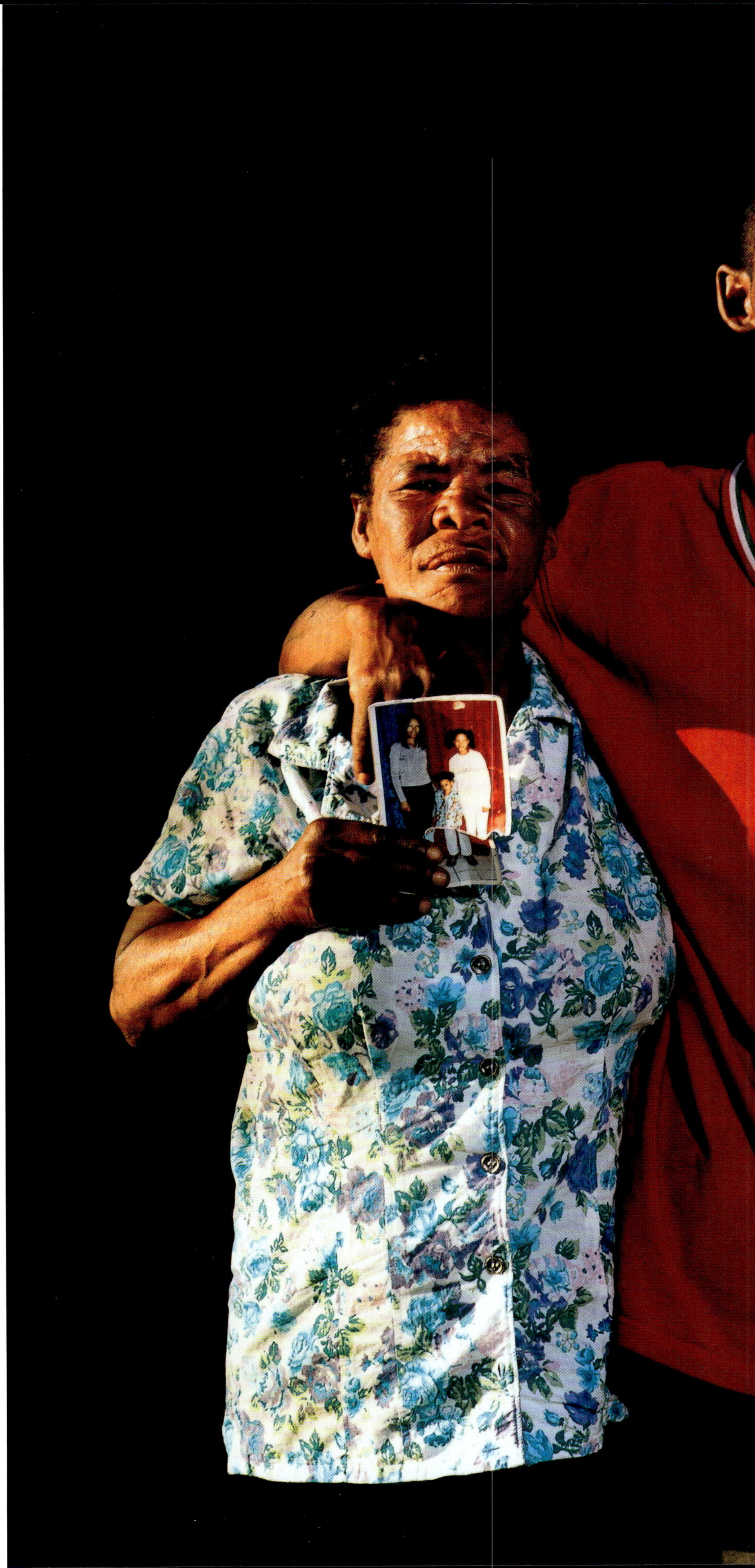

0

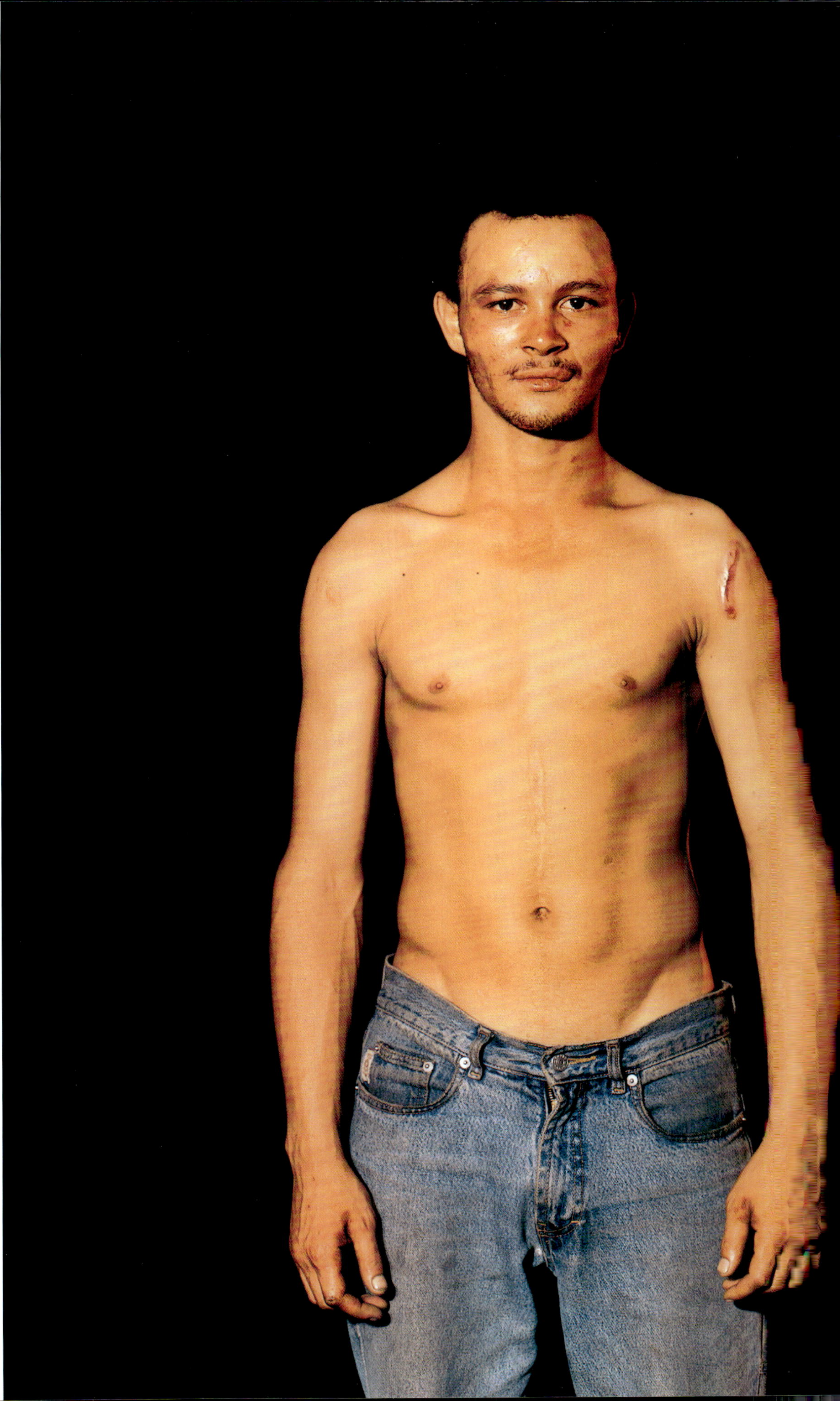

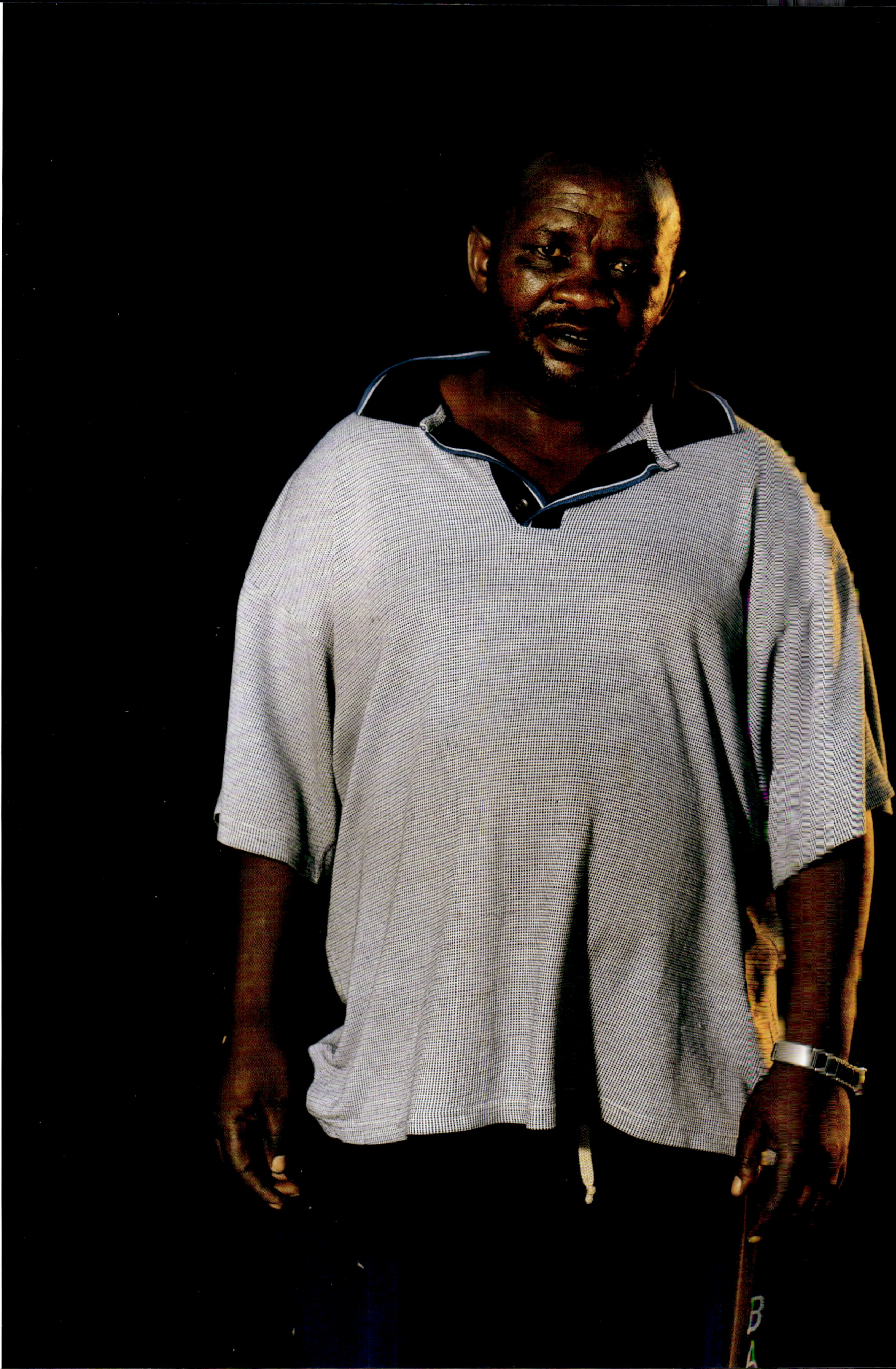

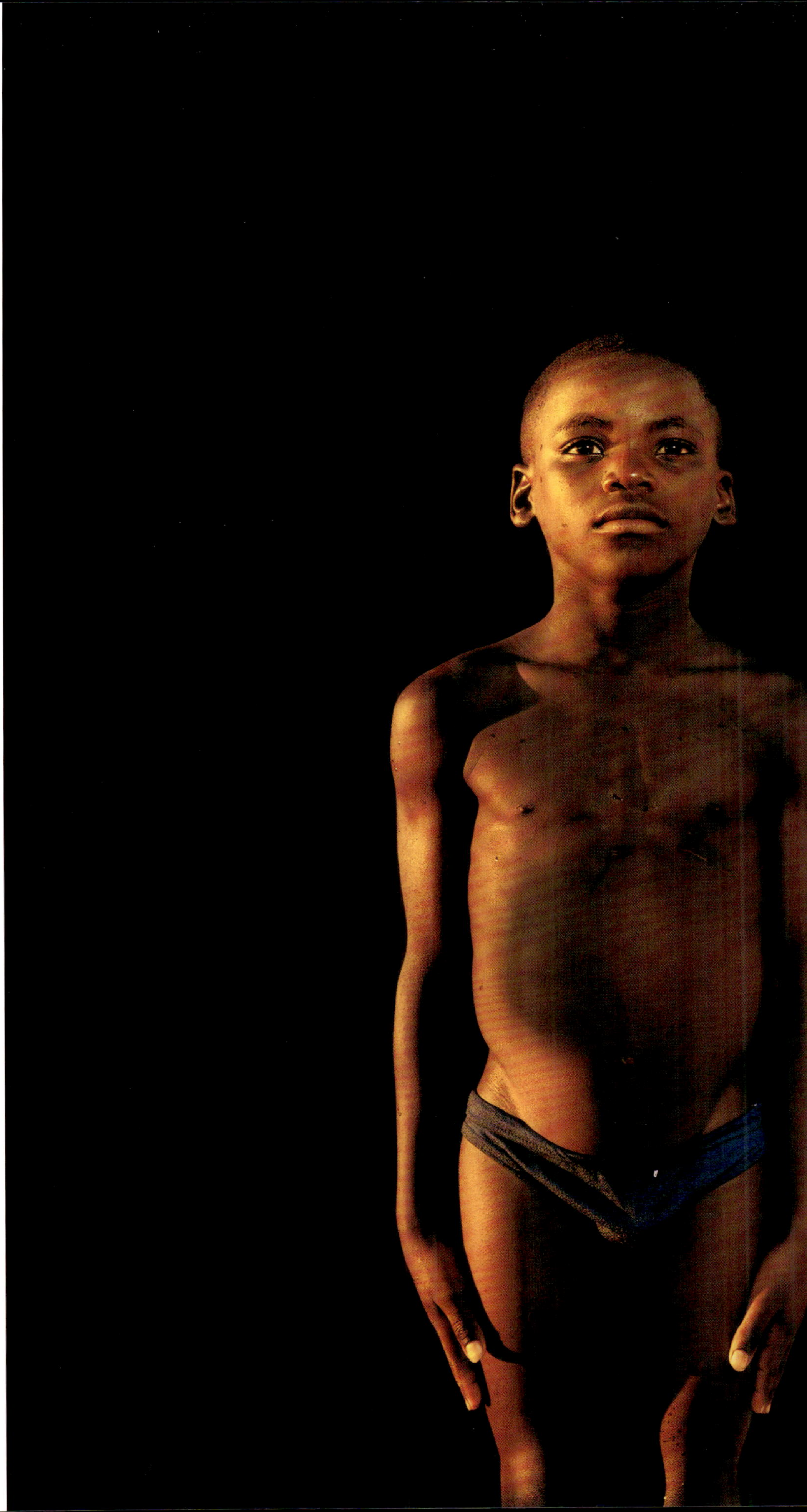

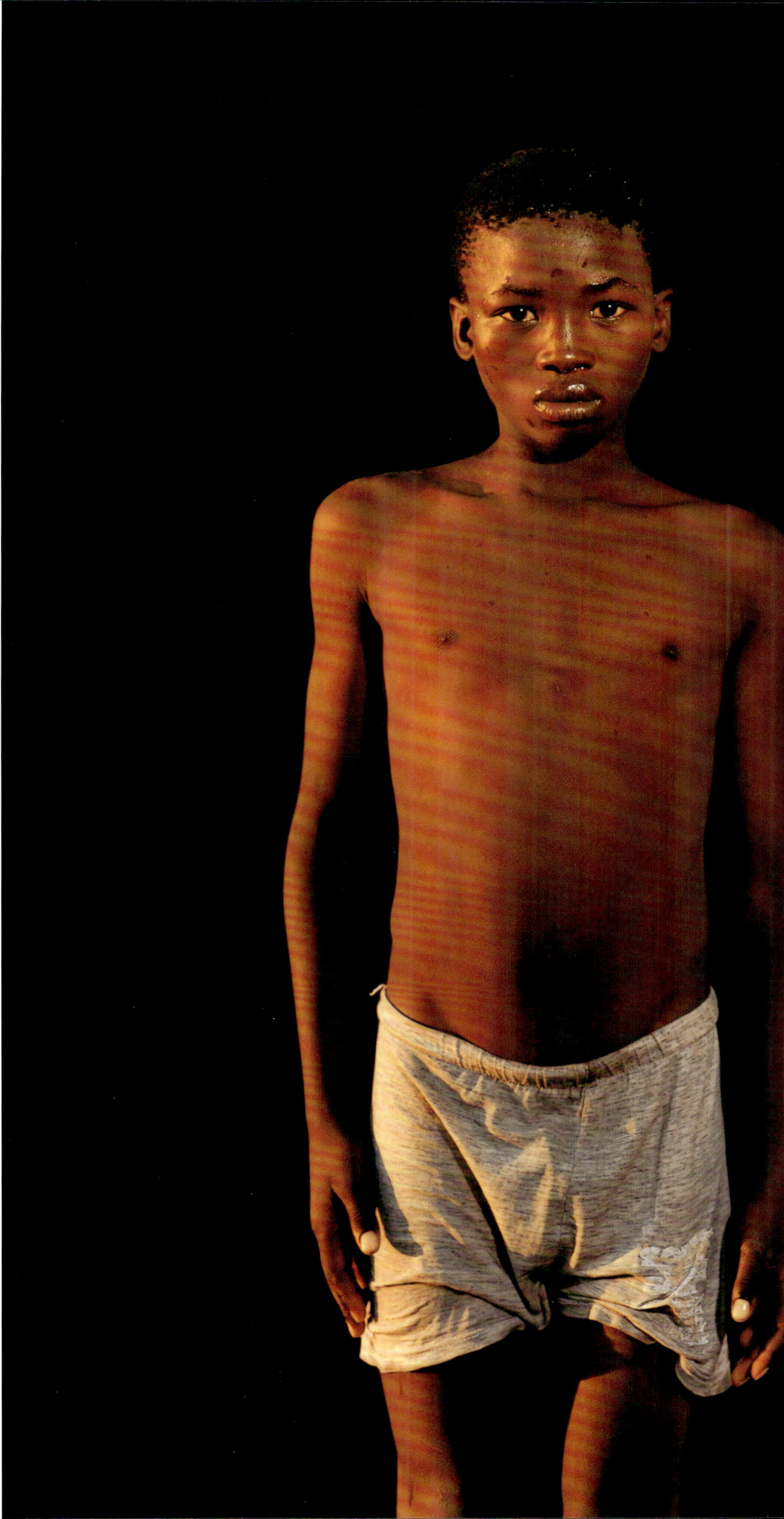

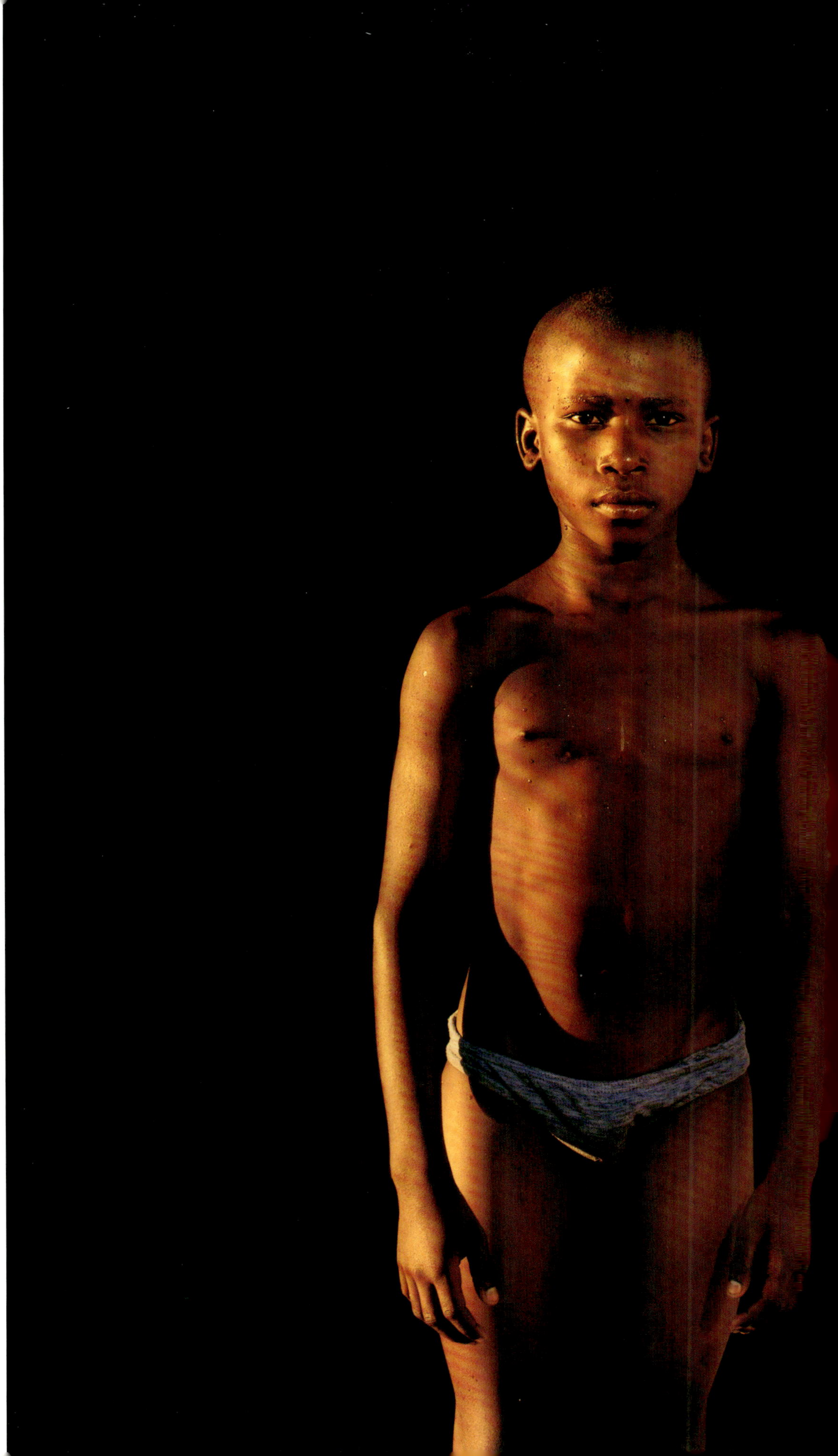

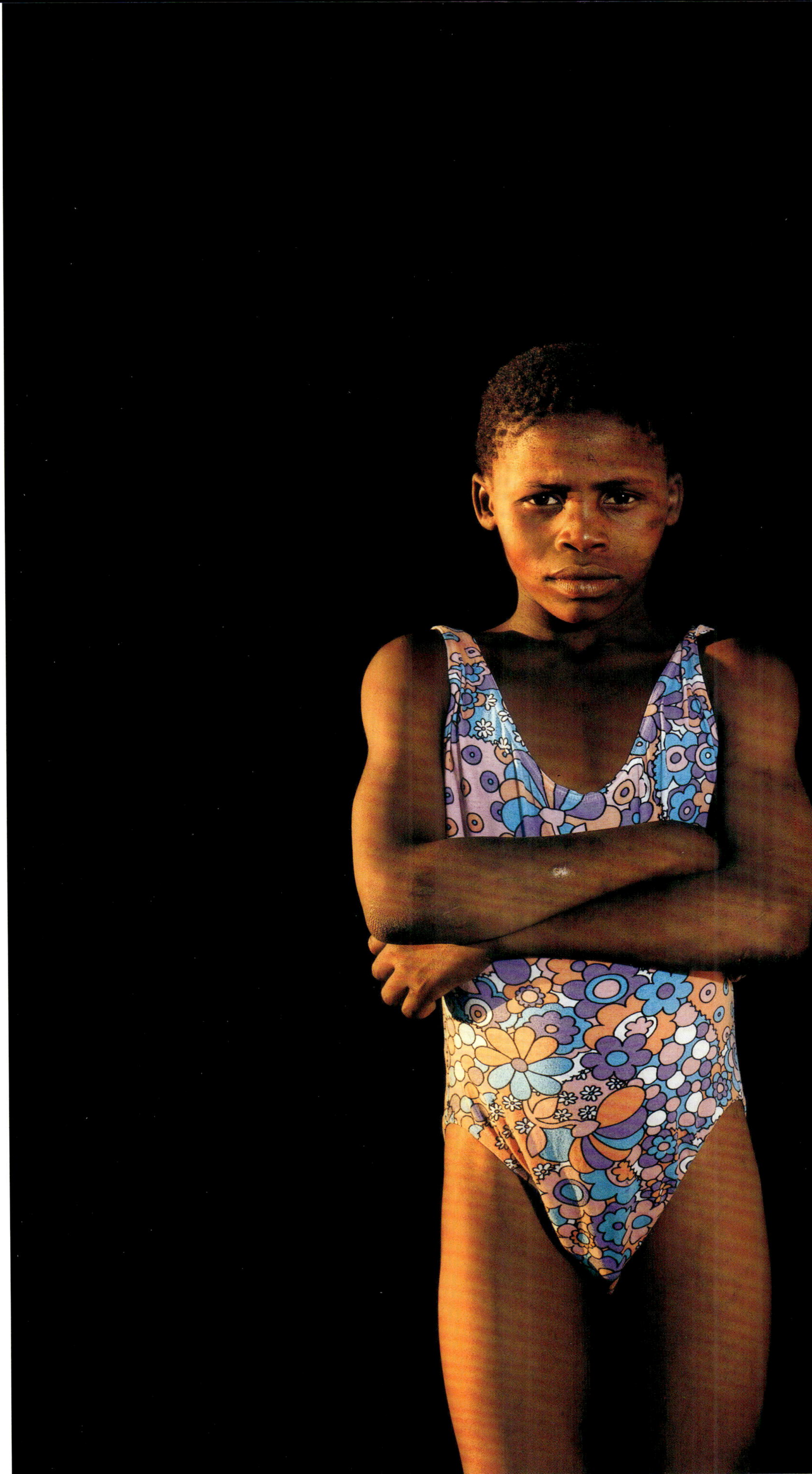

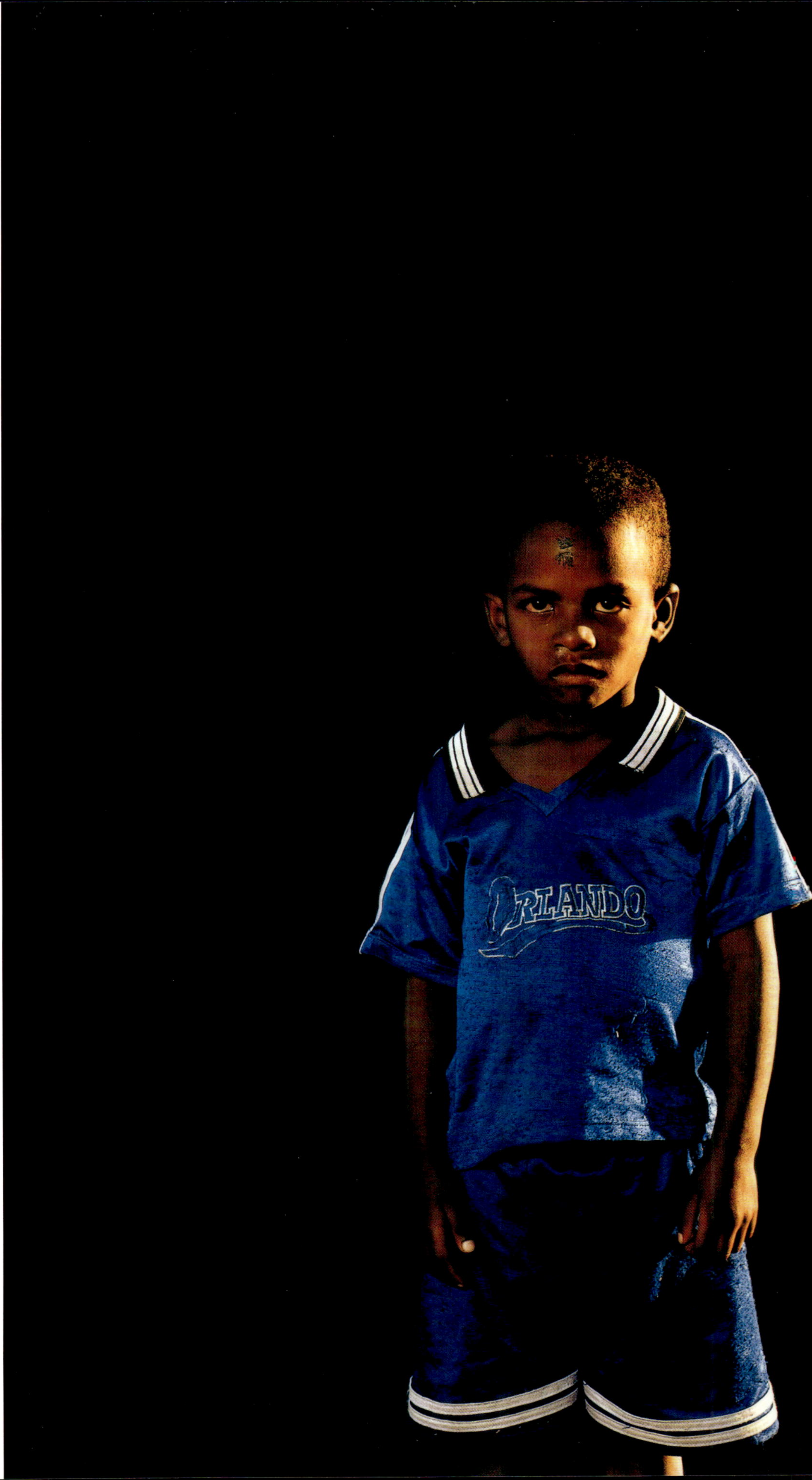
ORLANDO

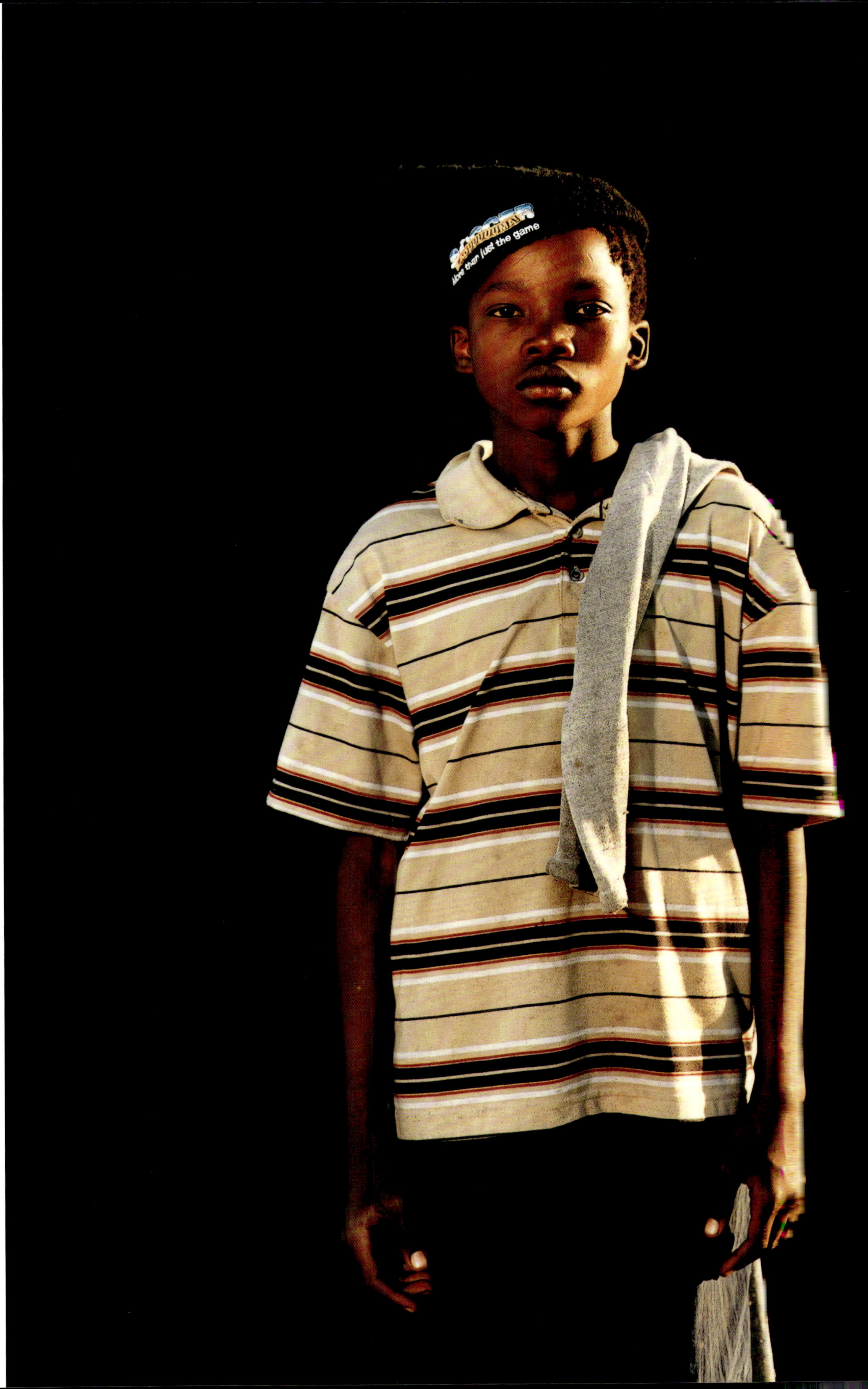
More than just the game

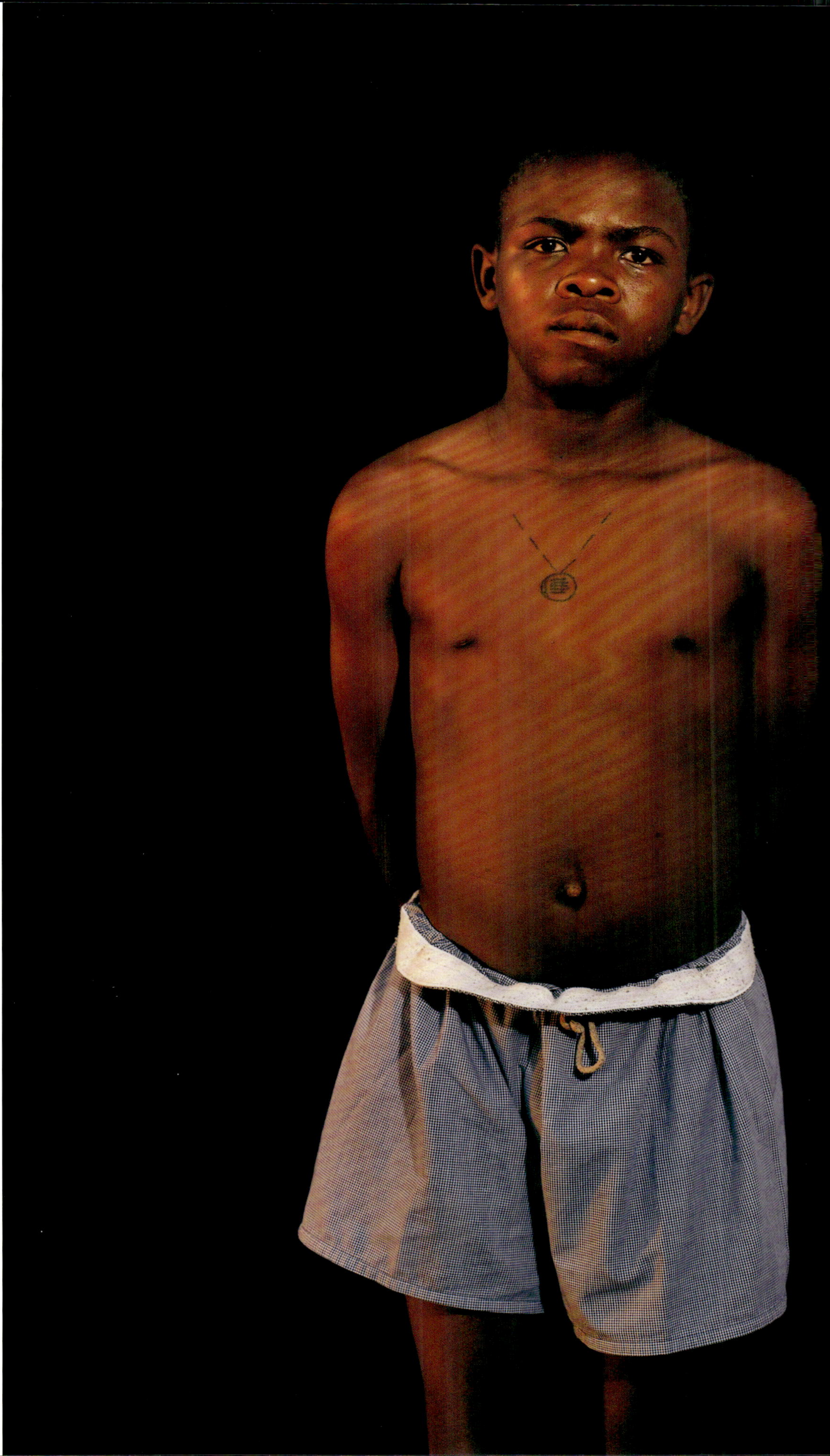

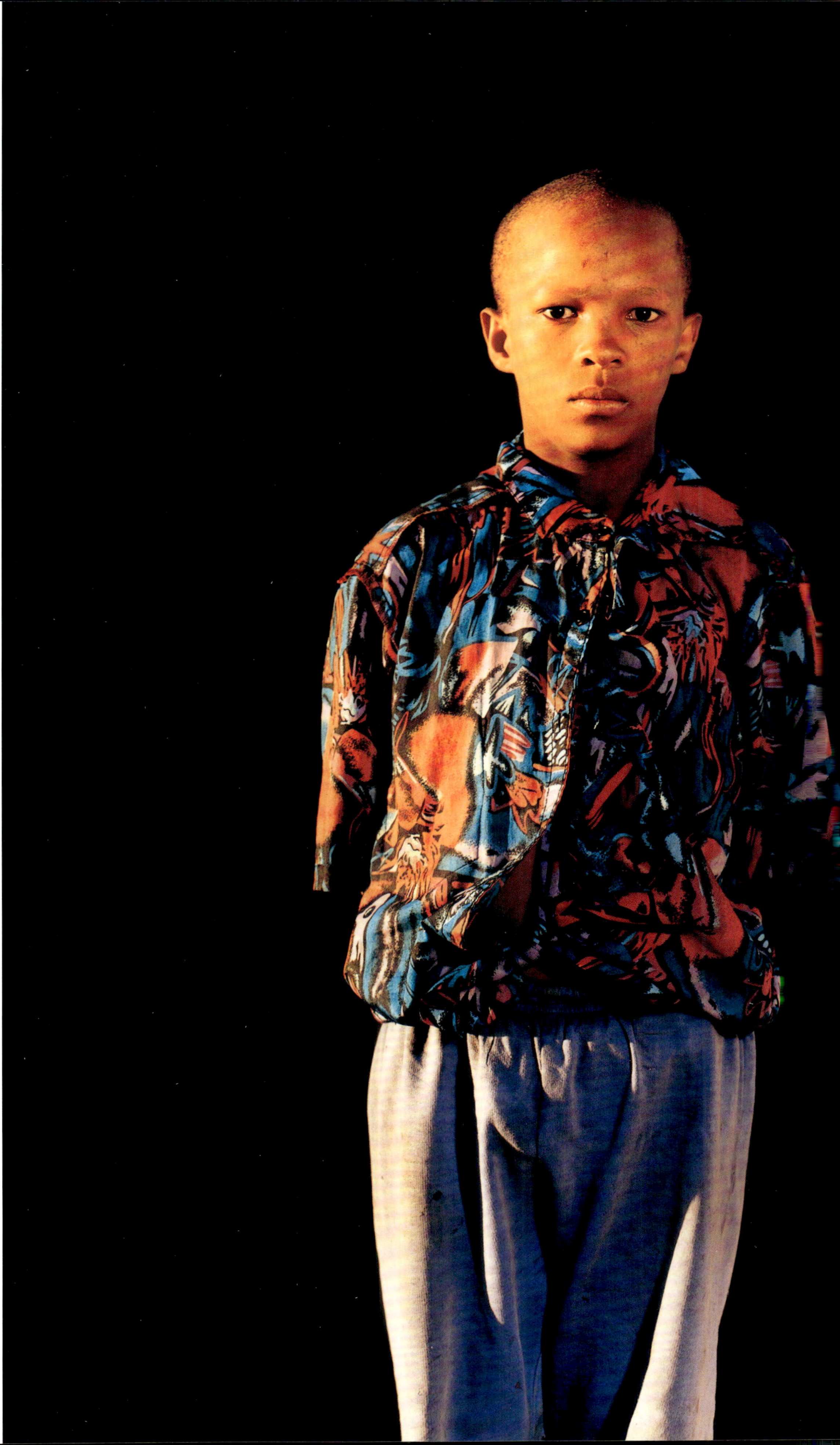

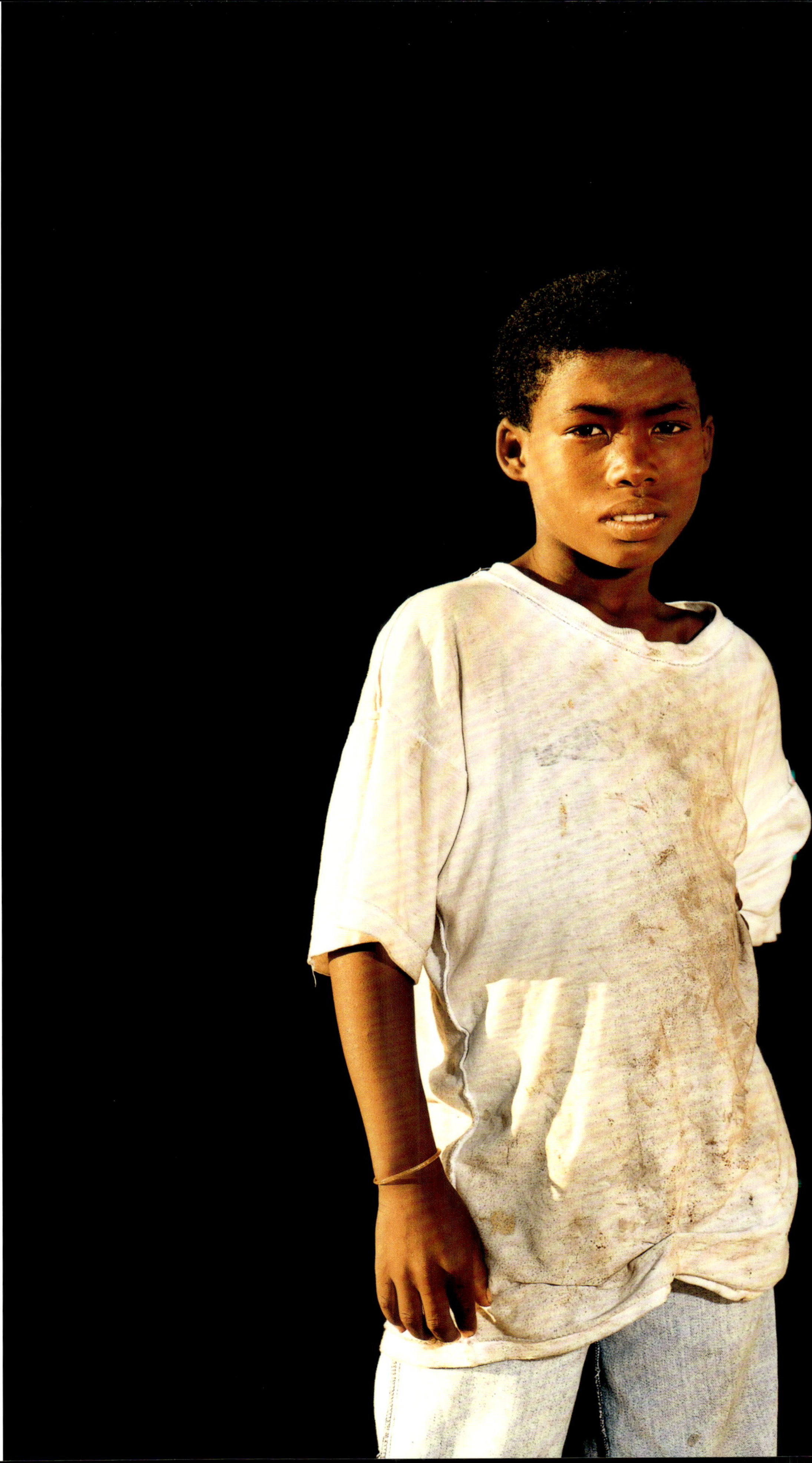

1

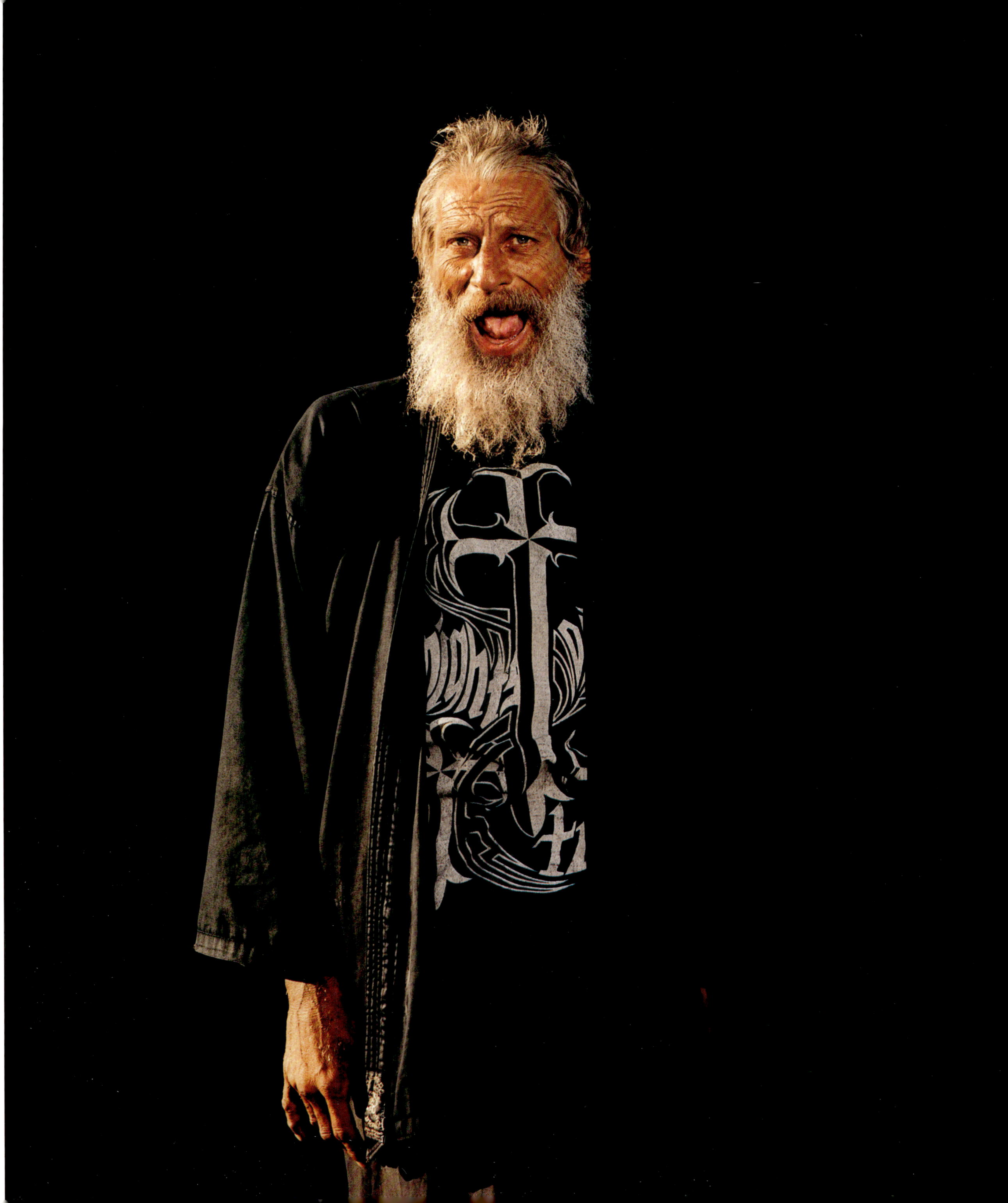

1

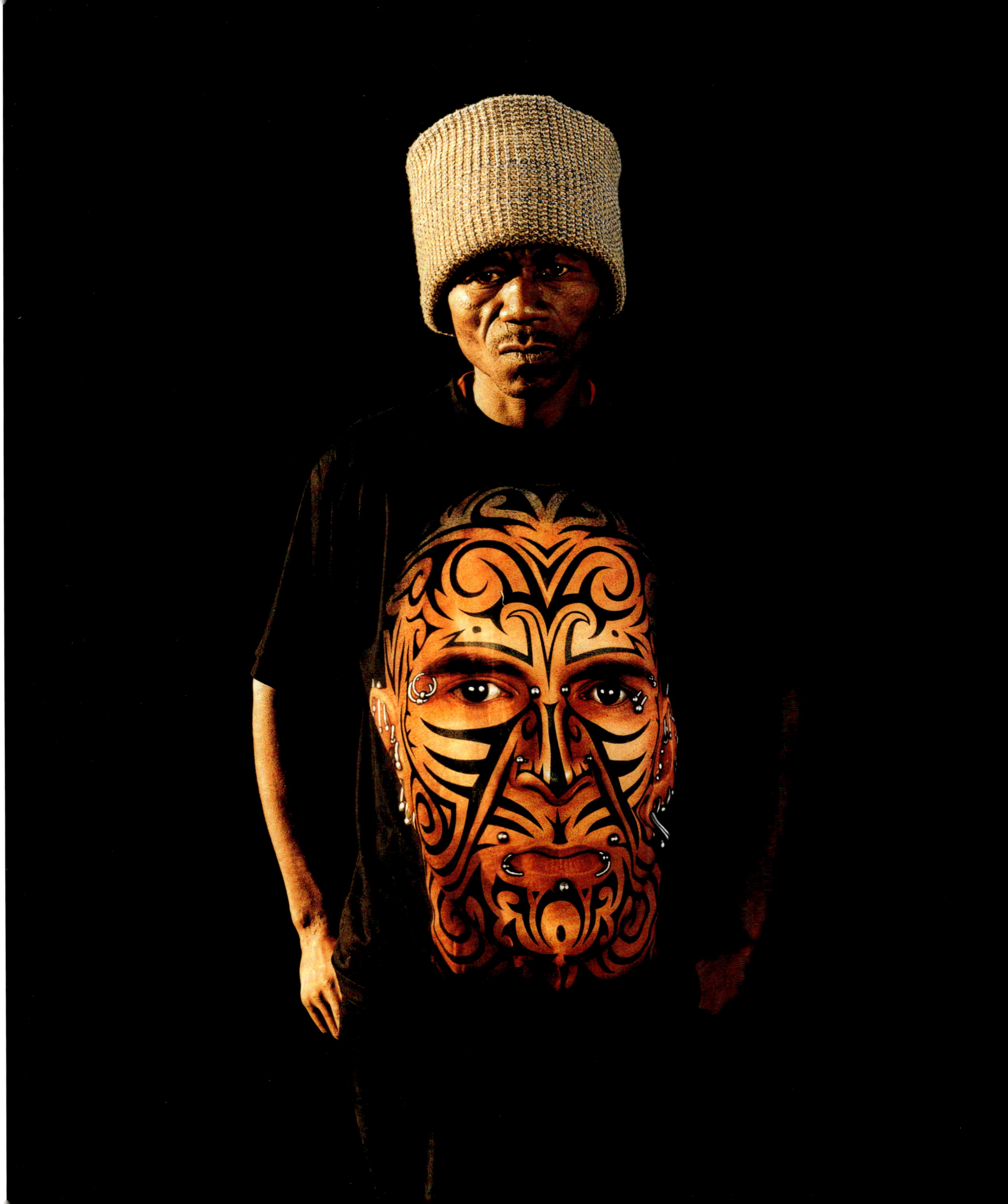

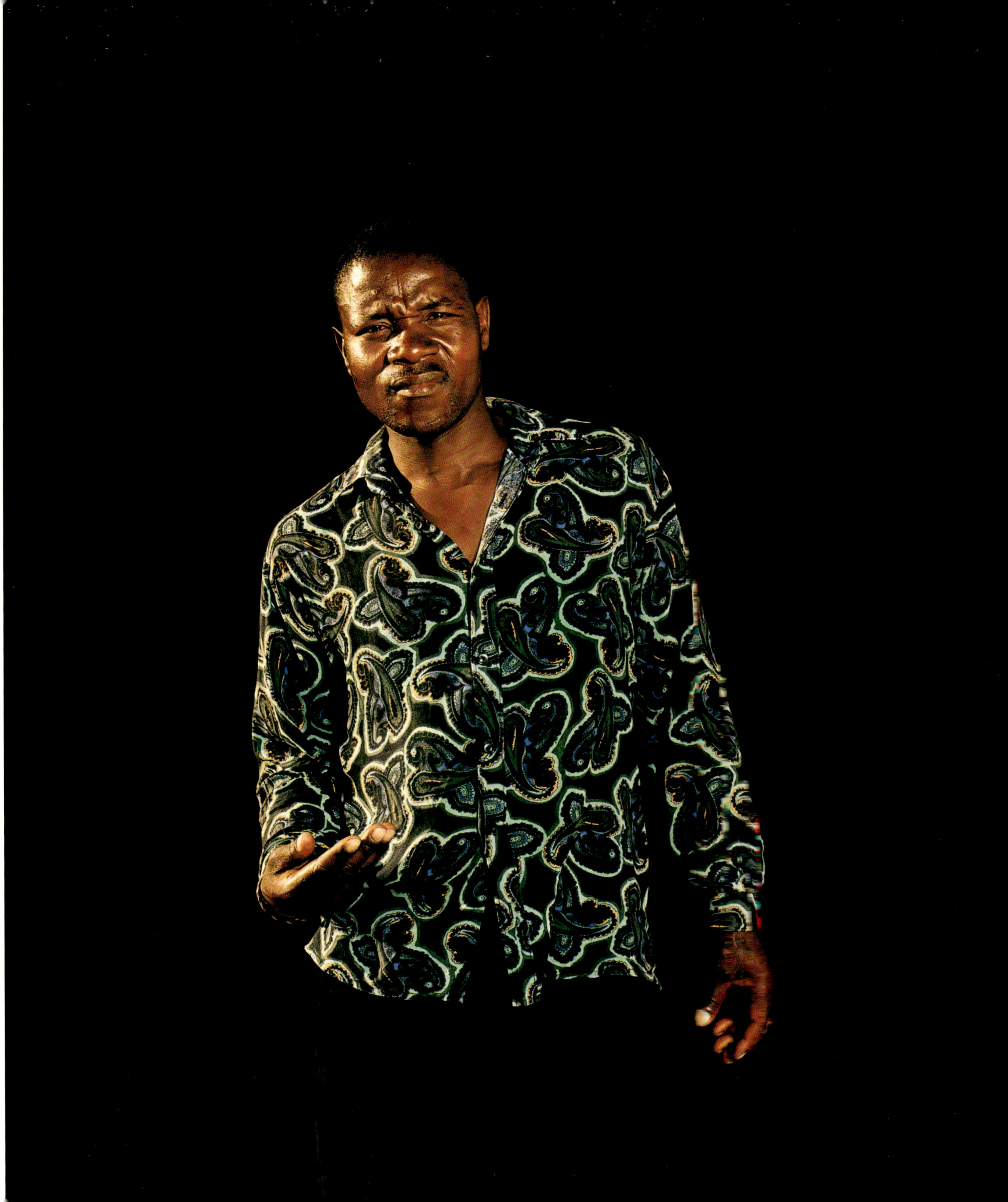

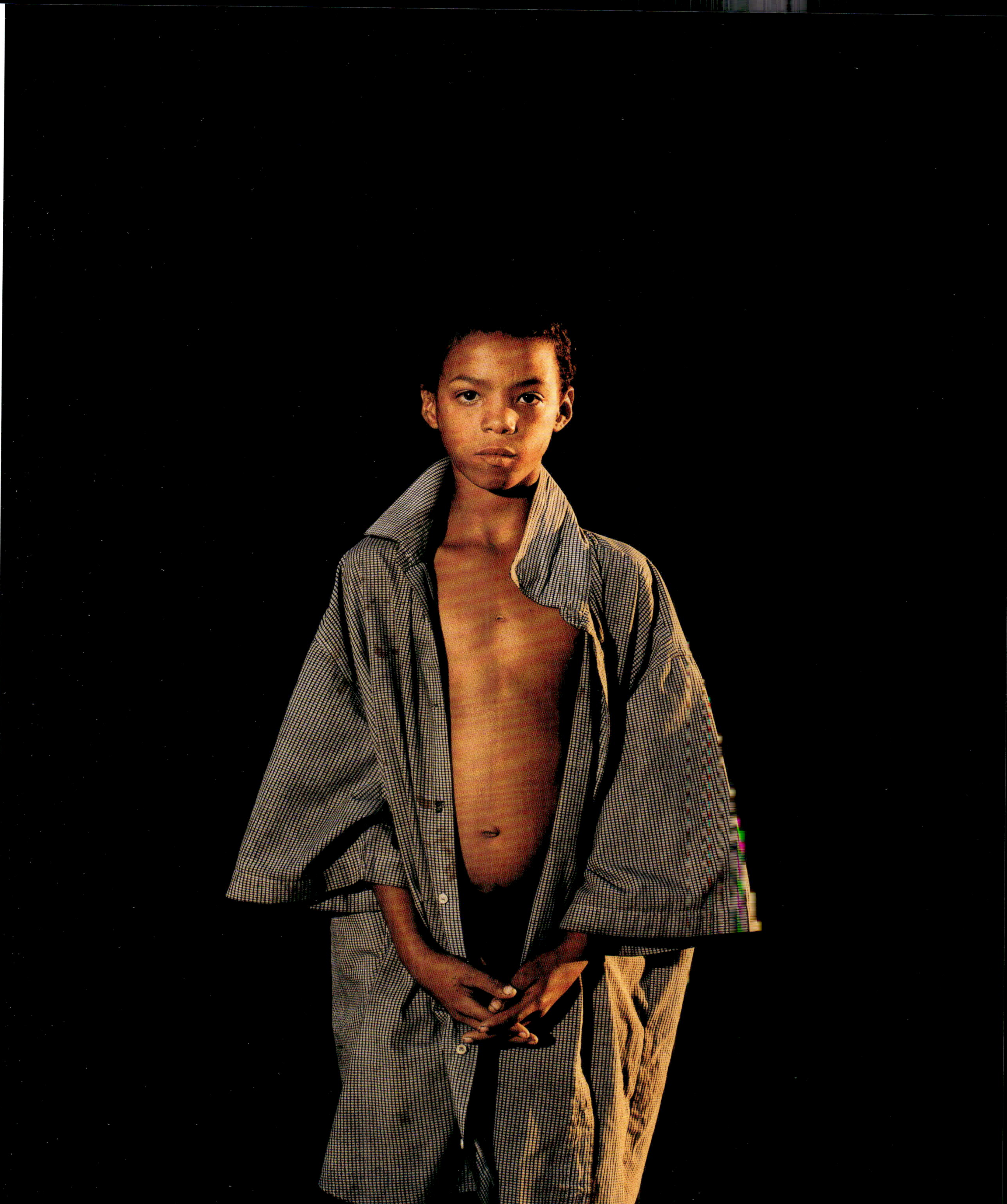

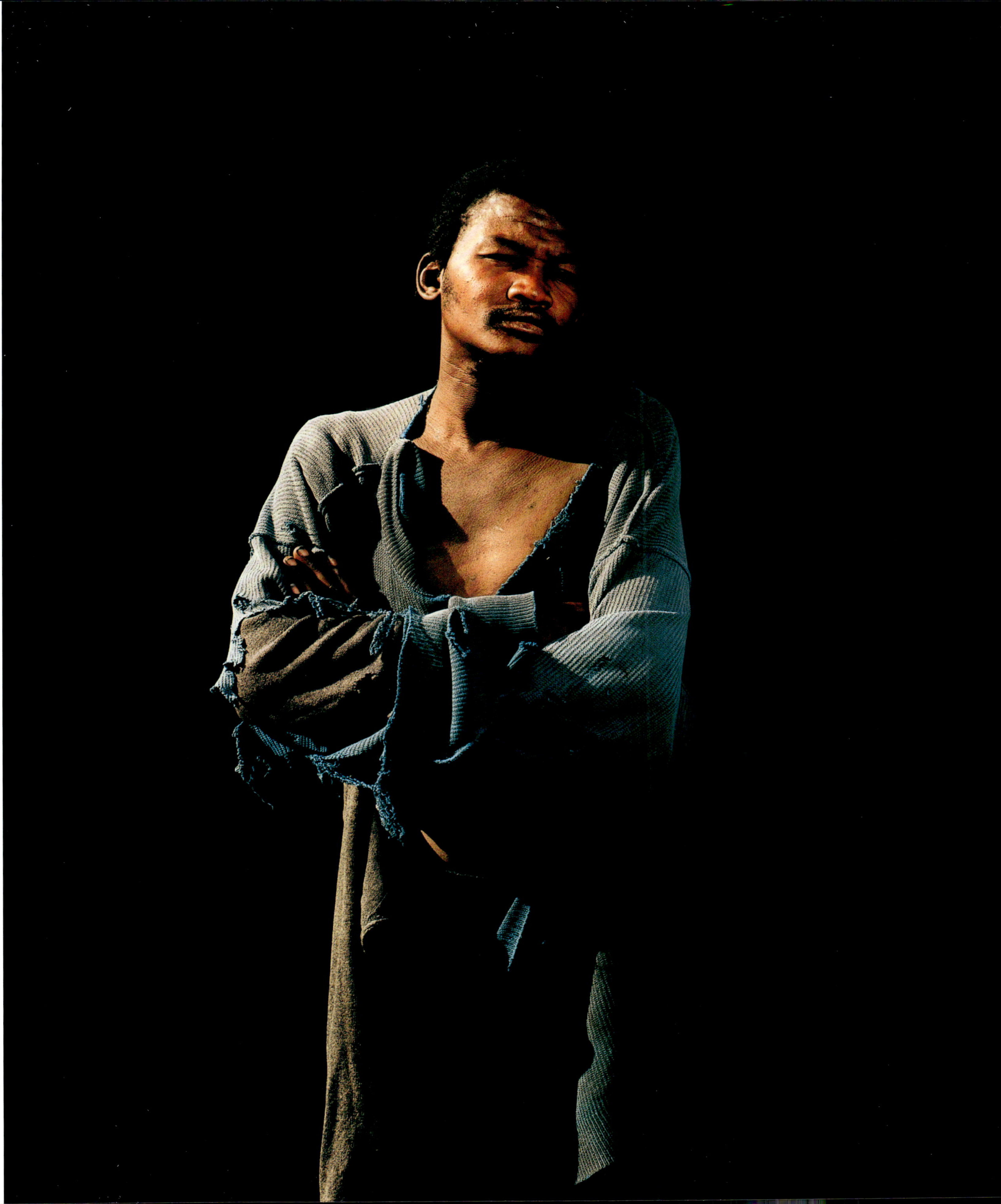

1

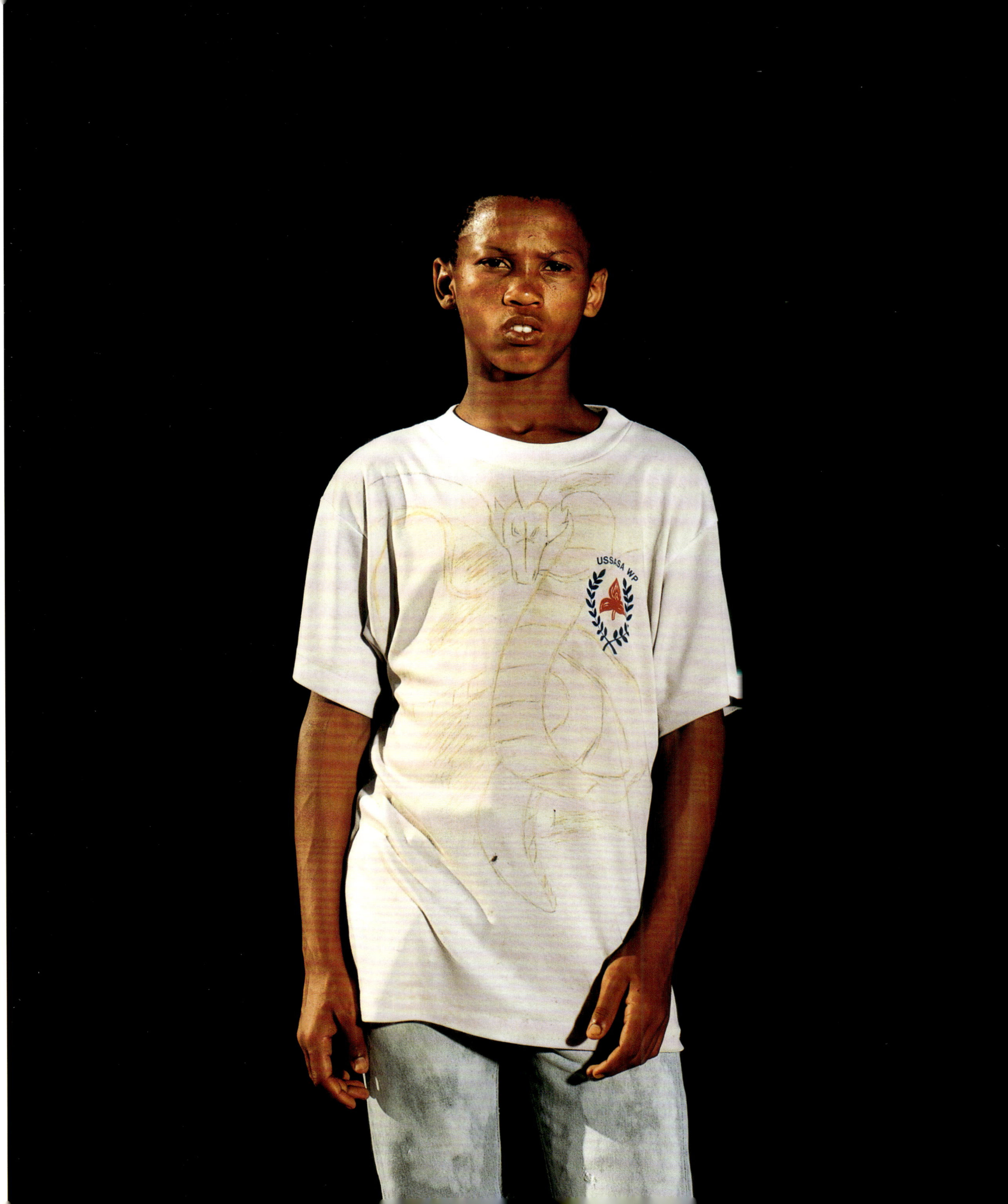
USSASA WP

1

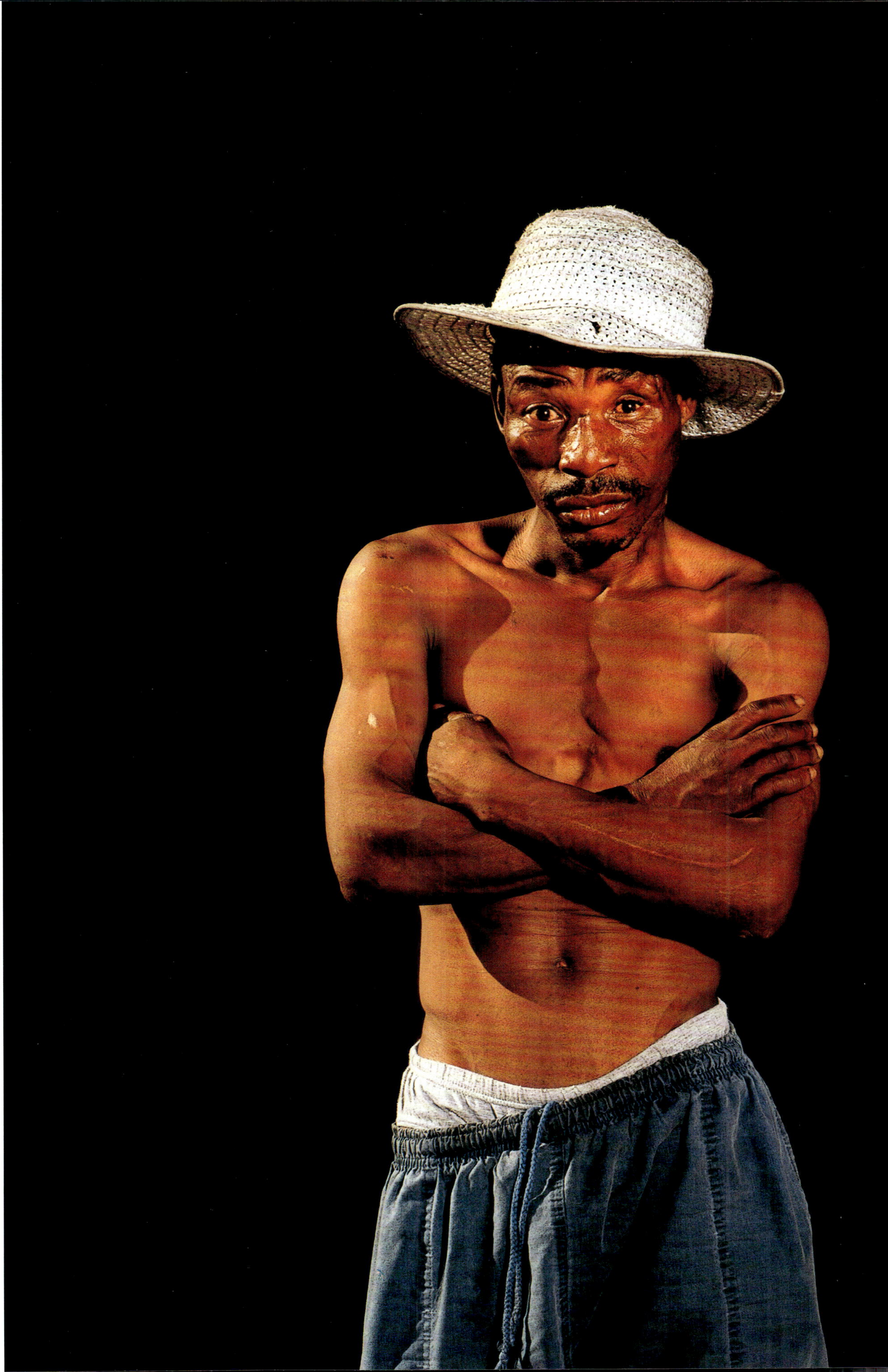

1

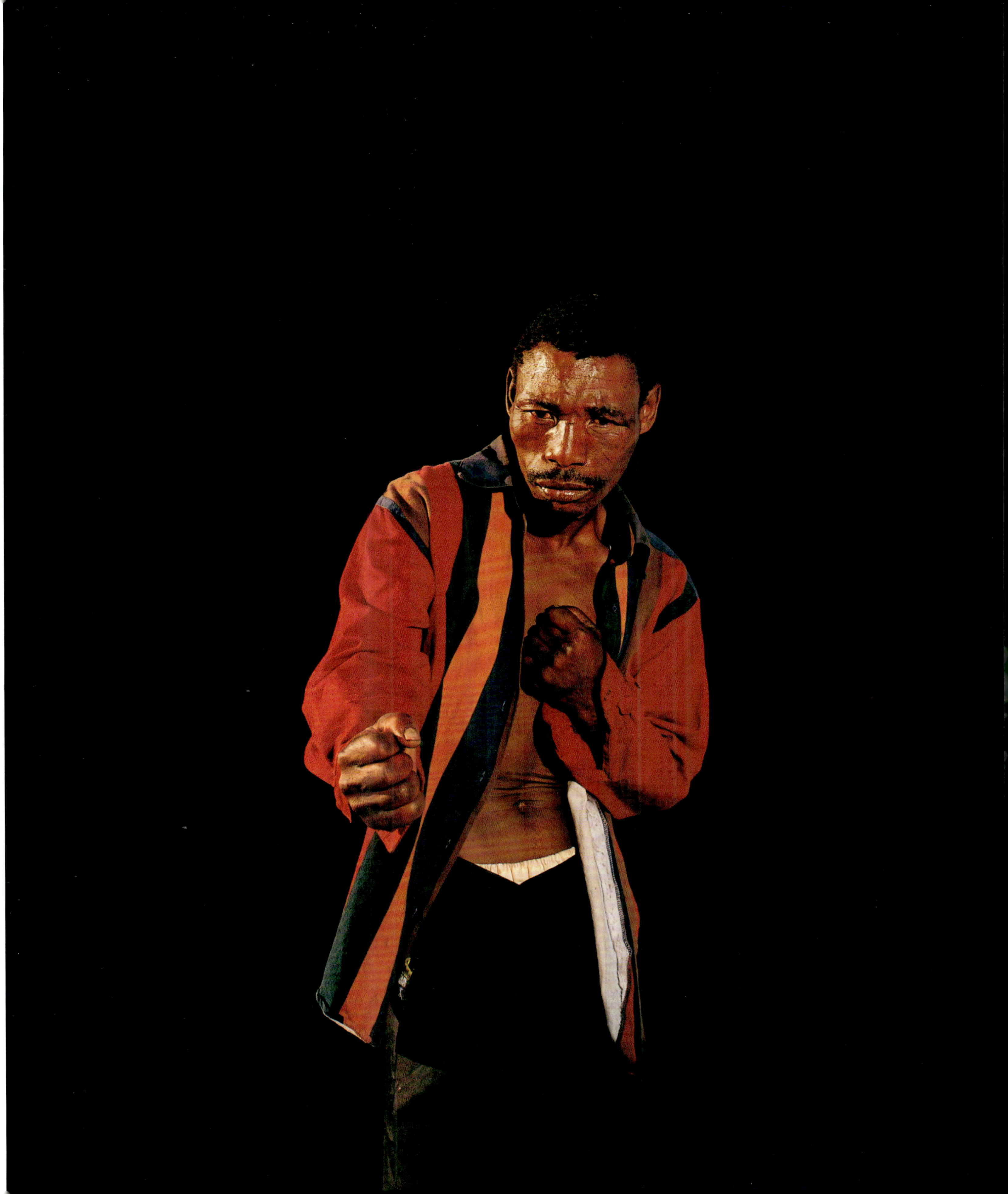

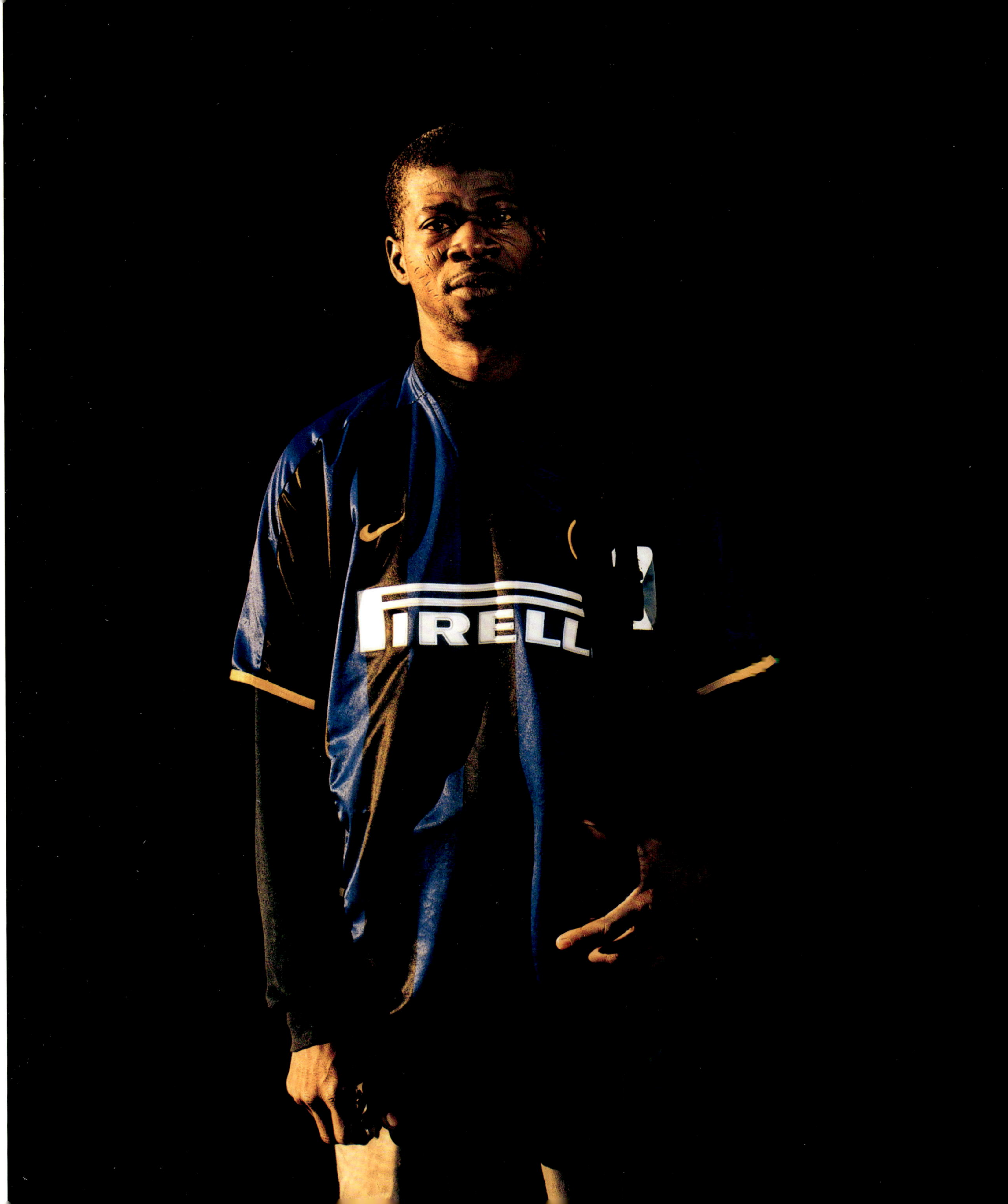

7

LIVE LONG
ALISON GREEN

It is well known that the invention of still photography made portraiture democratic. Whereas painted portraits had belonged to the very rich, within a few years of the invention of the camera demand for photographic portraits exploded. Some measure of this is revealed in the claim made by one New York photographic studio that it was taking up to a thousand portraits *a day* in the 1850s.

Now we are used to being photographed all the time, whether without our knowledge or explicit consent—by security cameras and the like—or informally by friends and family. A portrait, however, is a particular kind of picture, not a snapshot or a candid image. It's a rare occurrence in anybody's life, unlikely to happen by chance. When Trevor Appleson arrived on a beach or in a car park in Cape Town, set up his portable studio and announced he would be taking portraits for the next few hours, he was not short of willing subjects. Many waited a long time; some elected to queue twice. Taking his or her place in front of a black curtain, standing in the generous Cape Town sunlight, each person in turn posed for Appleson's camera, waited for the countdown and—click—the picture was made.

A portrait is different from other kinds of pictures of people because the subject has made a conscious choice to be there. There is something ritualised about the process; certain gestures, poses and expressions repeat themselves despite the individuality of the sitter. A projection also takes place. Each person considers how he or she wishes to be seen, in other words, how he or she will be seen by others. In this sense, the desire to have one's portrait taken seems connected to an aspiration to be part of history, to be indexed, catalogued, even celebrated. The film critic André Bazin noted this when he wrote that sitting for a portrait is like having the last word in an argument with death.

There is another side, however, to the notion of preserving oneself for posterity, and this is where photography becomes a tricky art—a complex agreement between sitter and photographer. In his well-known book on photography, *Camera Lucida*, Roland Barthes spends some time discussing his own experience of having his picture taken by a well-known photographer. He arrives at a fascinating idea: being photographed triggers a process of self-imitation. In his words, "once I feel myself observed by the lens, everything changes: I constitute myself in the process of 'posing,' I instantaneously make another body of myself, I transform myself in advance into an image." Barthes sees this as a kind of death, a mortification which is at odds with a different desire—to see oneself as alive. There is, he thinks, a deep mismatch between the photographic image, which is still, and the fluid state of human subjectivity. We can extend this idea to say that there is a contradiction between wanting to see oneself represented in some totality and the fact that this desire is rarely satisfied. This begins to explain why portraits are endlessly fascinating to look at. The subject wants to project his or her 'self' outward, the image we imagine for ourselves. But such control over one's representation is an illusion. In contrast, reality spills out, revealing instead what is inevitably flawed or vulnerable about the person you're looking at.

From another perspective, the process of being represented has two senses. First, there is being turned into an image (a picture) and second, there is counting, or mattering. In many cases, Appleson photographed people who are otherwise not seen—workers, gangsters, drug users, and those simply impoverished. His photographs show us people at the moment they present themselves for the camera, and the politics of this is important. Appleson's space is neutral; everyone has the potential to be equal there. And yet, although Appleson's photographs are replete with the economic and social life of their South African setting, they are not a political art, but nor do they make politics into something aesthetic. They create a space for self-representation and lead us to the specific, and therefore human, realities to be found there.

Originally from New York, Alison Green is a London-based art historian, critic and sometime curator.

PULLING IMAGES OUT OF THE DARK
OSSIAN WARD

The pioneering daguerrotypists of the 1830s often set up portrait studios outside—on rooftops or in the street—in order to make use of the maximum amount of daylight. Soon after the advent of portrait photography came the invention of basic lighting systems that would allow photographers to move indoors, which in turn necessitated the use of various coloured or painted backdrops, to create the illusion of naturalistic landscapes or exteriority. Certainly the studio allowed photographers to exercise greater control over their light and their images, but the growing demand for portraits meant that many early portrait photographers spent their time travelling from town to town to village, producing cheap photographs for those living outside the big cities.

The world of commercial photography—that of the studio photographer, the professional portraitist or the itinerant photographer with his bag of cameras, light stands and canvas backdrops—remains largely unsung in the history of the medium as an art form, much less even than the so-called 'amateur' photographer. However, the quirkily painted backdrops and portable photography booths of yesteryear have greatly influenced the practice of Trevor Appleson, who has carried his own modest studio around his native South Africa since 2000, setting up his temporary shoots in convenient spots where pedestrians can stop and be photographed. The sight of a compact metal frame being unfolded, erected and then covered in black cloth, whether it is on a beach, a busy dockside walkway or in a rundown suburb of Cape Town, is usually enough to attract the attention and curiosity of his potential subjects. Appleson invites passers-by to pose as they would for a formal portrait, except here there are no props, no trappings of status or standing and no idealising constructions of identity—they are just told to be themselves.

The ubiquitous high-street photography studio, with its shop window full of soft-focus babies cuddling soft toys or preened teenagers flashing toothy grins, fulfils a similar function to the eighteenth-century society portrait painter in that it provides the opportunity to commission an image of oneself for posterity. The traditional role of a private, indoor photography booth differs radically from the open-air, public scenario of Appleson's peripatetic portraiture. In fact, the action of parting with money for a portrait is not only refused in the artist's free-for-all approach, but the contract is often reversed when Appleson hands over a modest cash incentive to the less well-off volunteers or a donation to a local outreach programme to benefit the street kids. This system has more in common with the hiring of models for commercial photography, although obviously his portraits refute advertising's standard notions of beauty and there is no corporate client to appease. Consequently, Appleson has no duty to represent the sitters in any prescribed way or to leave behind any physical evidence of his intervention. Almost as soon as he has arrived and set up his nomadic studio, he has packed up and has gone again—mirroring the fleeting action of the camera's shutter and its ability to capture a discrete, finite aperture in time.

From the 1920s to the 1950s a grumpy, dour professional photographer—who mysteriously changed his name from Mike Meyer to Mike Disfarmer in the middle of this period—took thousands of portraits at his unprepossessing photographic studio, mainly of locals and visitors to the remote farming community of Heber Springs in Arkansas. "He wasn't friendly or talkative," remembered one sitter. "Instead of telling you to smile, he just took the picture," said another. "No 'cheese' or anything. You didn't even know when the picture was taken." Although Disfarmer's enclosed and intimidating studio space does not relate to Appleson's outdoor arena for portrait-making, there is a close visual correlation between the centrally composed compositions and dark draperies visible in both, as well as in the disquieting intensity of the expressions of many of their sitters. Despite documenting so many birthdays, engagements, graduations and anniversaries, Disfarmer's famously frosty nature perhaps explains his clients' alternately stony-faced or petrified appearances; maybe his lack of engagement meant they were caught unawares and unprepared for the instantaneous act of self-presentation. Some of Appleson's characters also glare, scowl or exude indifference. However, this is more a reflection of each individual's personality than of the artist's lack of rapport with his sitters, given that after his initial enthusiastic interaction with a new subject, Appleson quickly distances himself and gets down to the business of taking the picture, creating an ambiguous insider/outsider relationship with his subjects (as Disfarmer did also), to which we will return in due course.

Apart from the passing resemblance in composition and associated methodologies, what these two disconnected practitioners really share is the tacit objective of portraying 'community'. The inhabitants of Disfarmer's small-town backwater—categorised into men, women, children, military, families and couples—would surely have receded into anonymity were it not for his act of mass portraiture, just as Appleson seeks to document loose groupings of his own devising that would not otherwise exist. Although the beach-goers, homeless people, students, fruit-packers, policemen, security guards and bank clerks in Appleson's series of photographs do not conform to a strict typological study of a tribe or a specific collection of people, his project recalls August Sander's monumental undertaking began in the 1920s, *People of the Twentieth Century*, in which he grouped around 600 portraits of fellow Germans under seven archetypal categories: *The Farmer, The Skilled Tradesman, The Woman, Classes and Professions, The Artists, The City* and *The Last People*. Sander's aim, "to see things as they are and not as they should or could be", also applies to Douglas Huebler's conceptual project, *Variable Piece 70*, begun in 1971, in which he intended to "photograph the existence of everyone alive".

Any photographic inventory of human beings falsely presupposes that society can be envisaged as a comprehensible totality, but this did not stop Victorian anthropologists and ethnographers from attempting to photograph and 'collect' whole peoples in order to classify them by race, creed and colour. The typological classifications developed in physiognomy, criminology and ethnography that assisted colonial expansion in the nineteenth century would return a century later with the introduction of apartheid in South Africa in 1949. Under the Population Registration Act, all South Africans were classified as white, coloured or Bantu (the apartheid name for Africans), although the imprecise term 'coloured' led to eight new categories as defined by the Coloured Proclamation Act of 1959 and, subsequently, to some notorious and ridiculous tests, including one in which a pencil was twirled in a person's hair to see whether or not it sprang back into place, thereby determining their racial identity. Such attempts at ethnic categorisation were ultimately futile, as Appleson's project confirms. In this monograph, for example, it is unclear whether some of the ten or so white faces among the approximately 100 portraits might not actually be of mixed-race heritage and would thus have corresponded to one of the eight apartheid definitions of 'coloureds' which included 'Cape Coloured', Muslim, Chinese, Indian and 'Other Coloured' (the actual demographics suggest that white people compose 20% of the South African population, double the percentage depicted in this book). However, rather than a means of assisting the colonisation and enslavement of people, photography during apartheid instead became a weapon to challenge social and political oppression in South Africa, through the work of the so-called 'Struggle' photojournalists, such as Peter Magubane.

Since the beginning of the end of apartheid in 1990, contemporary South African photographers and artists have been seeking an antidote to representations of black South Africans as victims of apartheid or as political insurgents within their own country. Zwelethu Mthethwa's portraits of shantytown residents taken throughout the 1990s were an attempt to redress the balance of harsh, desolate black-and-white documentary photography by presenting colourful, uplifting imagery of South Africans, or as he says of his own work: "Colour restores people's dignity. I think these photographs preserve and show a humanness of the occupants in their private spaces. They restore their pride and affirm their ownership." The subjects of Mthethwa's portraits still appear poor because of their cramped living conditions and informal interiors constructed from advertising hoardings, yet his depictions are sympathetic to the sitters and perhaps in some way enact a redefinition and rehumanising of the official terminology 'coloured'. Much of this empathy in Mthethwa's work can also be found in Appleson's practice, because he too is bound to his subjects through a shared nationality—despite the fact that Appleson was categorised as white under the terms of apartheid.

Diane Arbus once noted the difficulties of ingratiating herself with her subjects: "If I were just curious, it would be very hard to say to someone, 'I want to come to your house and have you talk to me and tell me the story of your life'. I mean people are going to say 'You're crazy.' Plus they're going to keep mighty guarded. But the camera is a kind of license. A lot of people, they want to be paid that much attention and that's a reasonable kind of attention to be paid." As an insider, rather than an outsider as Arbus often found herself, Appleson uses his camera as a licence to investigate South African identity and representation, irrespective of his racial difference. Despite the fact that Appleson has photographed perhaps 1,000 people who are grouped to some degree by their similarities—for example in their uniform, in their employment or lack thereof—in many ways his work celebrates their difference.

Within the first 20 images of this book there appears: a wild-eyed homeless man wearing a tweed dress and a paint-spattered blue jacket, a small blond boy carrying his dog, four female bathers, a beachcomber with a sorry-looking quarter of watermelon and a beefy boat skipper baring his chest. The bizarre cross section of characters that makes up the various *Beaches* series partly arose because some images were shot on poor neighbourhood beaches while others were taken in more affluent locations such as Cape Town's Clifton 4th Beach, but it is also a measure of the multiplicity and incongruity of the individuals that make up South African society. Similarly, among the many portraits in the *Uniforms* series are poignant details of individuality from the varying blues, greens and greys of the shipbuilders' overalls to the different school logos and crests emblazoned on tracksuits, blazers and gym outfits. The repetitive nature of *Uniforms* is a vehicle of intensification for dissimilarity; there is endless difference in this sameness.

Although the clothing, gestures, postures and expressions mark all of Appleson's subjects out as individuals, they are still bound together by their nationality as well as by a less obvious kinship with one another—their relationship to the dark background of the portable studio.

Appleson's title '*Free Ground*' is an English translation of an Afrikaans word 'Vrygrond', which is the name of one of the most memorable locations for his portable studio portraits. Vrygrond is the oldest unofficial conglomeration of settlements and homes in the Cape area and sits on the beach, facing False Bay on the east coast of the peninsula. It was supposedly gifted to local fishermen and their families in the 1930s by an Italian aristocrat landowner, literally given as 'free land'. Under apartheid, however, the area was declared public land, meaning that the inhabitants no longer had any legal rights to dwell there. A hardcore of Vrygrond squatters avoided this persecution and continued to live in their makeshift tin and wood shacks on the beach, albeit with the more-or-less constant threat of eviction hanging over them. In 1996 the Cape Town City Council agreed to allow the 7,000 or so settlers constitutional rights to live on the land, but made no efforts to provide them with electricity, water or sewage facilities.

Given its origin and the economic impossibility of truly 'free' land, *Free Ground* could be read as ironic or absurd. However, it is better interpreted as an optimistic pronouncement on post-apartheid South Africa, as well as being a metaphorical musing on the specific nature of Appleson's process of portraiture. In fact, the etymological origins of the word 'photography', literally meaning 'light writing' in Greek, is especially apt for *Free Ground*, because for each shoot Appleson sets up his roving studio for just one hour at sunrise and one hour at sunset, to avoid the harsh light of the day.

In 1994 South Africa was reborn and could be said to have become free ground once more. Since only 12 years have passed since then, it is still an extraordinarily young democracy by Western standards. This miraculous revolution and the heroic leadership of its idol, Nelson Mandela, should not mask the many issues that have yet to be dealt with in this fledgling nation: poverty, housing, corruption, HIV/AIDS, employment discrimination and land reattribution are just a few. Also, the country is still emerging from the mire of apartheid in artistic terms. There are still very few artists of the stature of Mthethwa or William Kentridge visible on the international circuit, partly due to South Africa's absence of almost 27 years from the Venice Biennale (to which it was finally invited back in 1993), and the geographical inaccessibility of its own contemporary art platforms such as the Johannesburg Biennial.

Appleson's work does display the occasional mark of overt Africanicity: one man proudly wears a lion's-head print on his shirt, another sports a green and yellow Cameroonian national football team shirt, a flash of traditional batik or 'Dutch wax' fabric is seen on the skirt of a woman holding a young brightly dressed child, while one white woman's bathing suit is emblazoned with orange and black tiger stripes. Yet, there are also confusions of national boundaries and signs of globalisation in one man's T-shirt of a Maori warrior from New Zealand complete with traditional face tattoos, and another's print of Reggae superstar Bob Marley, who was a symbolic figure for African unification and development but spent most of his life in Jamaica and the UK. Unlike the work of the revered mid-century Malian studio photographer Seydou Keita, who used various backdrops such as fringed bedspreads or heavily patterned textiles draped behind his subjects, which emphasised the specific condition of being African, Appleson's backdrop is inscrutably-pitch black, a tabula rasa, or even a conceptual free ground.

"There is as much difference between us and ourselves as between us and others," said the Renaissance thinker Michel de Montaigne, about our fraught relationships with ourselves, mankind and what would later be called the 'Other'. As stated earlier, Appleson's nationality, race and peripatetic process make his relationship with his subjects a similarly ambiguous amalgam of both insider and outsider, but for most viewers his sitters really are strangers who are geographically, economically and socially removed from our everyday spheres of experience. Karl Jung believed we are all connected by the 'two-million-year-old man' within ourselves, and Freud argued, in the course of his 1919 explorations of the uncanny *Das Unheimliche*, that foreignness is within us and that we should embrace "the fascinated rejection that the foreigner arouses in us". In his use of the black background to conceal a landscape or an exterior context for each portrait, Appleson invites us to consider each person individually, to welcome both the fascination and rejection that is produced by this 'Other' and take it as an opportunity to experience our own radical differences, our own strangeness.

Rineke Dijkstra, who also makes large-scale portraits of youngsters on beaches, as well as of teenage soldiers, students and bullfighters, reveals something of her photographic 'discovery' of a person in this statement: "When I make portraits of these people, I look at them, observe them. But it's really a question of choosing the right moment. It has to do with a kind of recognition which doesn't happen consciously. It happens between them and me, and it lasts just a fraction of a second." This revelatory moment, which also applies to the viewer's experience of work by Appleson, is somehow monumentalised by the landscapes of the moody grey skylines or beaches that frame each of her subjects and makes it seem, as she says, "As though they had been sitting there forever". On the other hand, Appleson's black background heightens the immediacy of our acquaintance with each portrait, whether it is someone flexing their muscles, blowing out smoke or running their hand through their hair. In effect the darkness starkly foregrounds their natural, unforced presence.

By drastically reducing perspectival space, the trademark black curtain adds to this intense frontality and closeness with the viewer. In his *Photography: A Middle Brow Art* of 1965 Pierre Bourdieu discusses how this claustrophobic foregrounding of the portrait photograph demands a certain posture: "It is certainly possible that the spontaneous desire for frontality is linked to the most deep-rooted cultural values. Honour demands that one pose for the photograph as one would stand before a man whom one respects and from whom one expects respect, face on, one's forehead held high and one's head straight." The fixed stare of the sitter—"adopting the most conventional posture, seeking as far as possible to control the objectification of one's own image"—is best seen in Appleson's images of authority figures such as policemen and security guards. Far from signifying Bourdieu's friendly deference or a reciprocal respect, however, this stiff pose and insistent rebuttal of our gaze can actually provoke a certain unease or a contract of conflict as advocated by Jean Baudrillard: "The photographic act is a duel; that is to say, it is a challenge to the object and the object's defiance of that challenge."

Among the most defiant characters in *Free Ground* are the gangsters and homeless people whose scar-lined and substance-ravaged faces recall portraits by social documentarists such as Lewis Hine, Roman Vishniac and Jacob A. Riis, who described himself as a mediator between the horrors of the Manhattan slum and respectable society in his 1890 book, *How the Other Half Lives: Studies Among the Tenements of New York*. While early documentary photography reveals how far apart we are from the 'Other', street photographers such as Garry Winogrand and Philip-Lorca diCorcia bring us into close contact with ordinary individuals. This is even more true of Appleson who presents all of his subjects in exactly the same way, on their own 'free ground'. The flattering combination of flash and sunlight highlights the features of each face equally; none are represented as victims. *Free Ground*'s almost utopian emphasis on equality and individuality (another metaphor for recent events in South African history) is all the more interesting when considered with regard to a recent court case in which Philip-Lorca diCorcia was sued for exhibiting strangers' portraits in his 1999 series, *Heads*. Although unsuccessful, this lawsuit charts the way in which artistic expression and individual privacy rights might have an impact on future street photography, signifying a steady erosion of photographic freedom. Appleson, a sympathetic mediator, blurs the boundaries between street, documentary and studio photography through his portable, black cloth, the 'free ground'.

The blackness of the backdrop could be interpreted in numerous ways. It could represent a veil, like the black hood that traditional Victorian plate photographers would retreat underneath, which has sinister associations with the hood of Death himself. Or it could relate to Malevich's radical reduction of the act of painting to one simple black square, either "The embryo of all possibilities", as he called it, or the end point of art, as symbolised by the black squares that were draped over his hearse and used to mark his graveside. However, even though Roland Barthes was at great pains to highlight the photograph as a reminder of death—as the ultimate, modern *memento mori*—it is also an admission of the opposite: that we are alive.

In the same breath, Barthes described photography as a "kind of primitive theatre, a kind of *Tableau Vivant*", which has more relevance to the rudimentary stage set created by Appleson's portable studio, in which each person acts, pretends, performs or, in some cases, succumbs to stage fright and stands stock-still in front of the drape. The dark background also acts as a framing device (used by myriad photographers including Jeff Wall and Hiroshi Sugimoto) and as a partition, similar in function to a traditional Chinese screen which creates "a zone of emptiness in the apparent continuity of the visual world", according to Darian Leader. In fact, psychoanalyst Leader's 2002 book, *Stealing the Mona Lisa*, describes a similar phenomenon to the curiosity aroused by Appleson's roving studio in his description of the spectators flocking to see the empty space left behind after Leonardo's most famous picture was surreptitiously removed from the Louvre's wall in 1911. This non-reflective, nowhere field with no history, no language, no race and no colour allows Appleson to effectively make something out of nothing. He is pulling images out of the darkness and, more importantly, out into the light.

Ossian Ward is an editor and writer on contemporary art. Formerly editor of ArtReview, he has also been an editor at the V&A magazine and The Art Newspaper.

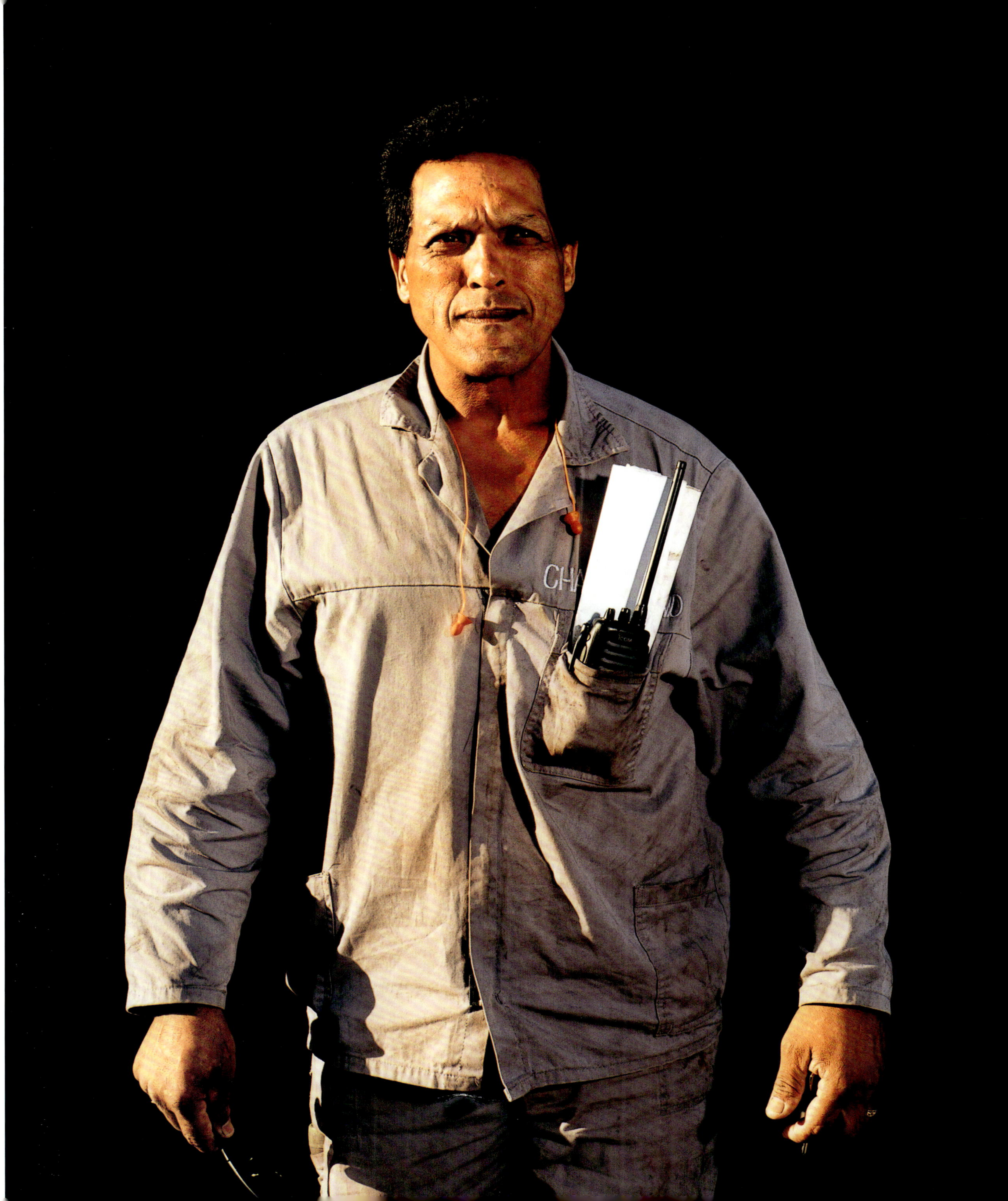

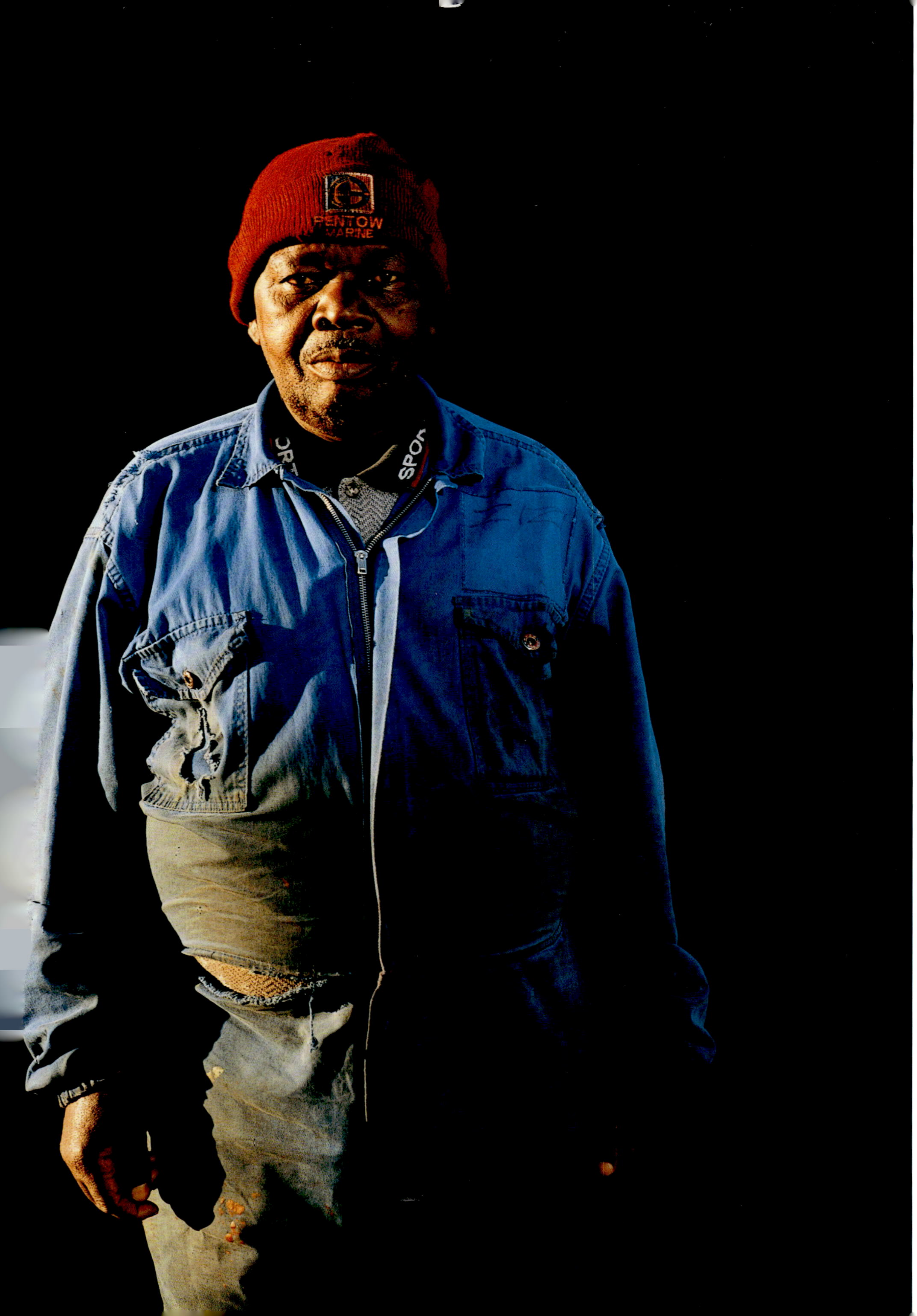
PENTOW

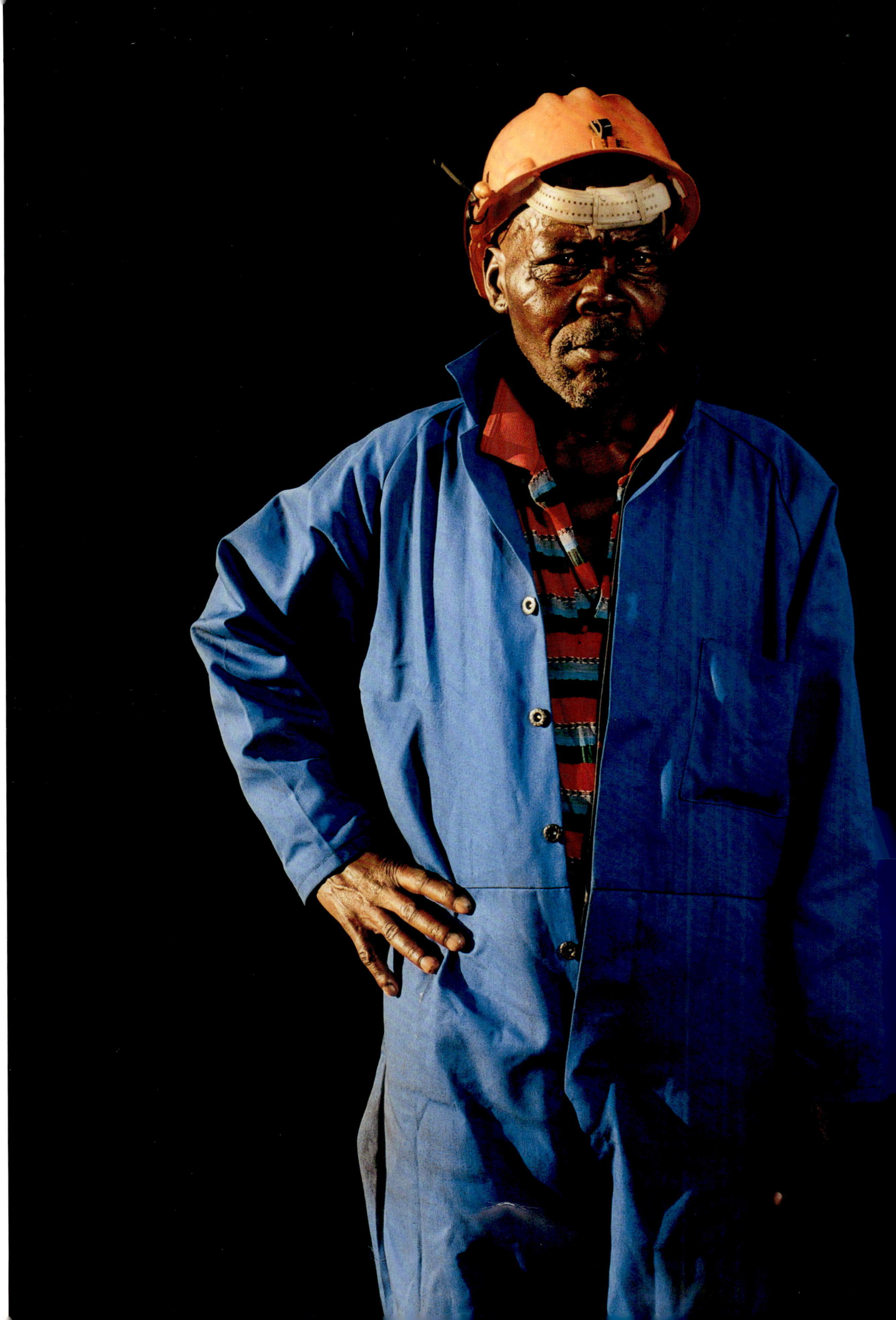

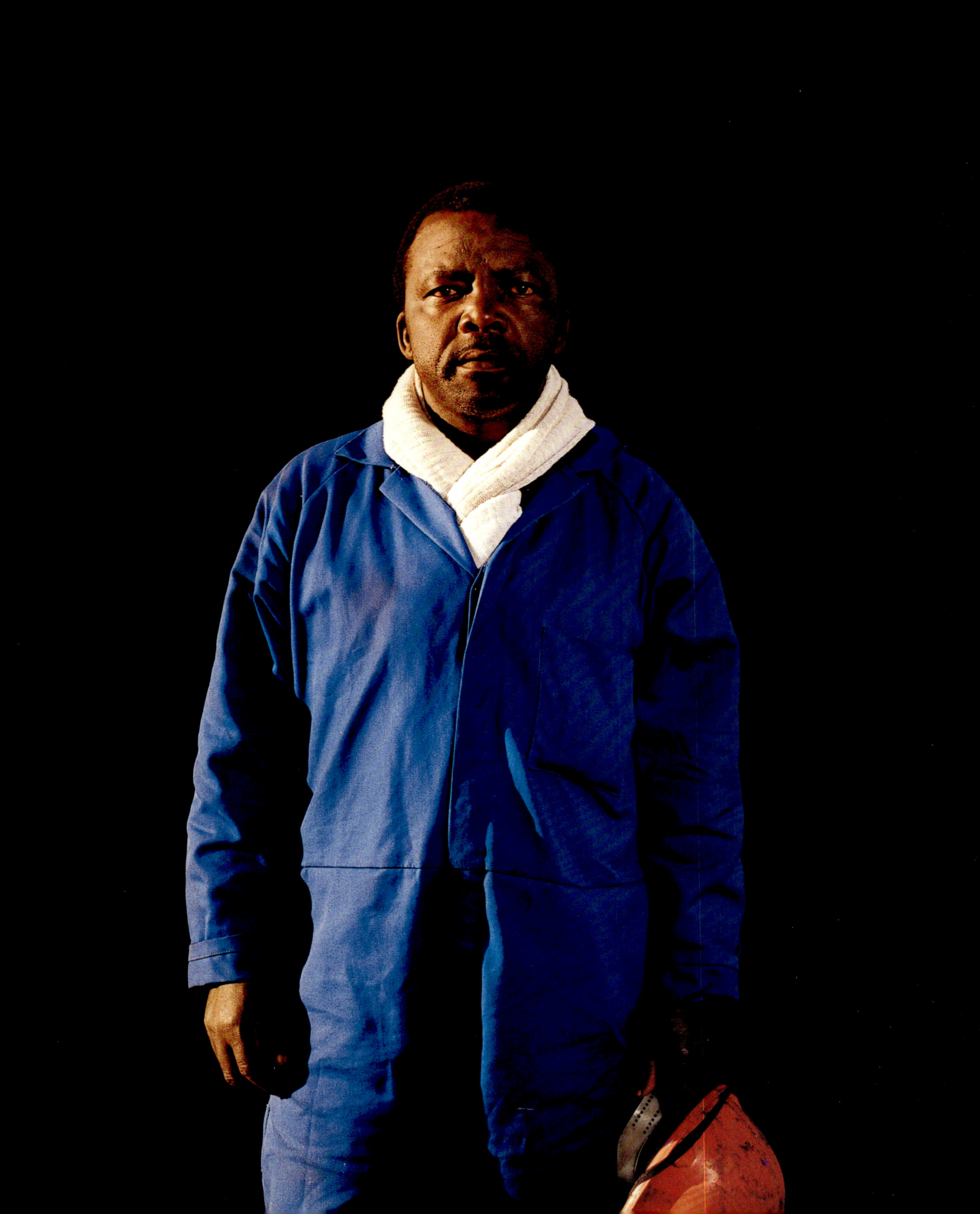

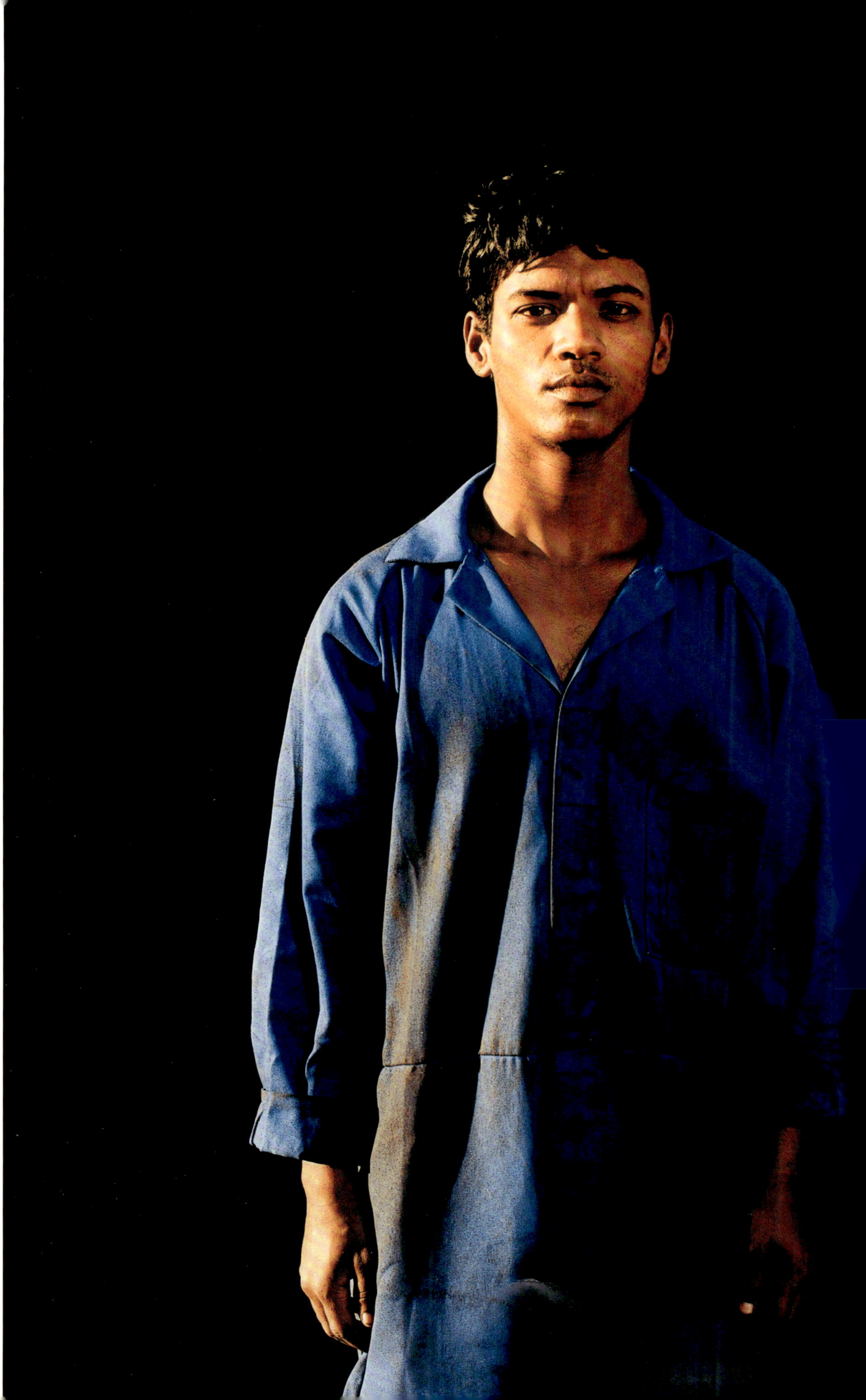

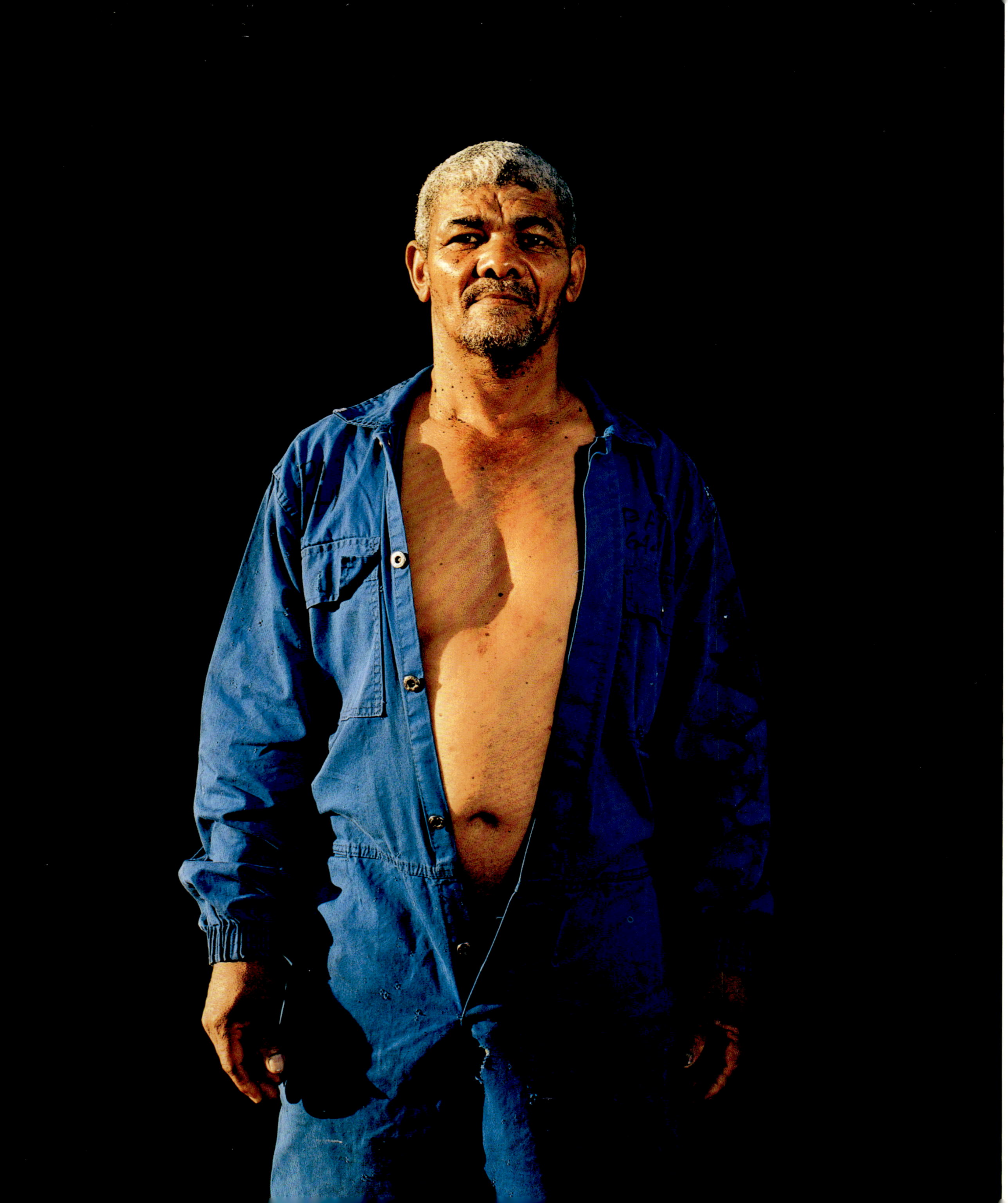

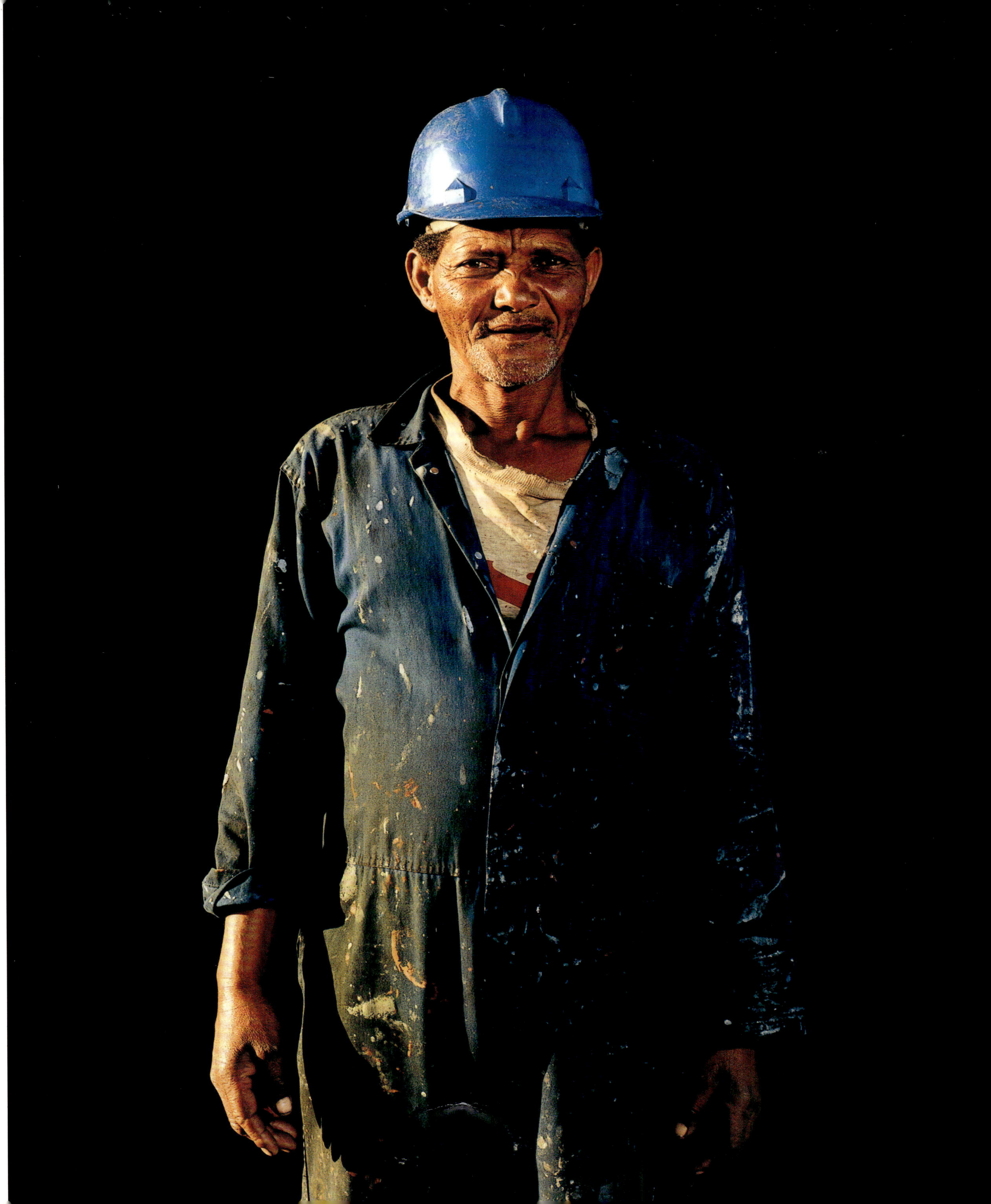

7

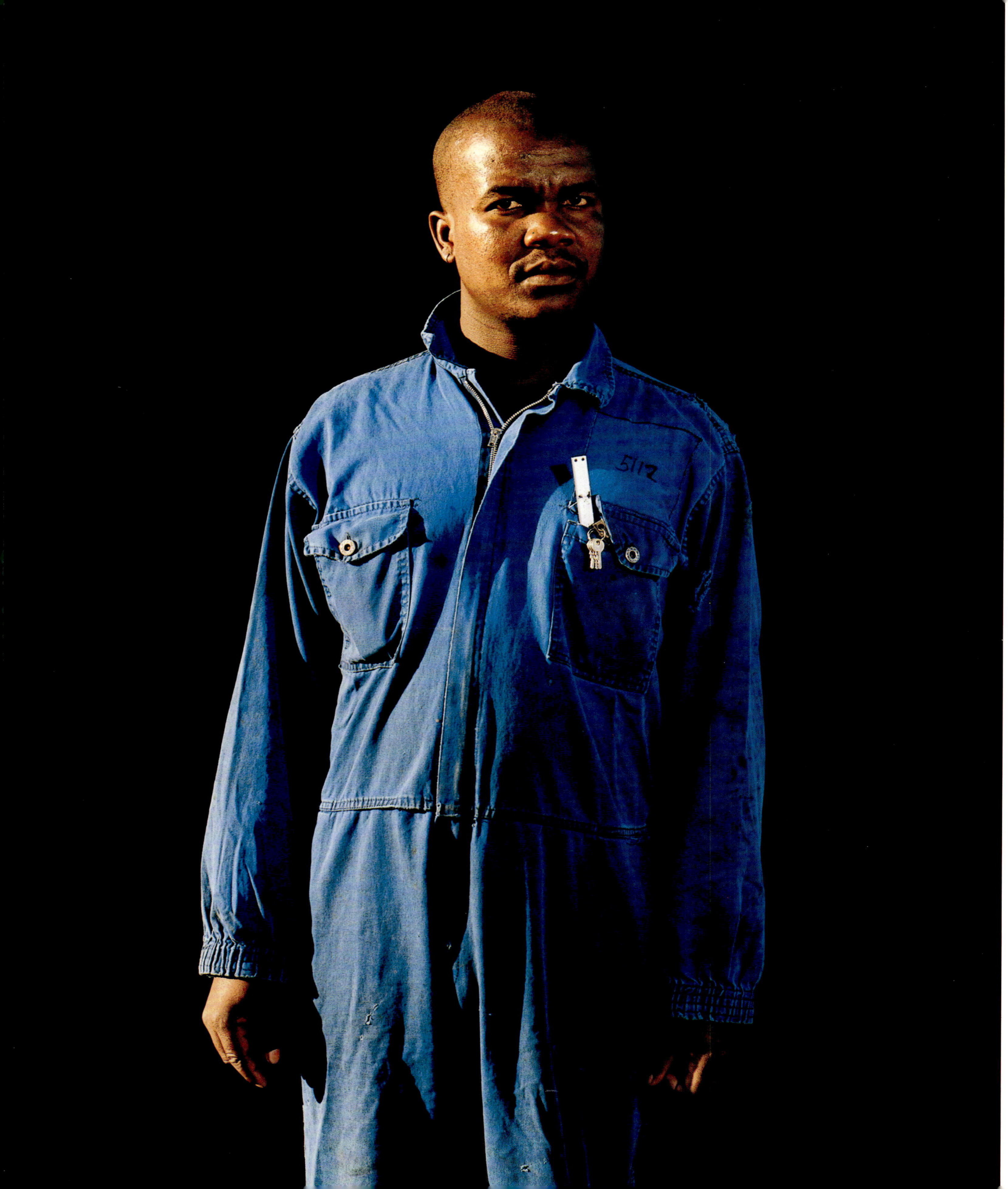
5112

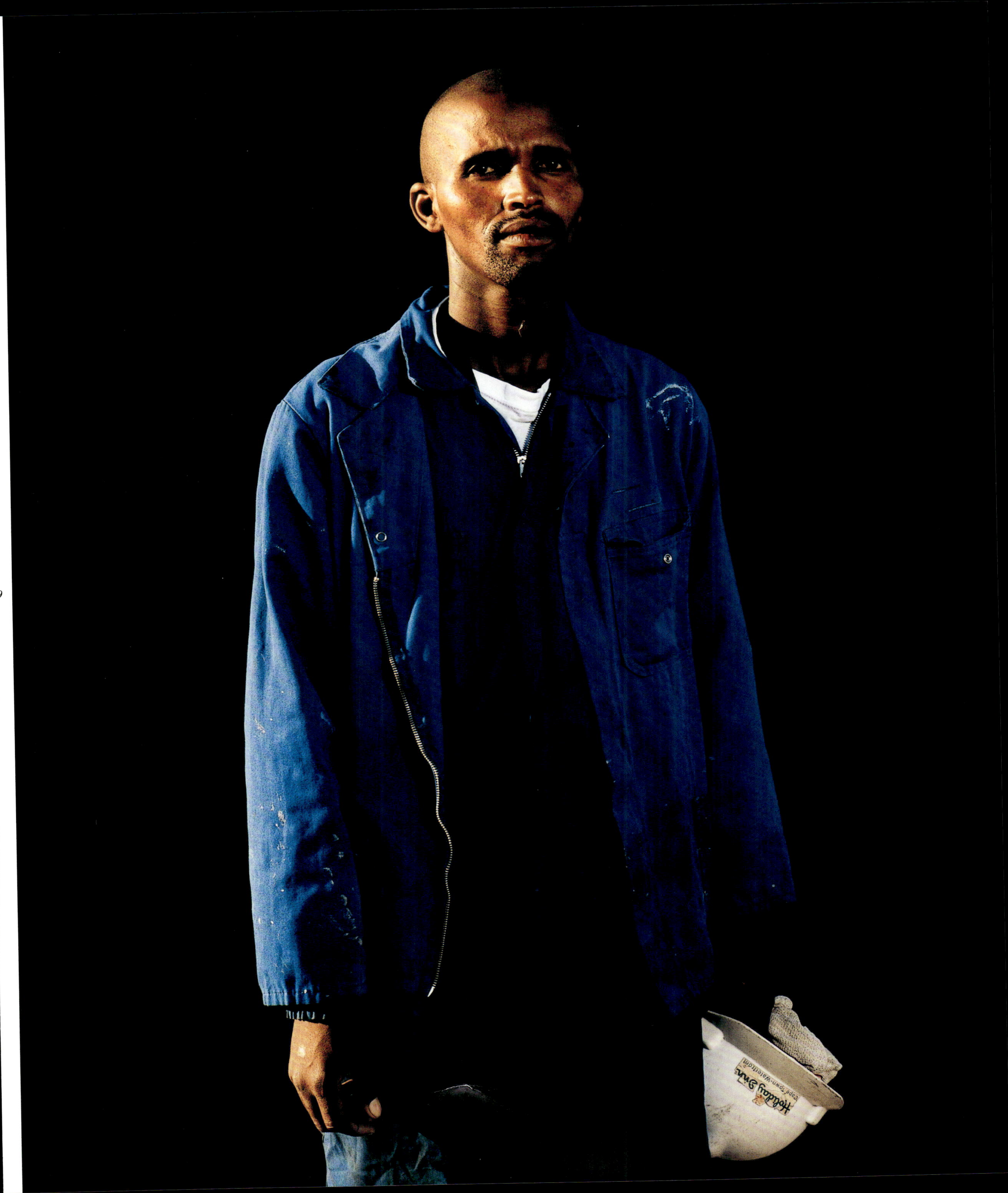

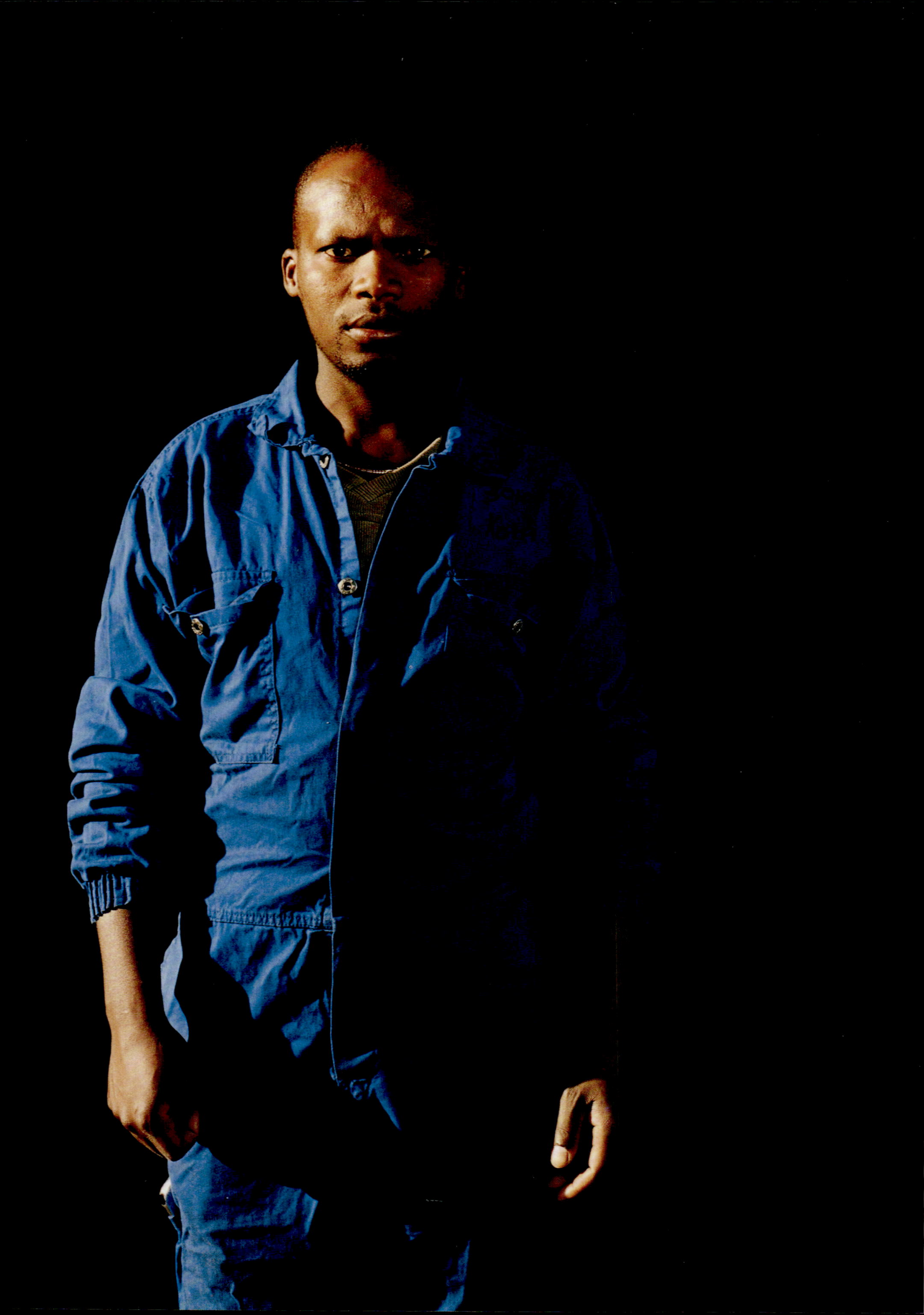

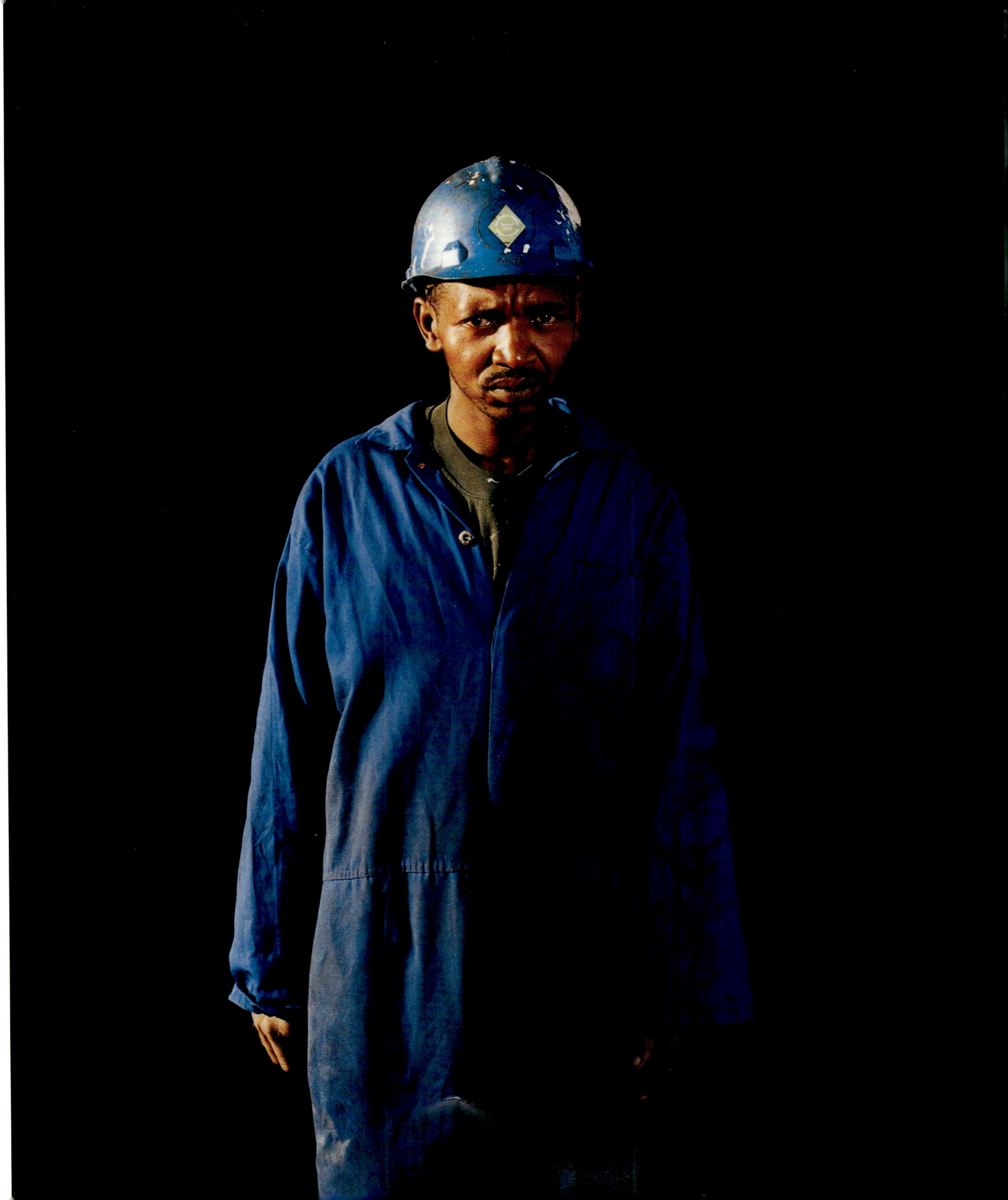

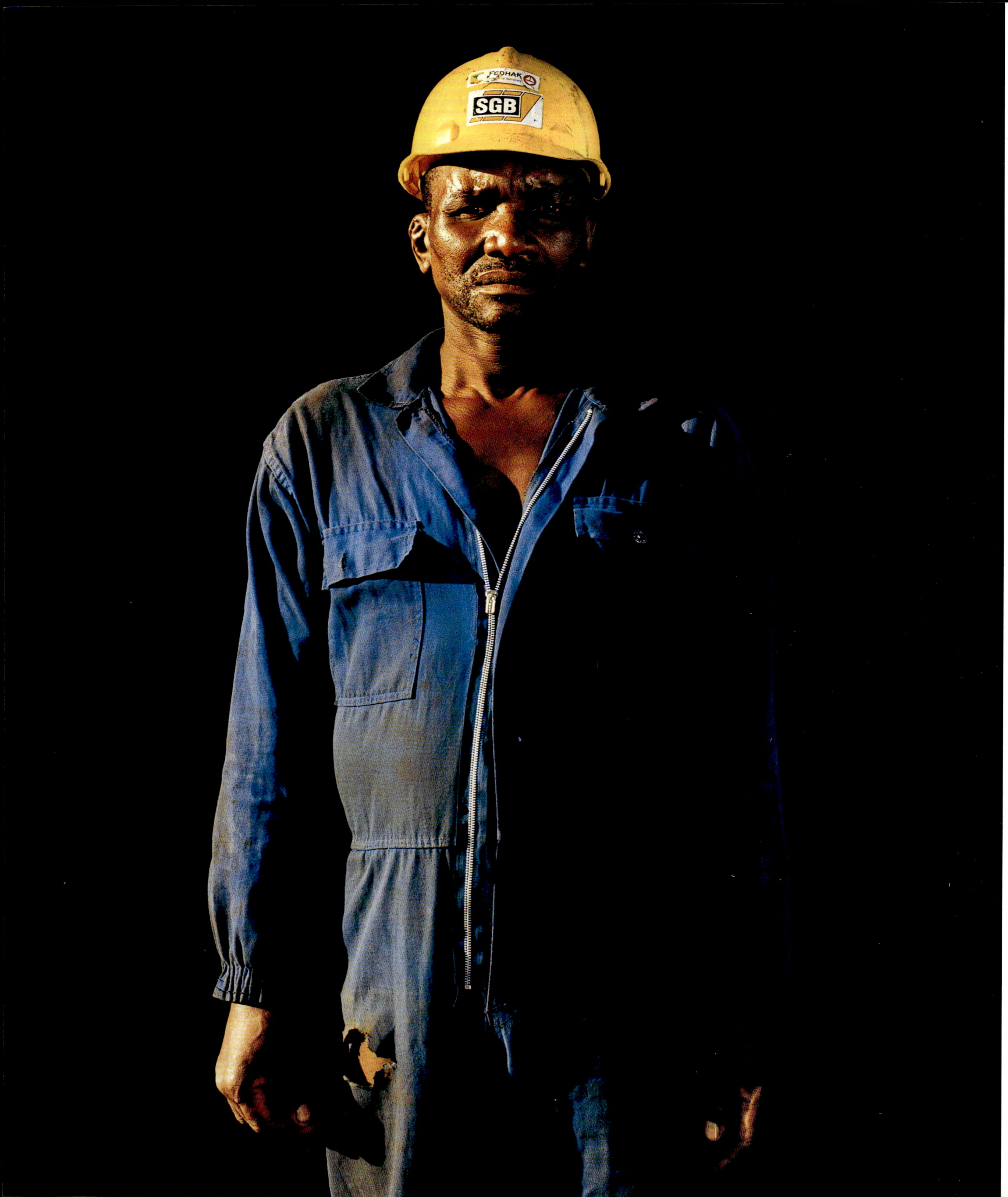
SGB

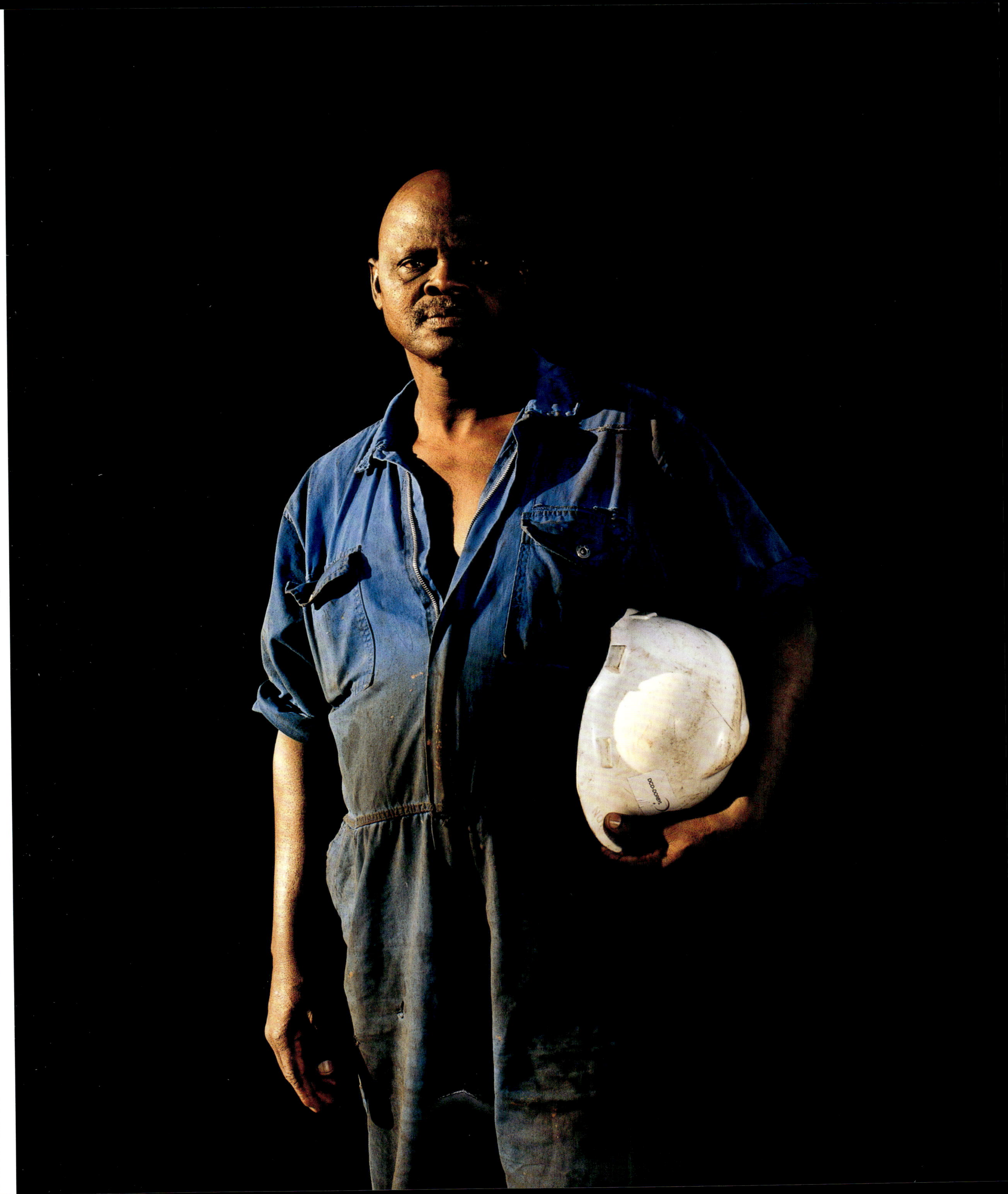

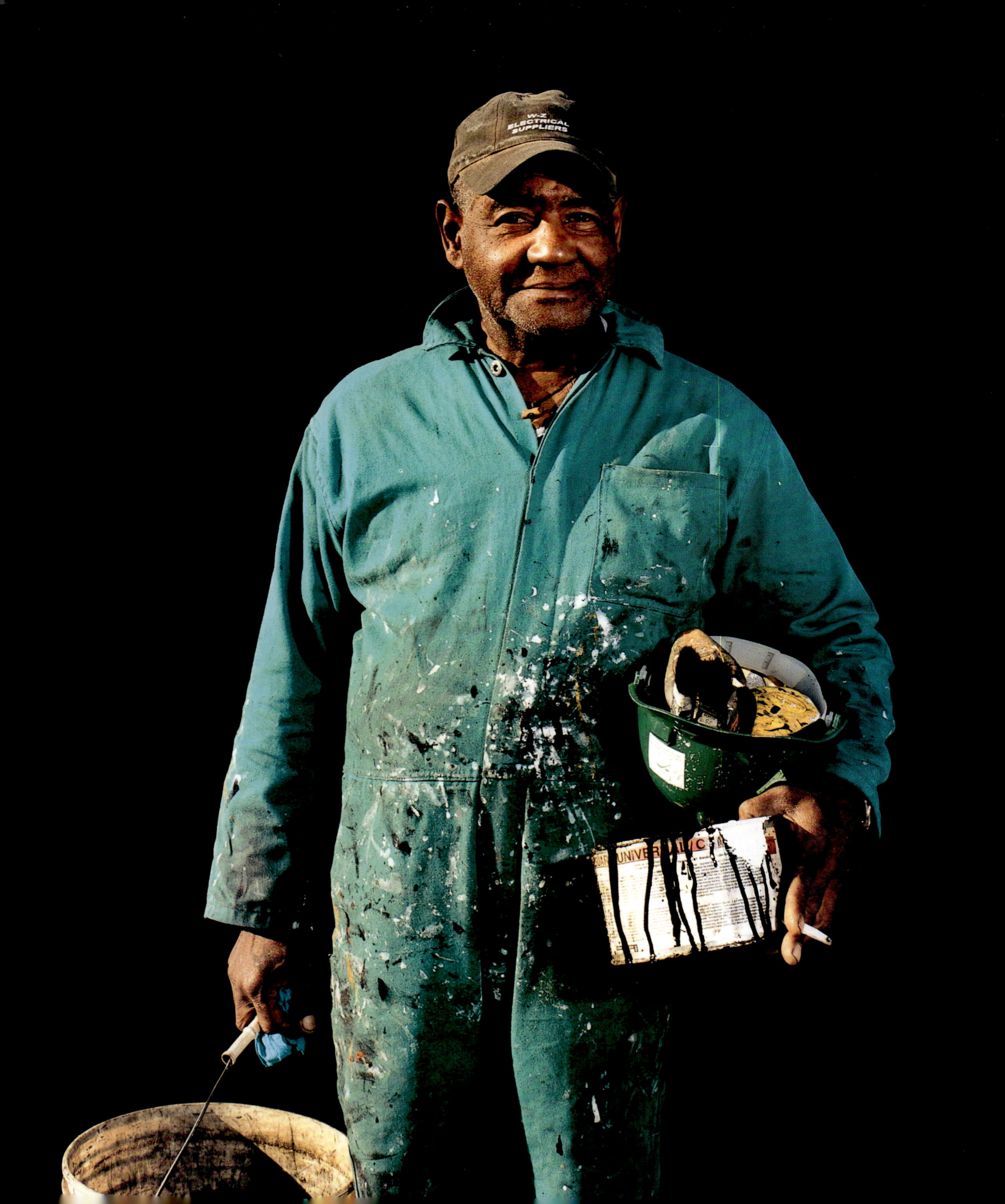
W-Z
ELECTRICAL
SUPPLIERS

5

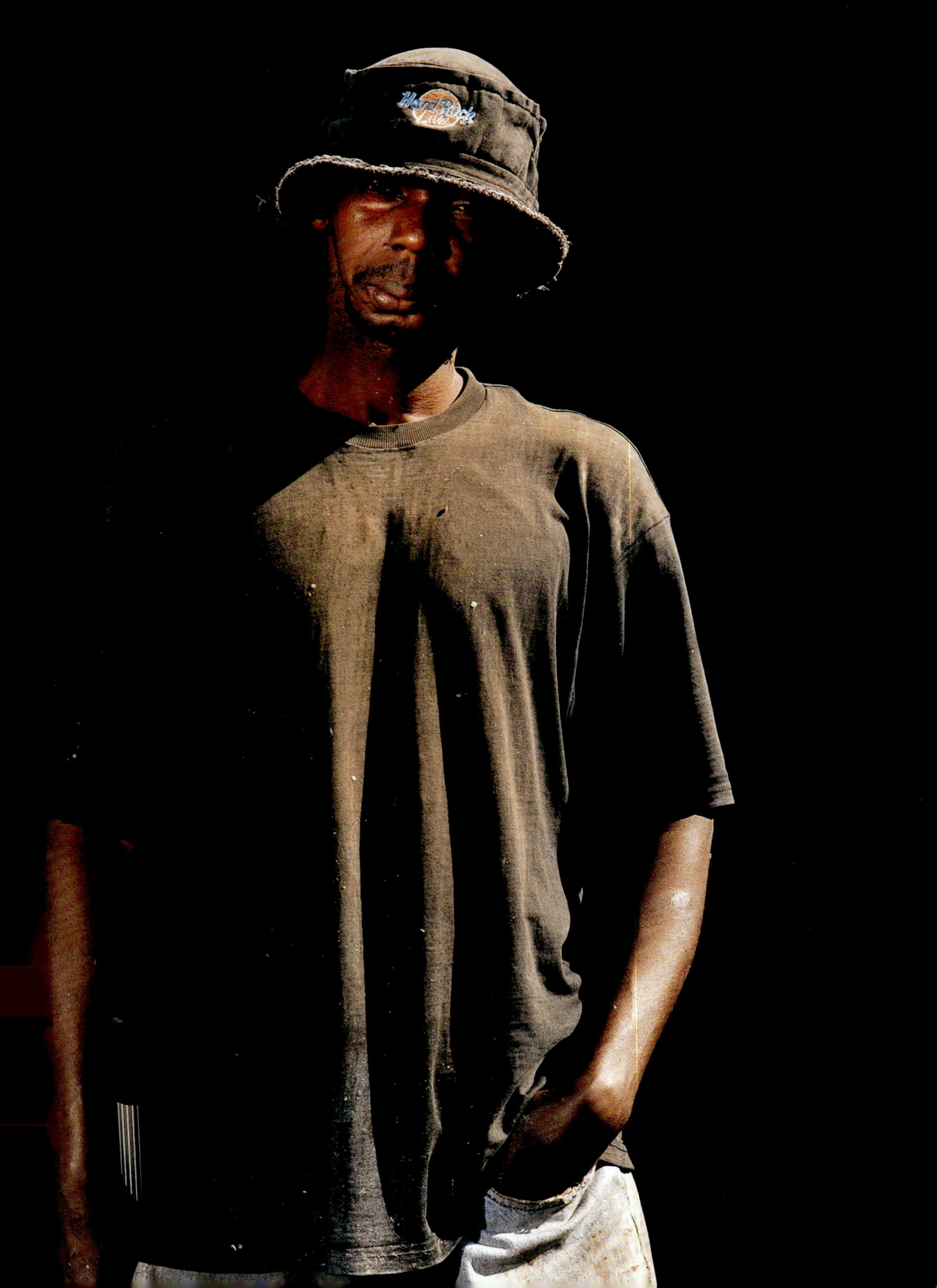
Hard Rock
Live

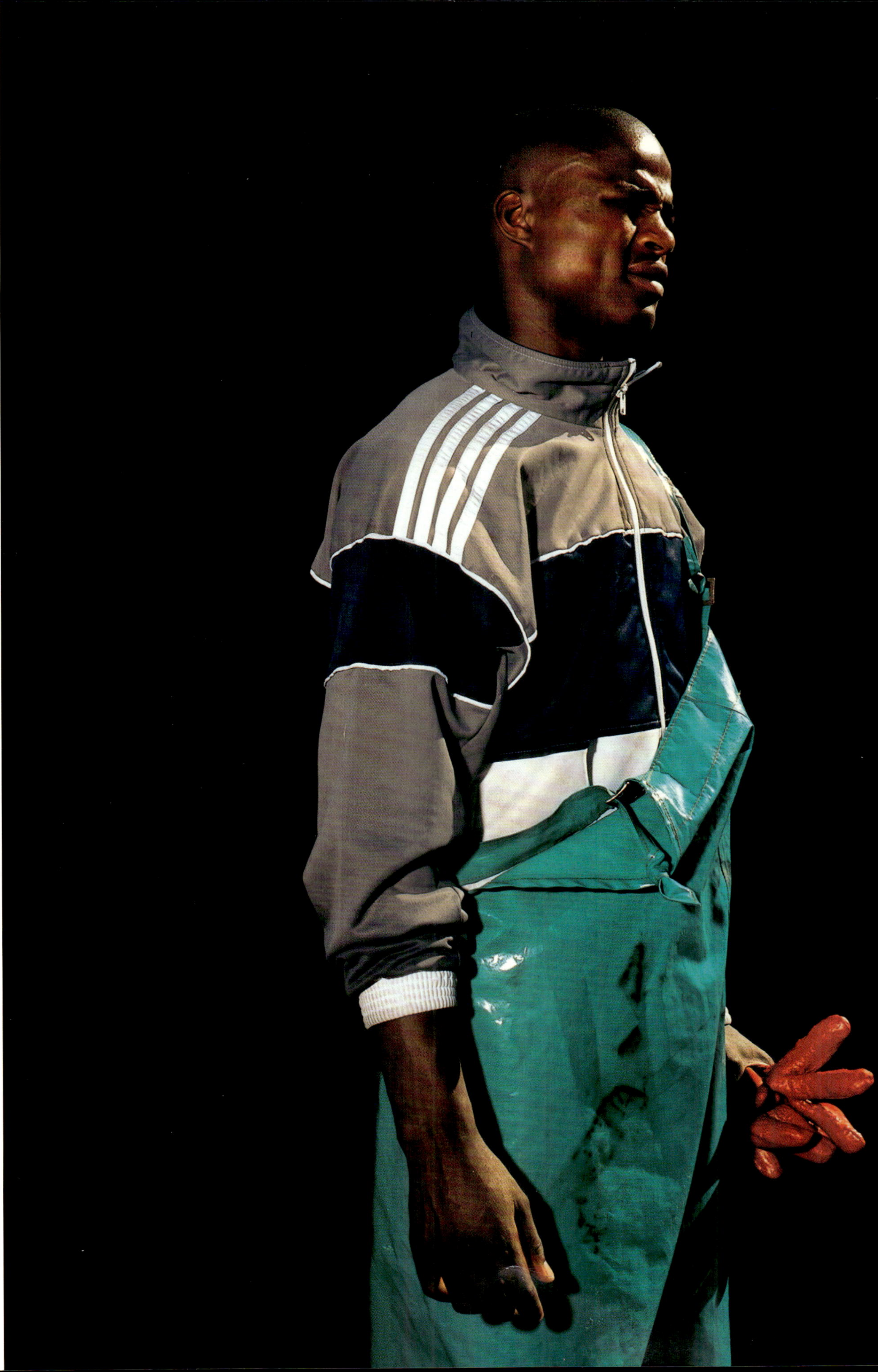

1

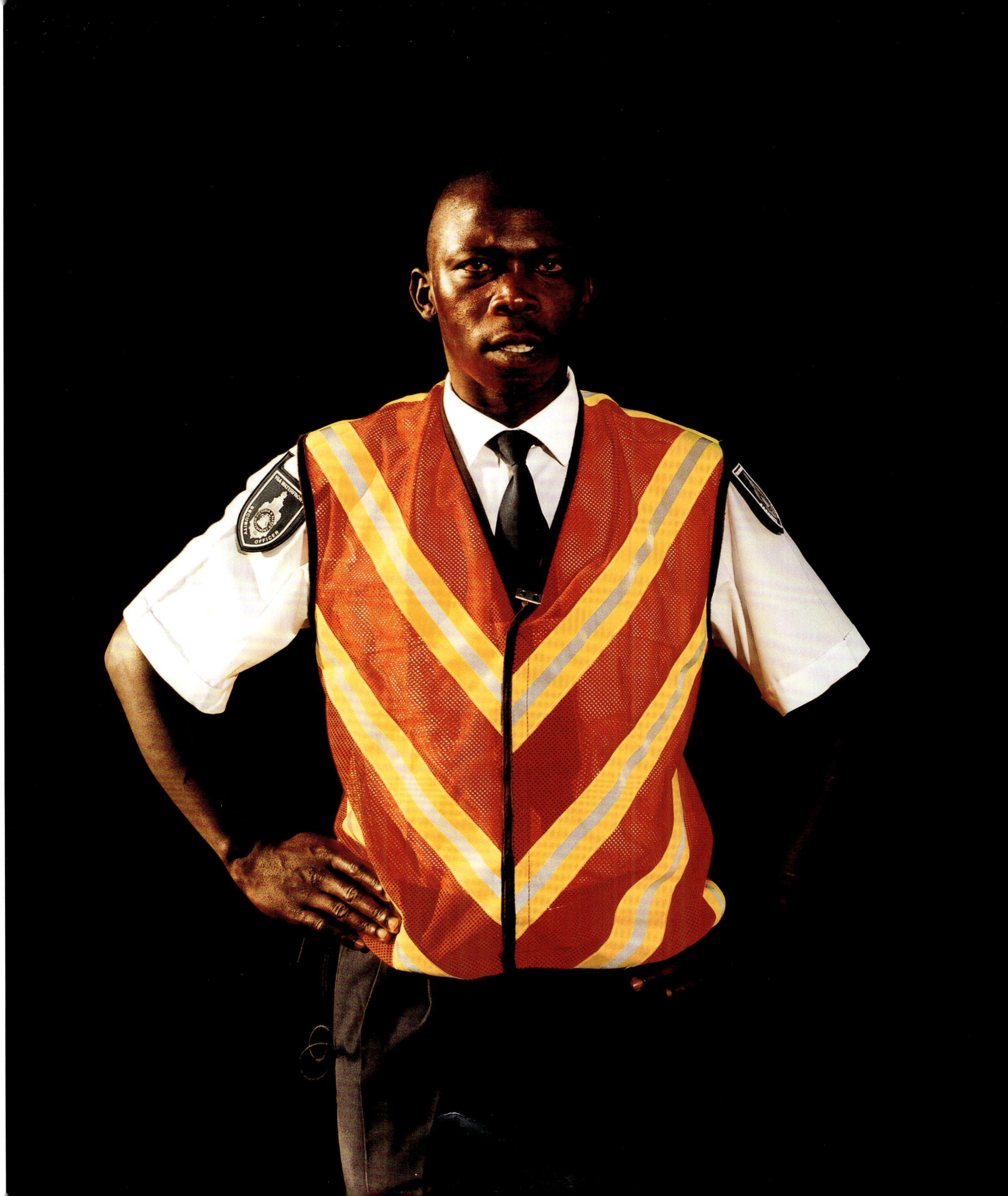
SECURITY
OFFICER

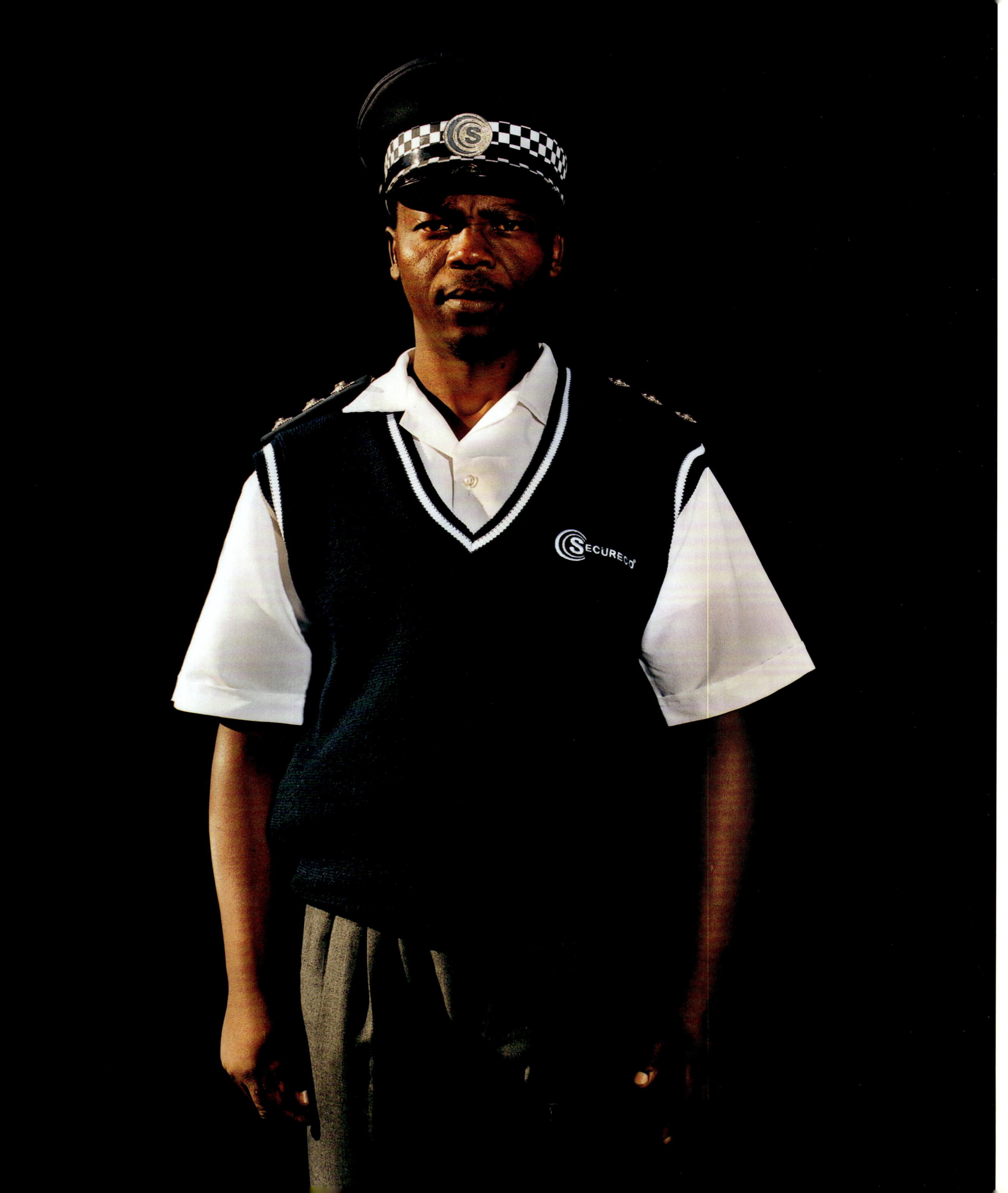
SECURECO

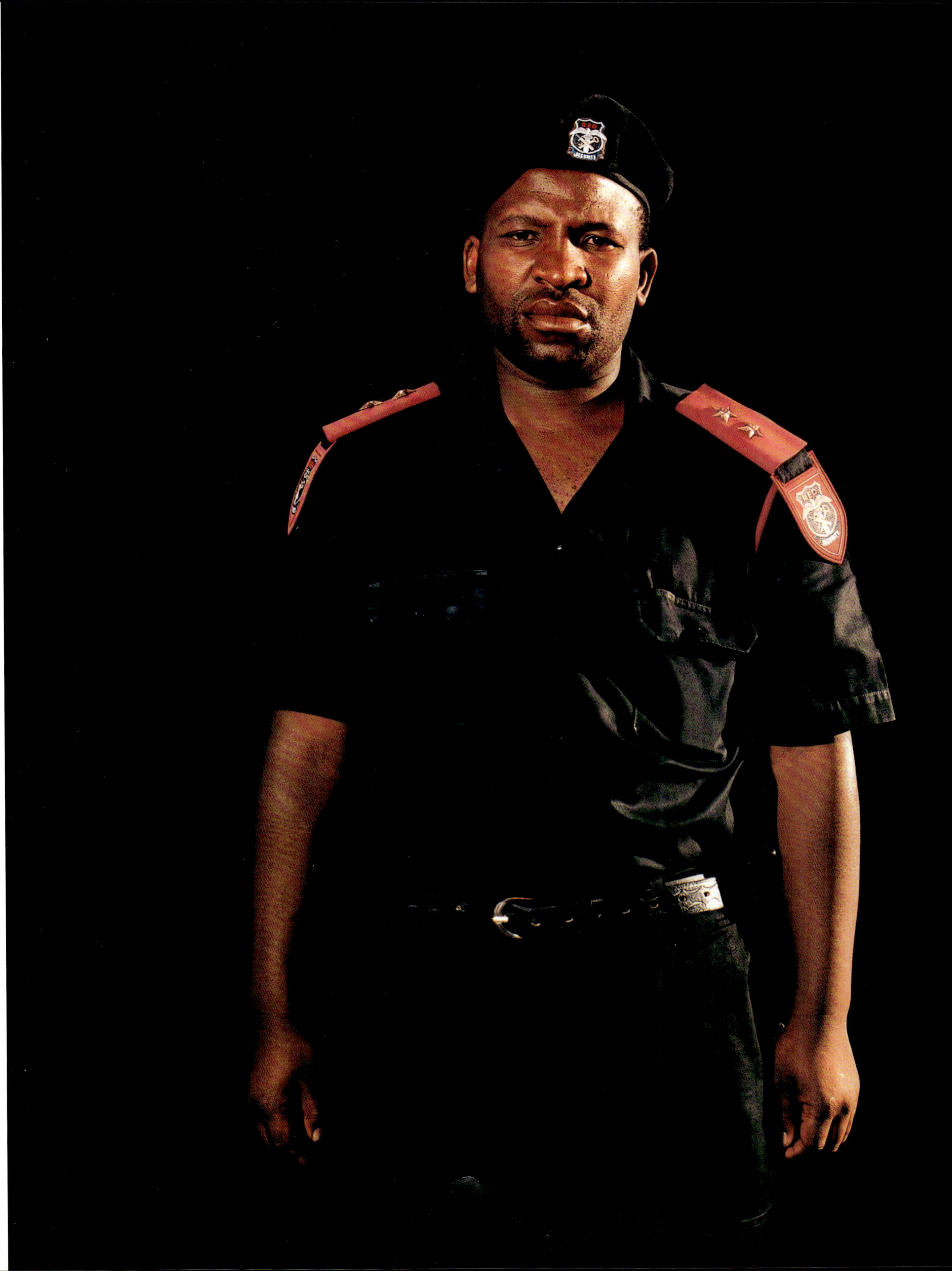

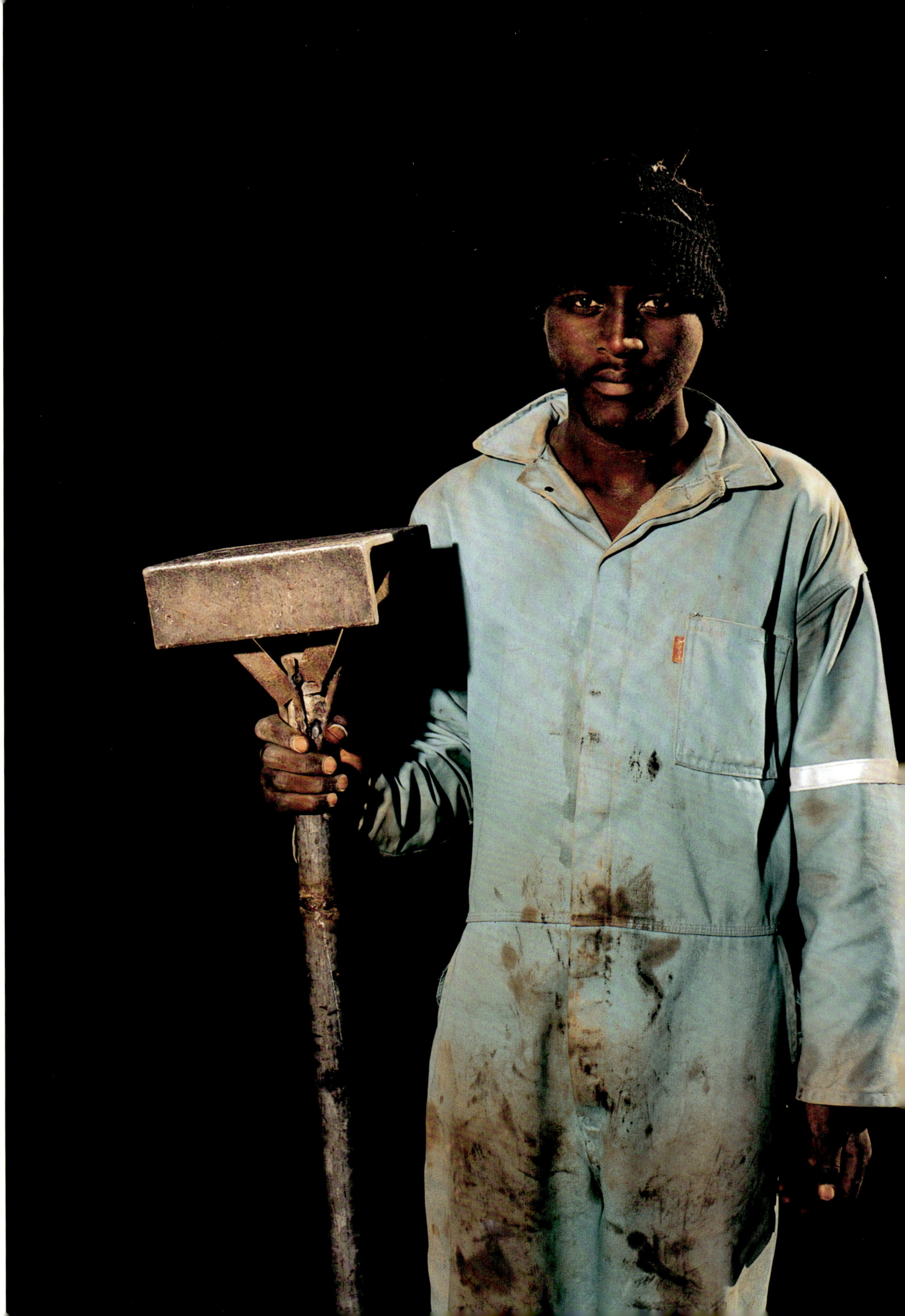

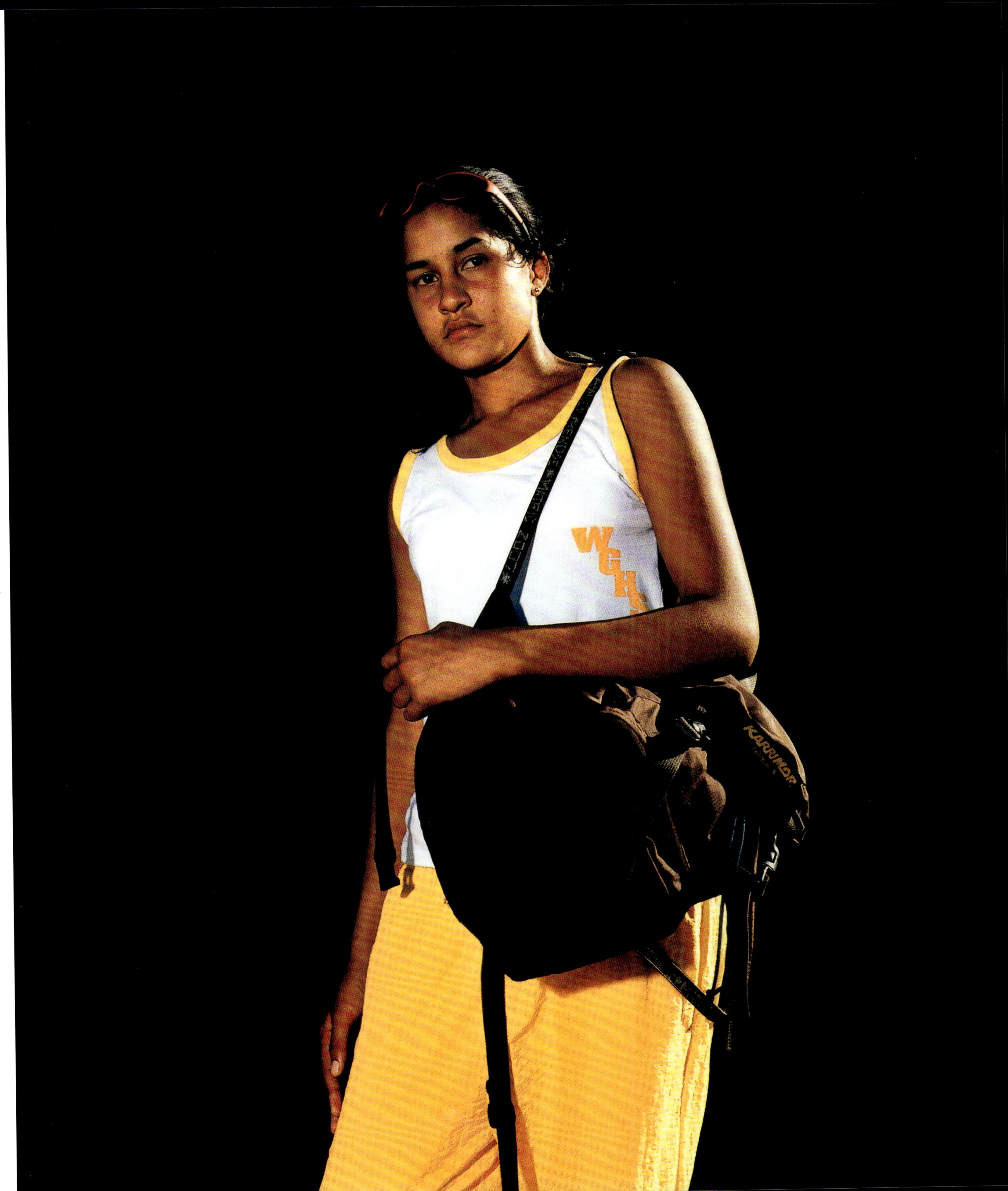
WGHS
KARRIMOR

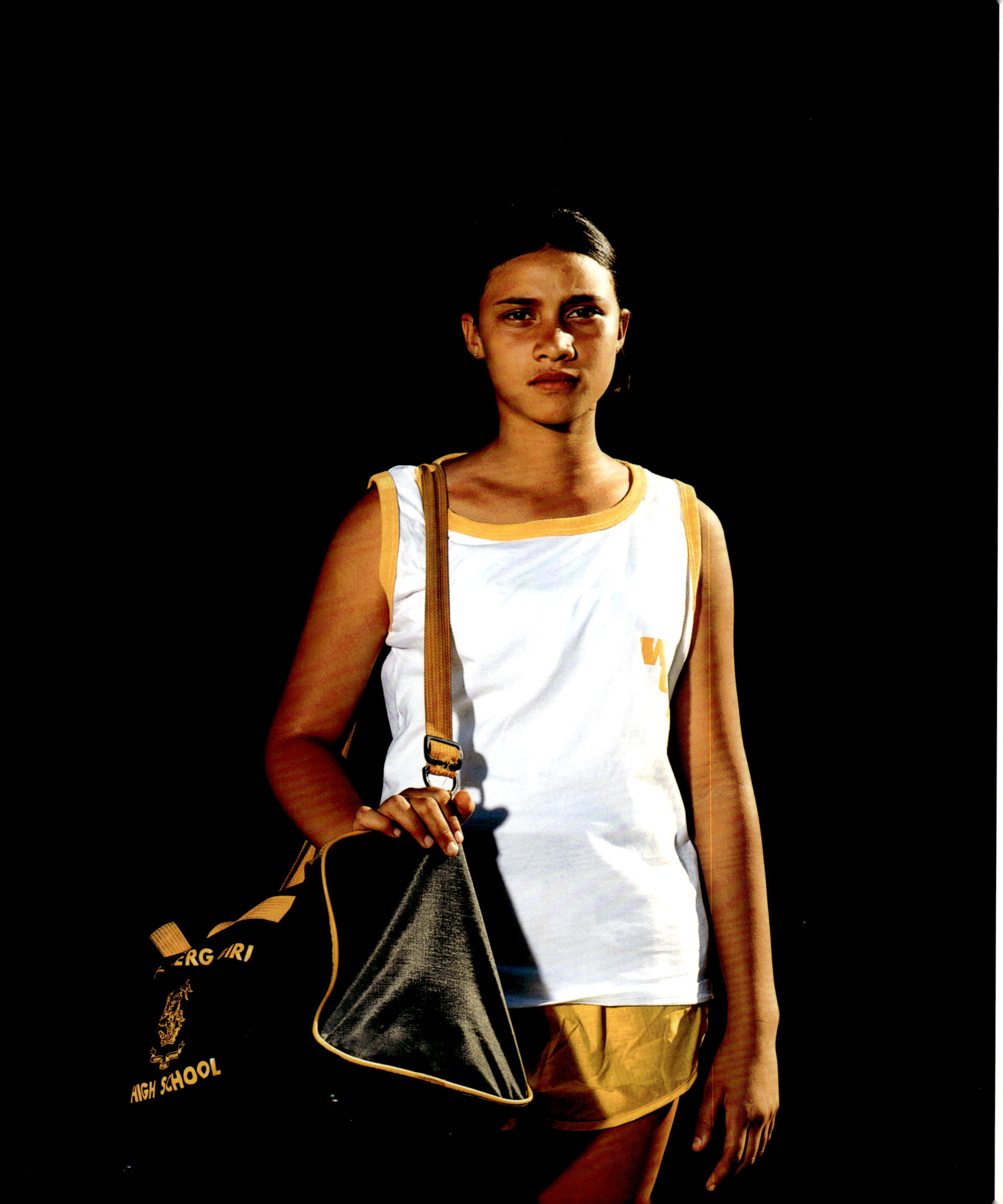
HIGH SCHOOL

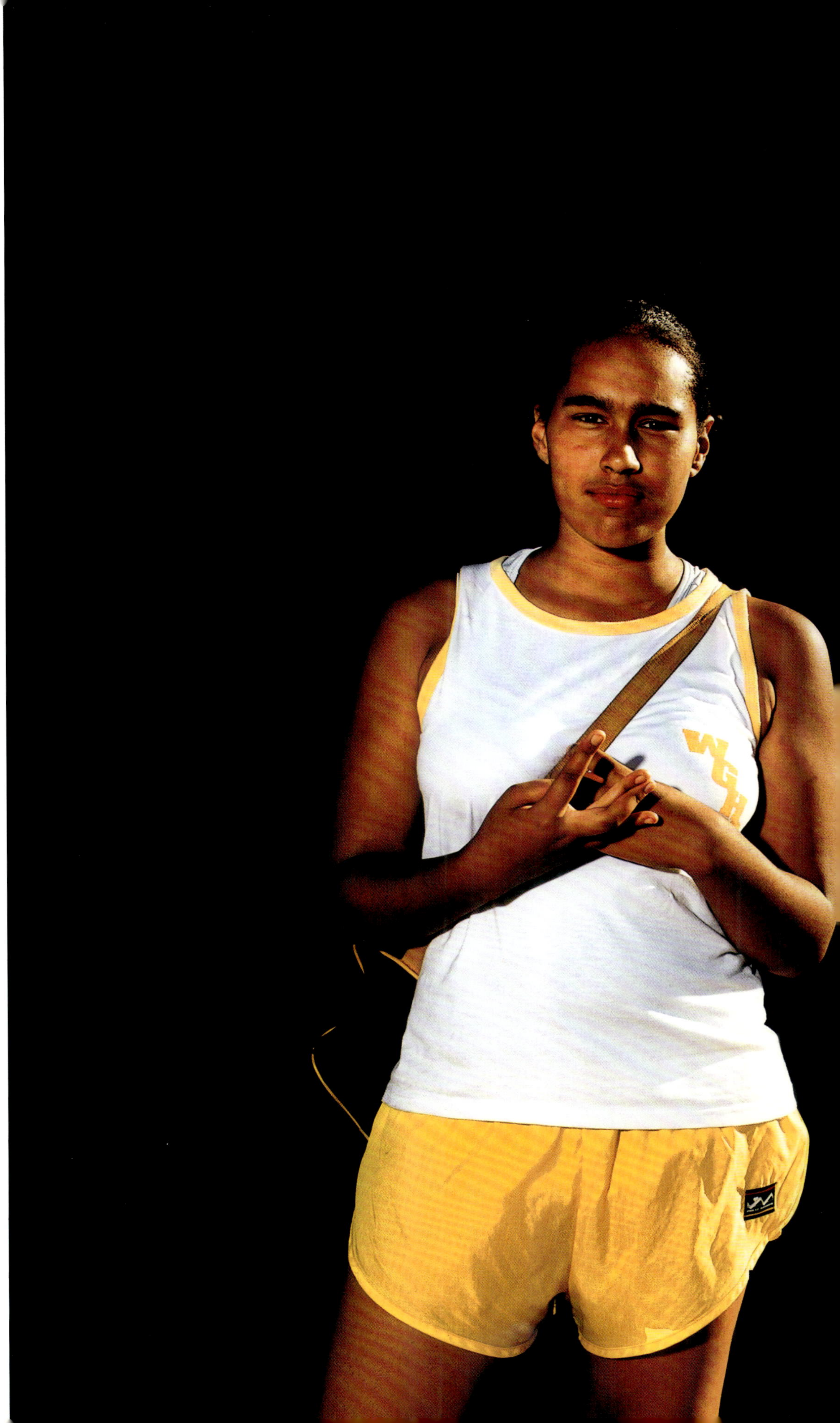
WGH

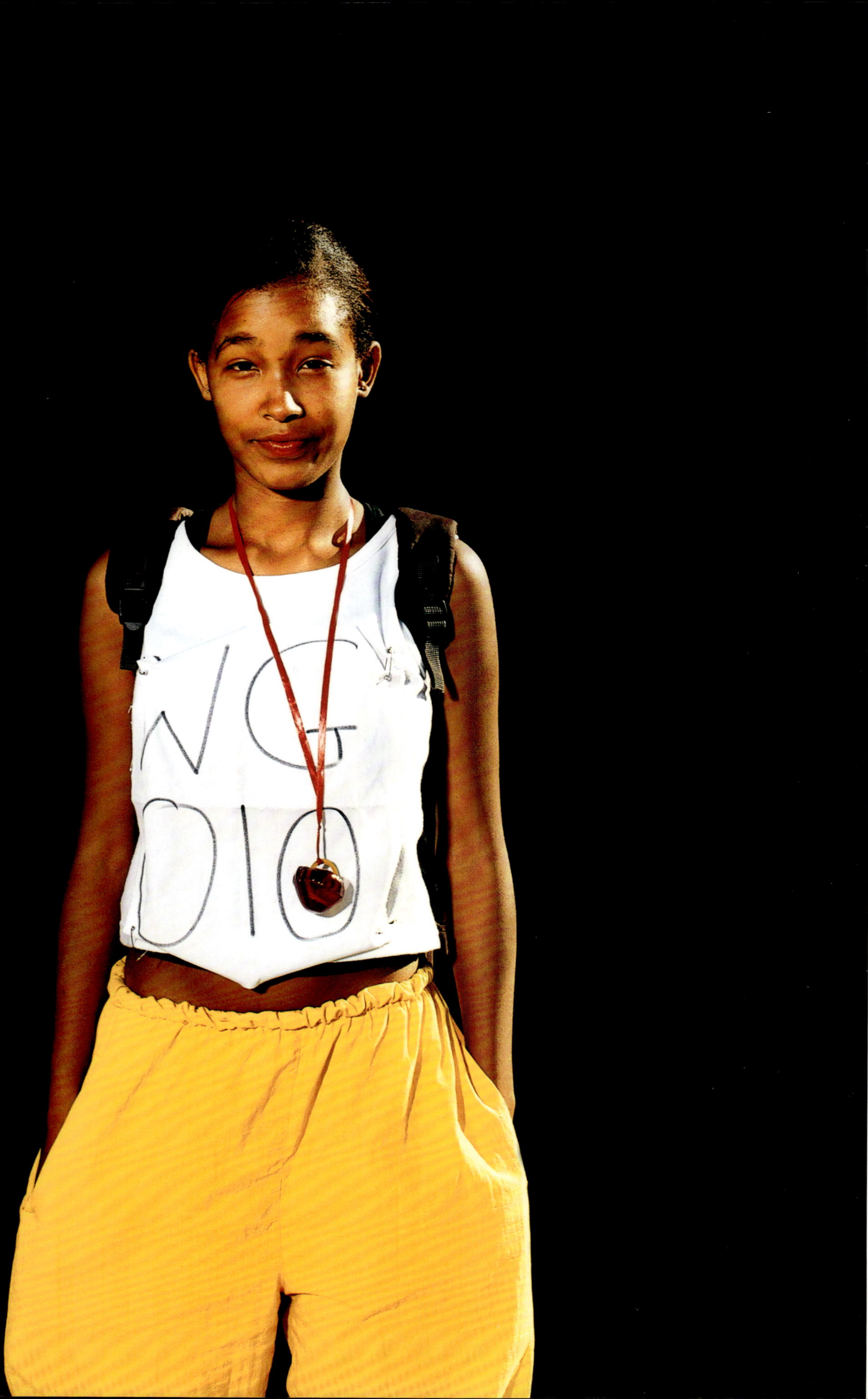

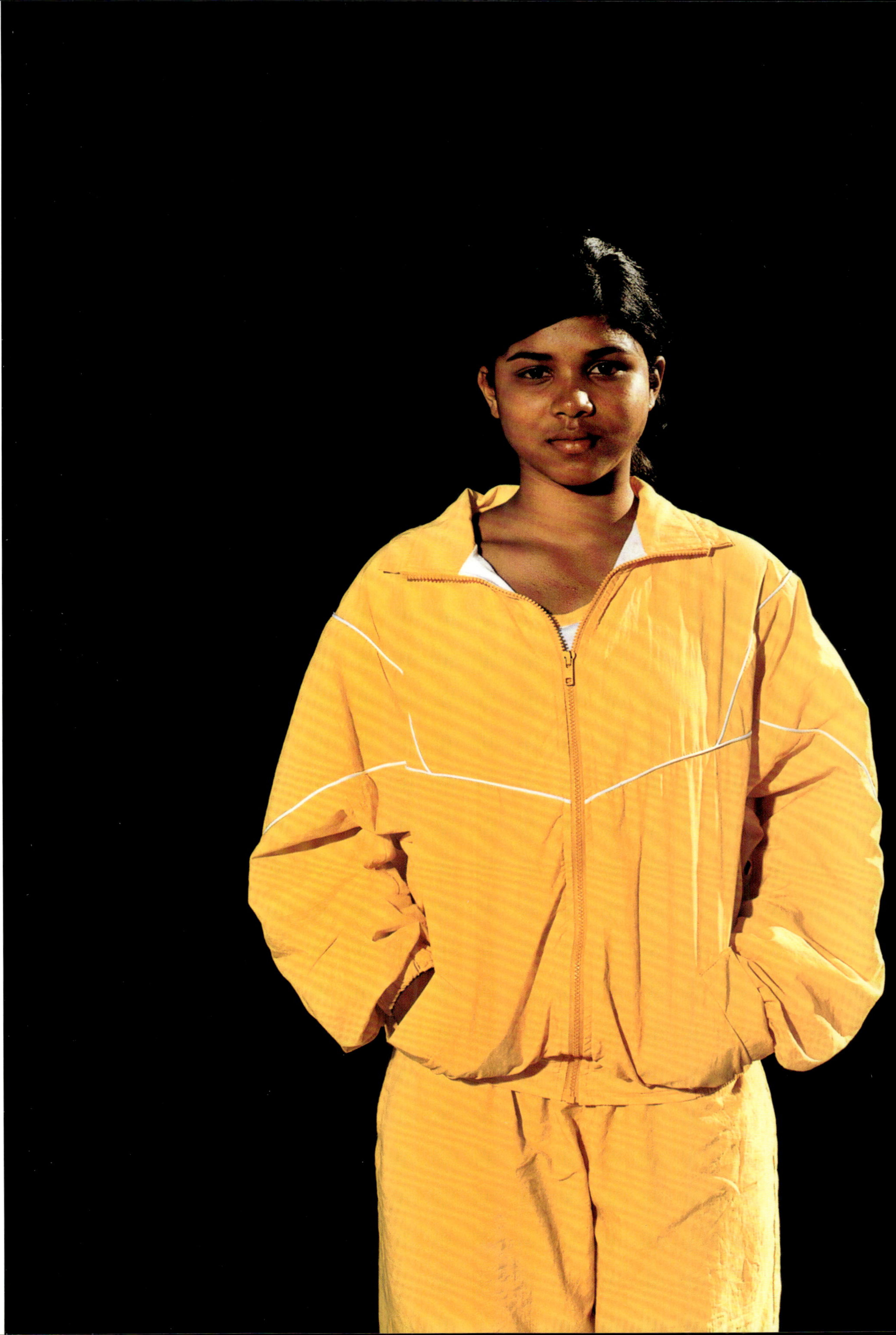

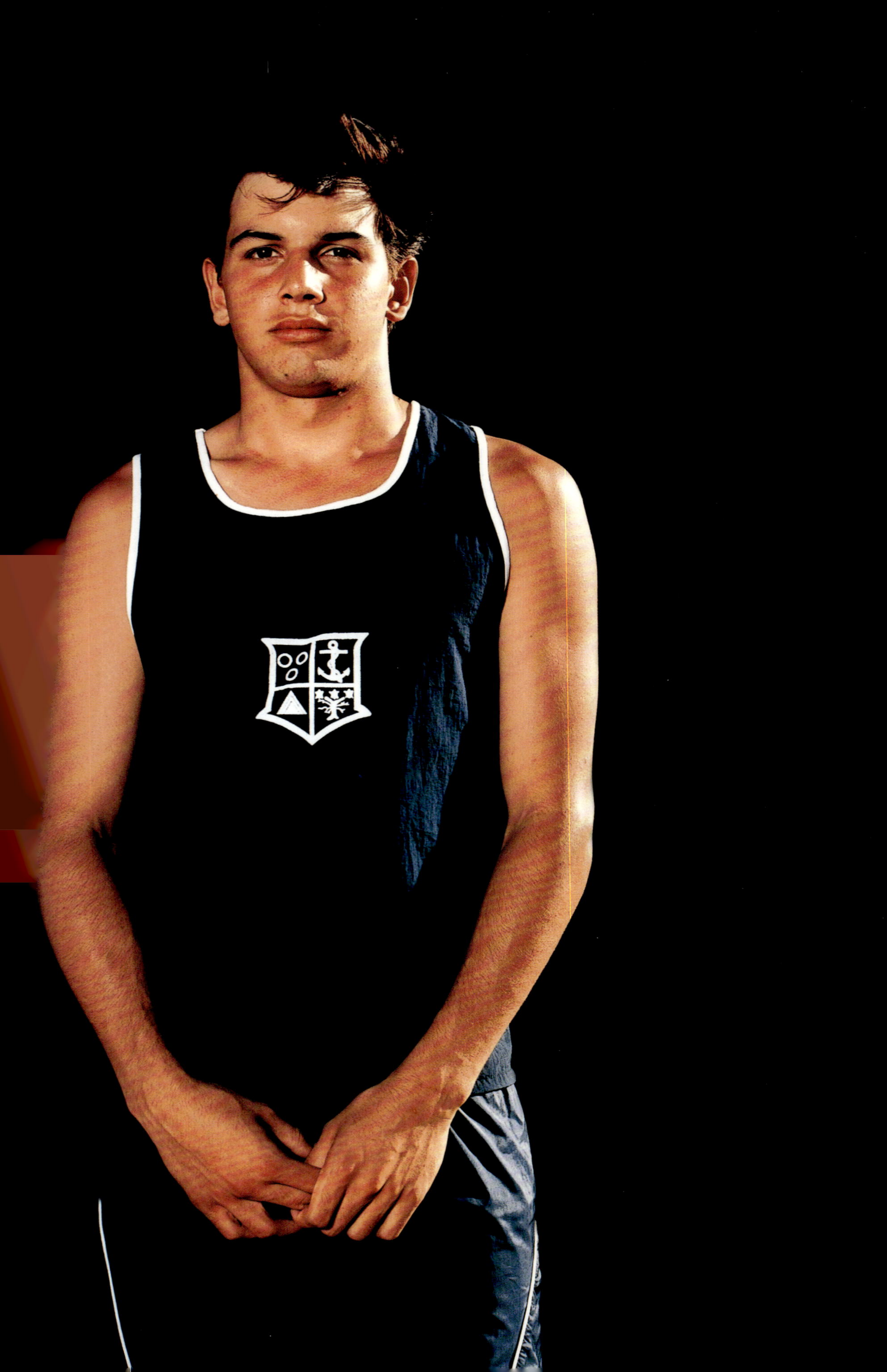

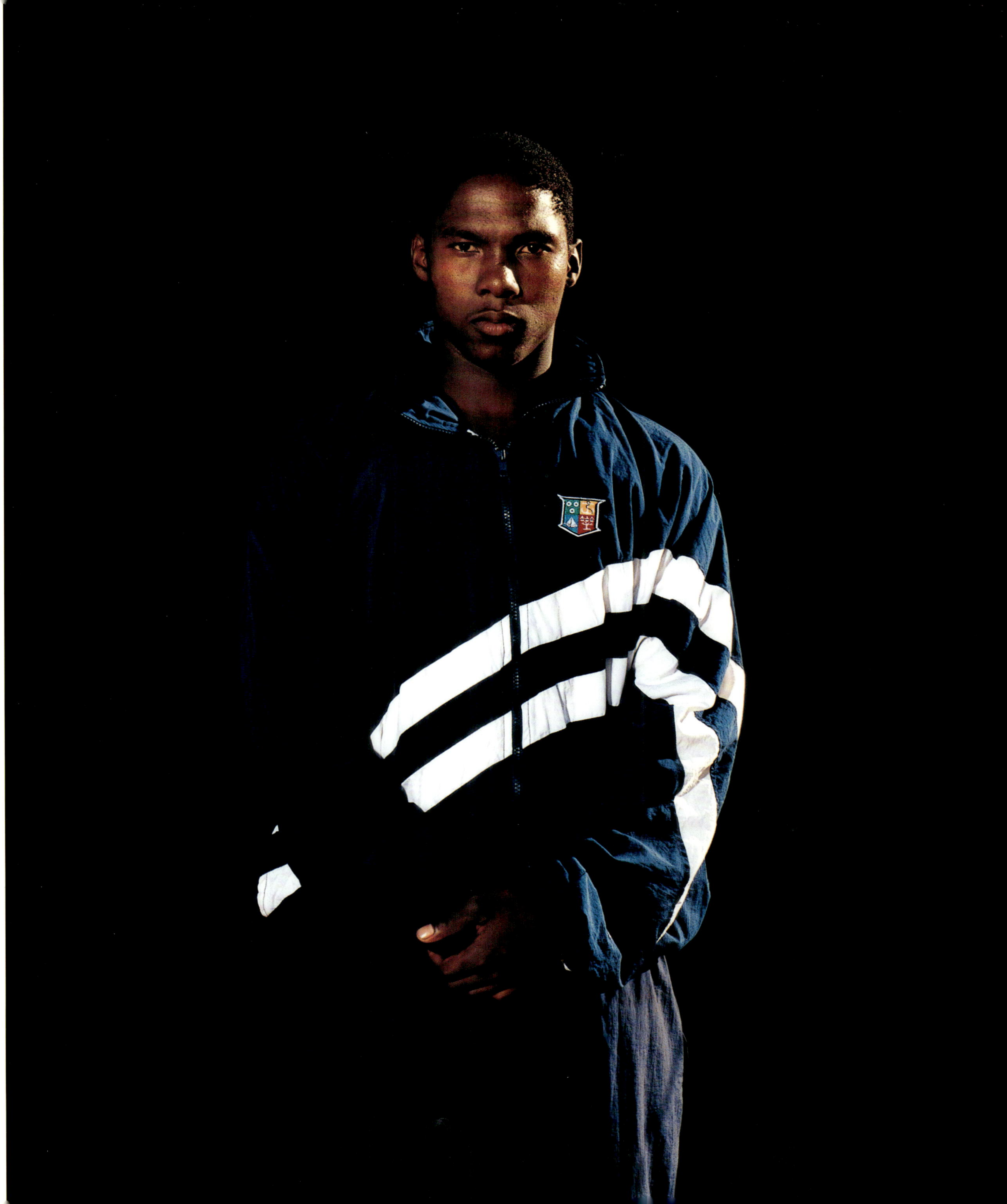

1

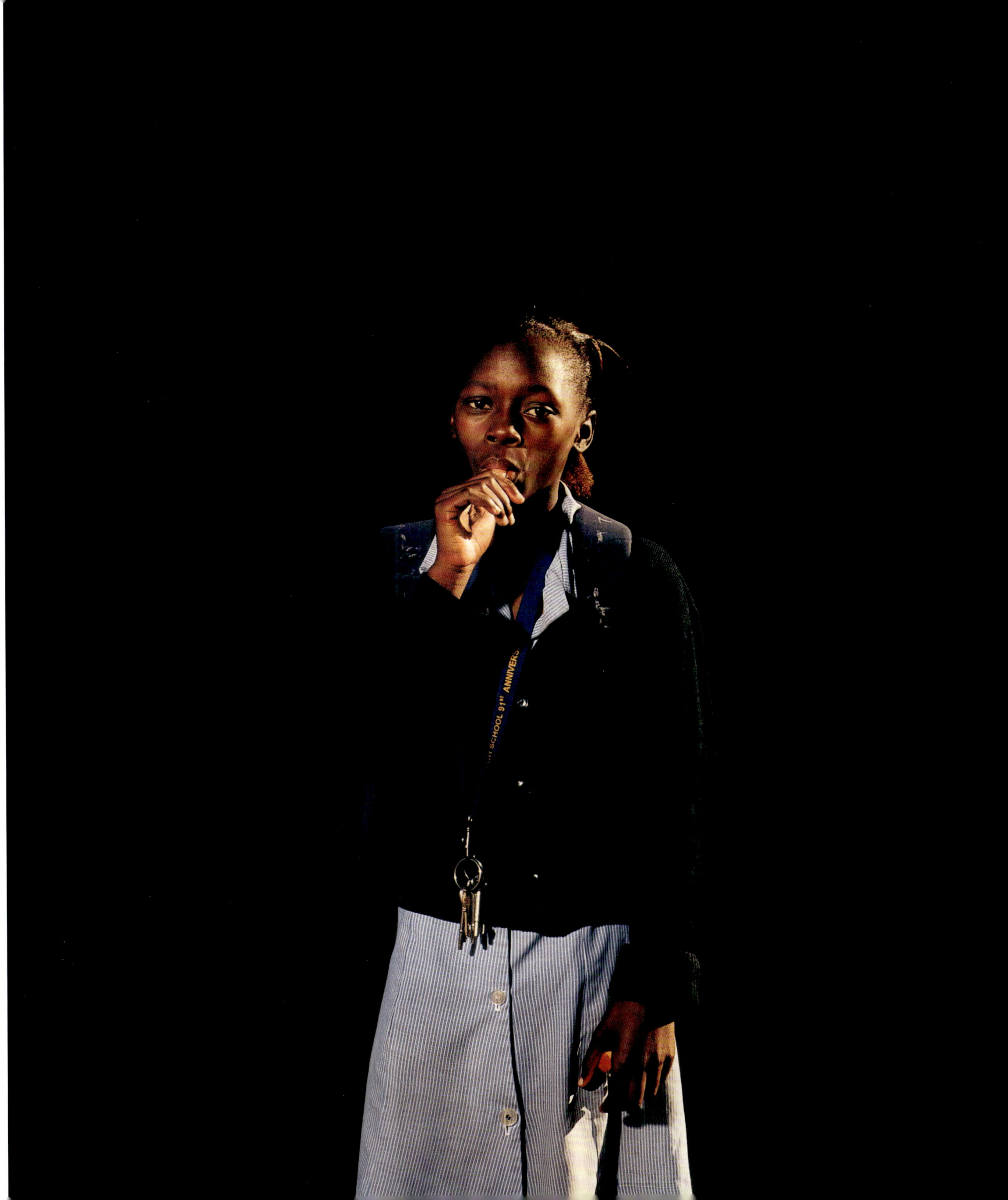
SCHOOL 91ST

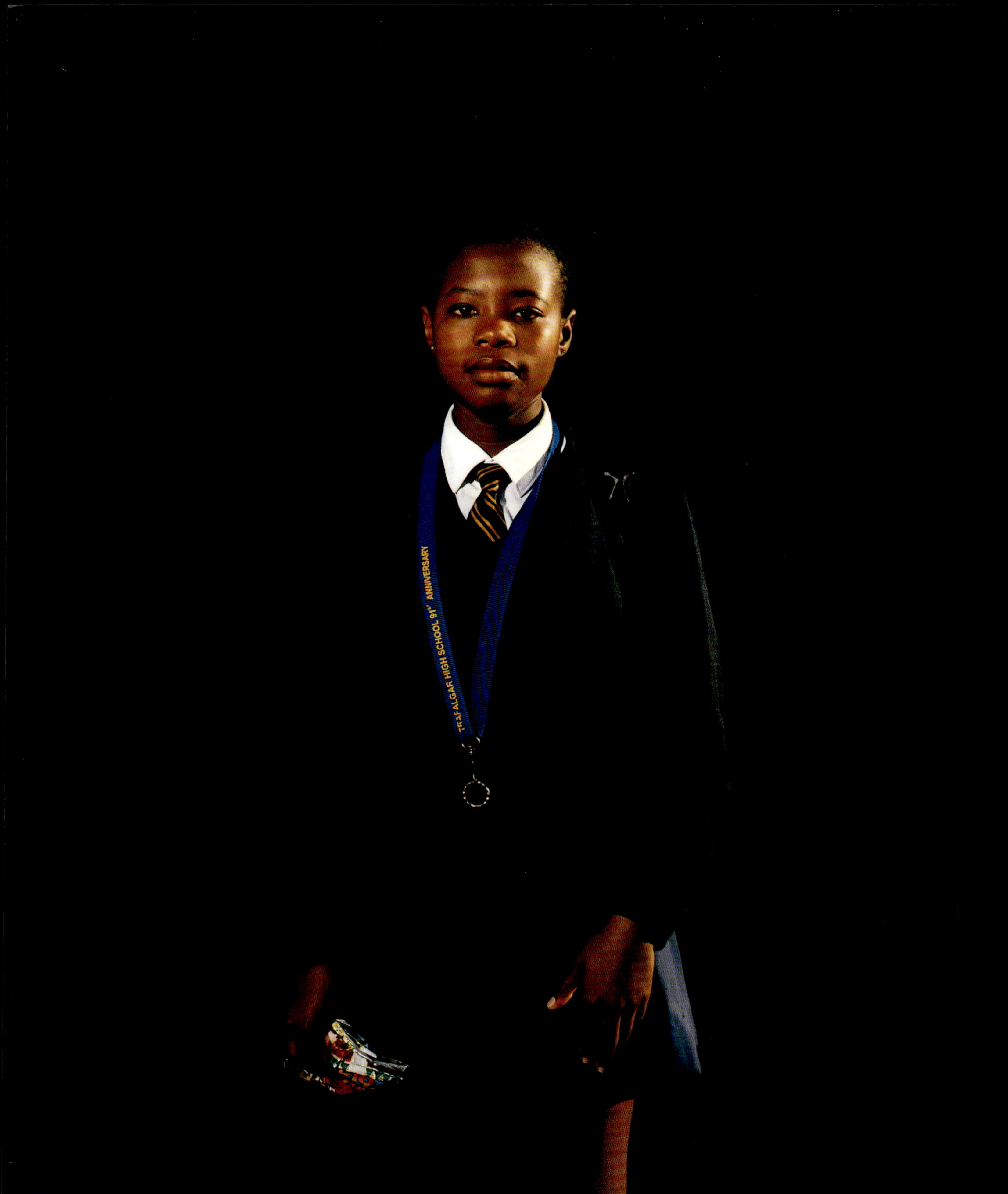
TRAFALGAR HIGH SCHOOL 91st ANNIVERSARY

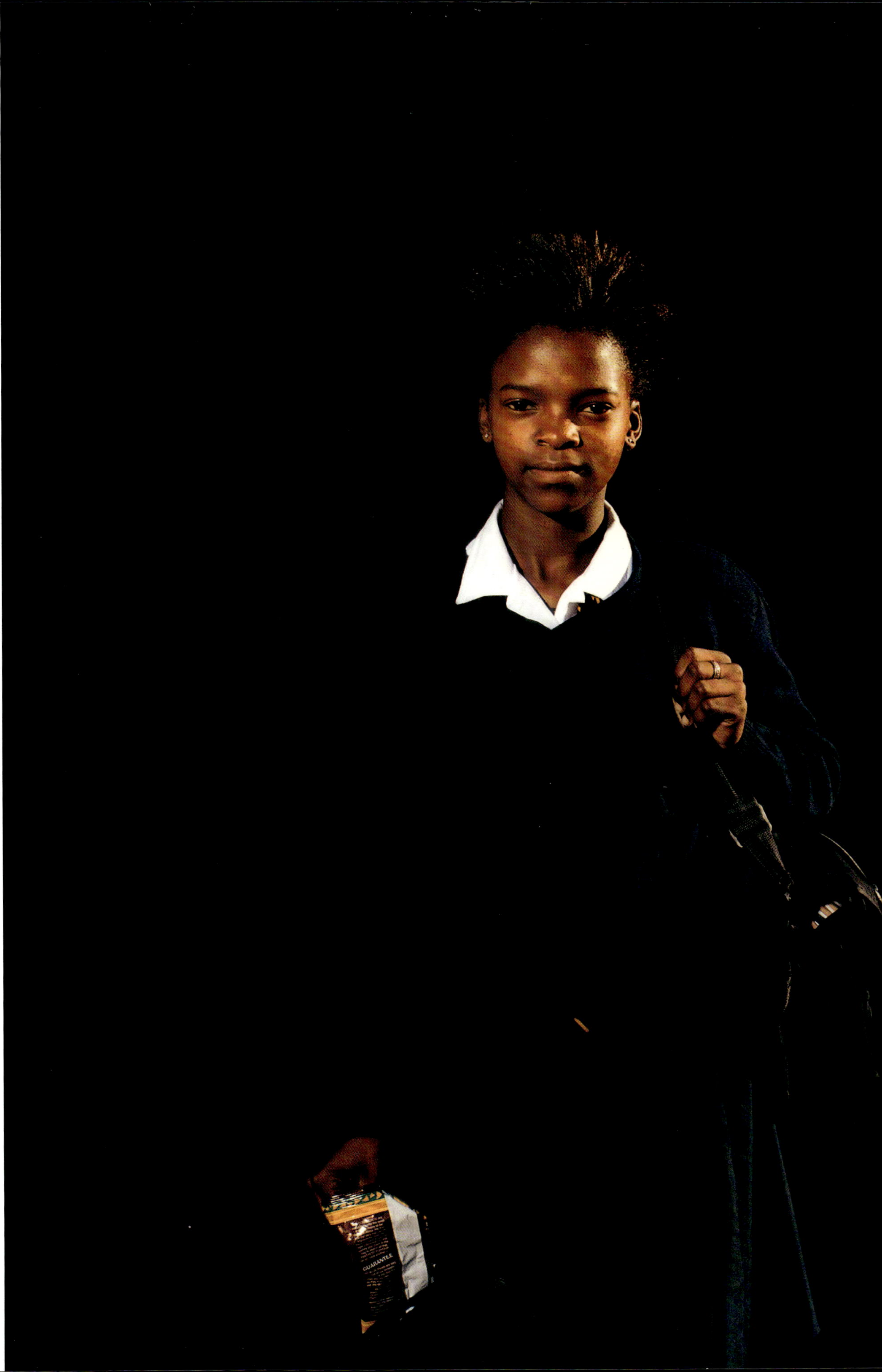

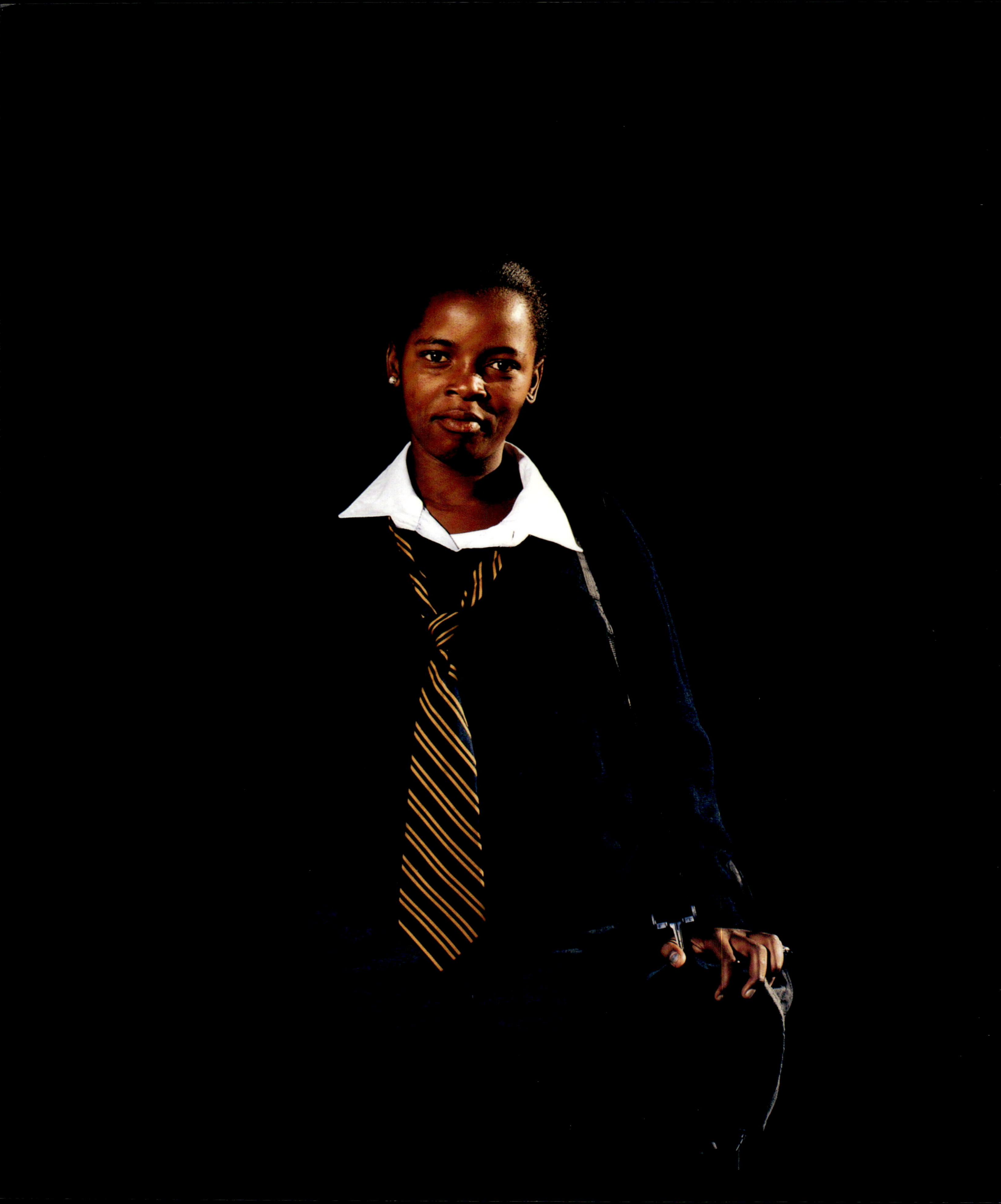

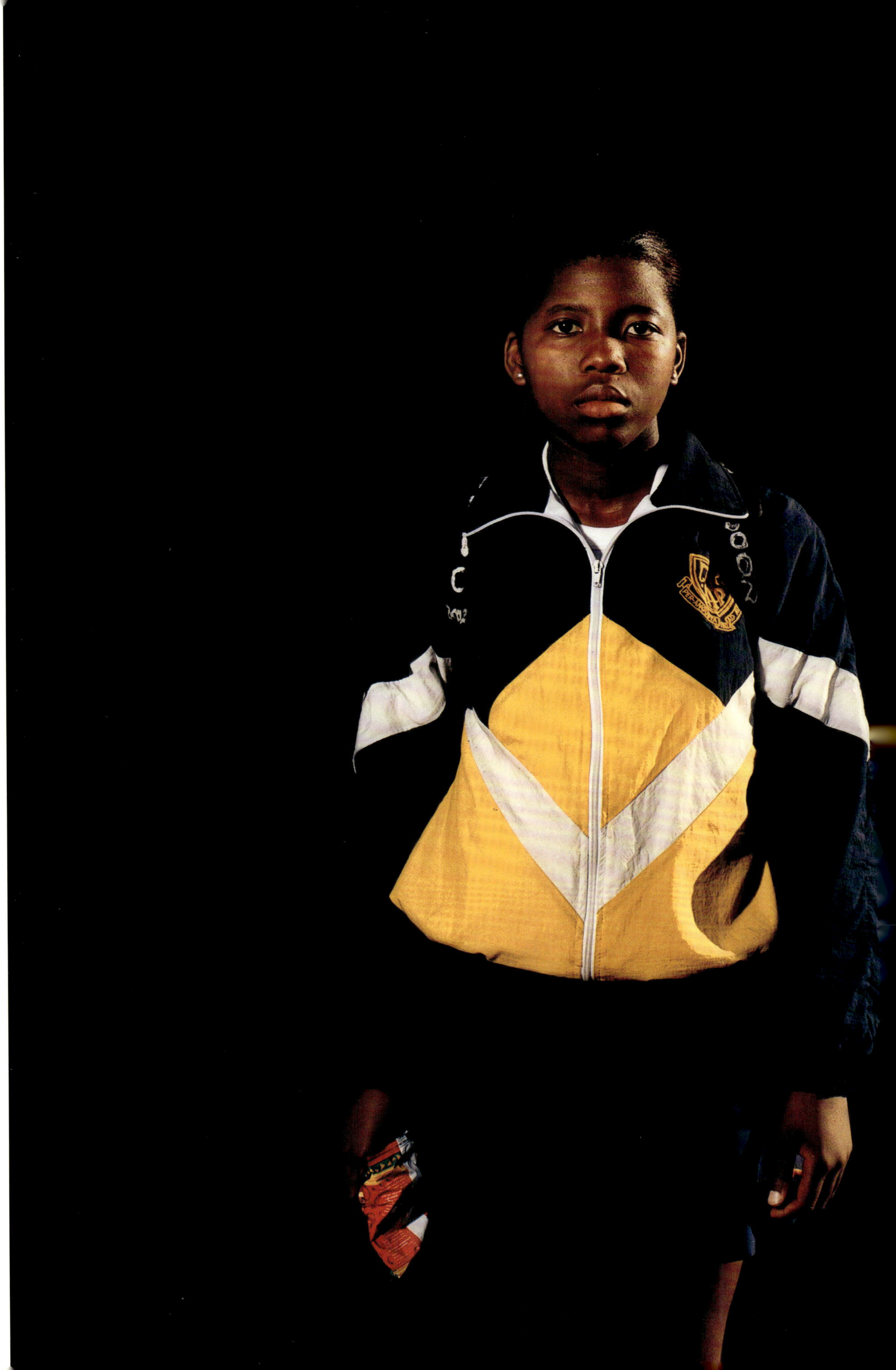

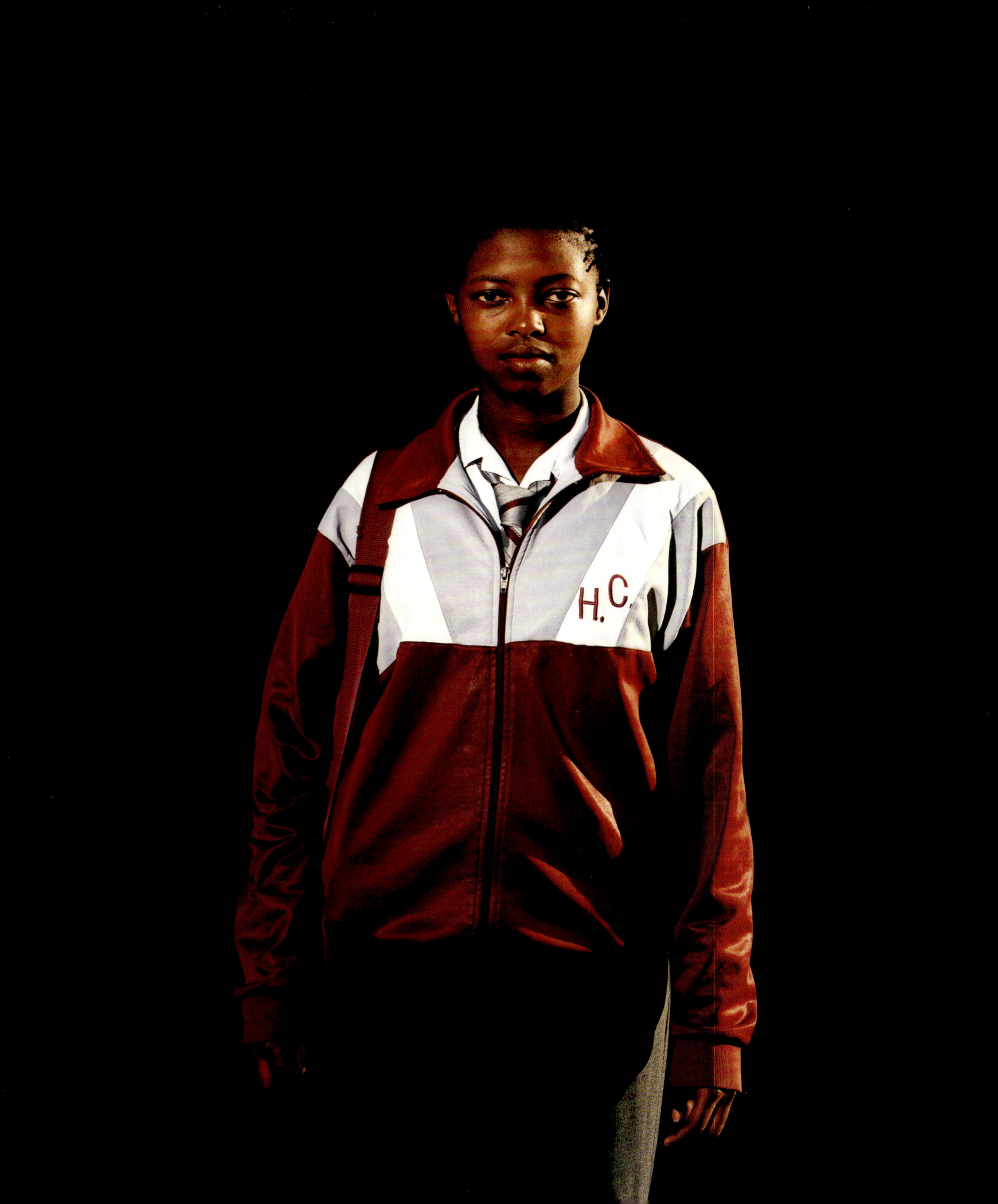
H.C.

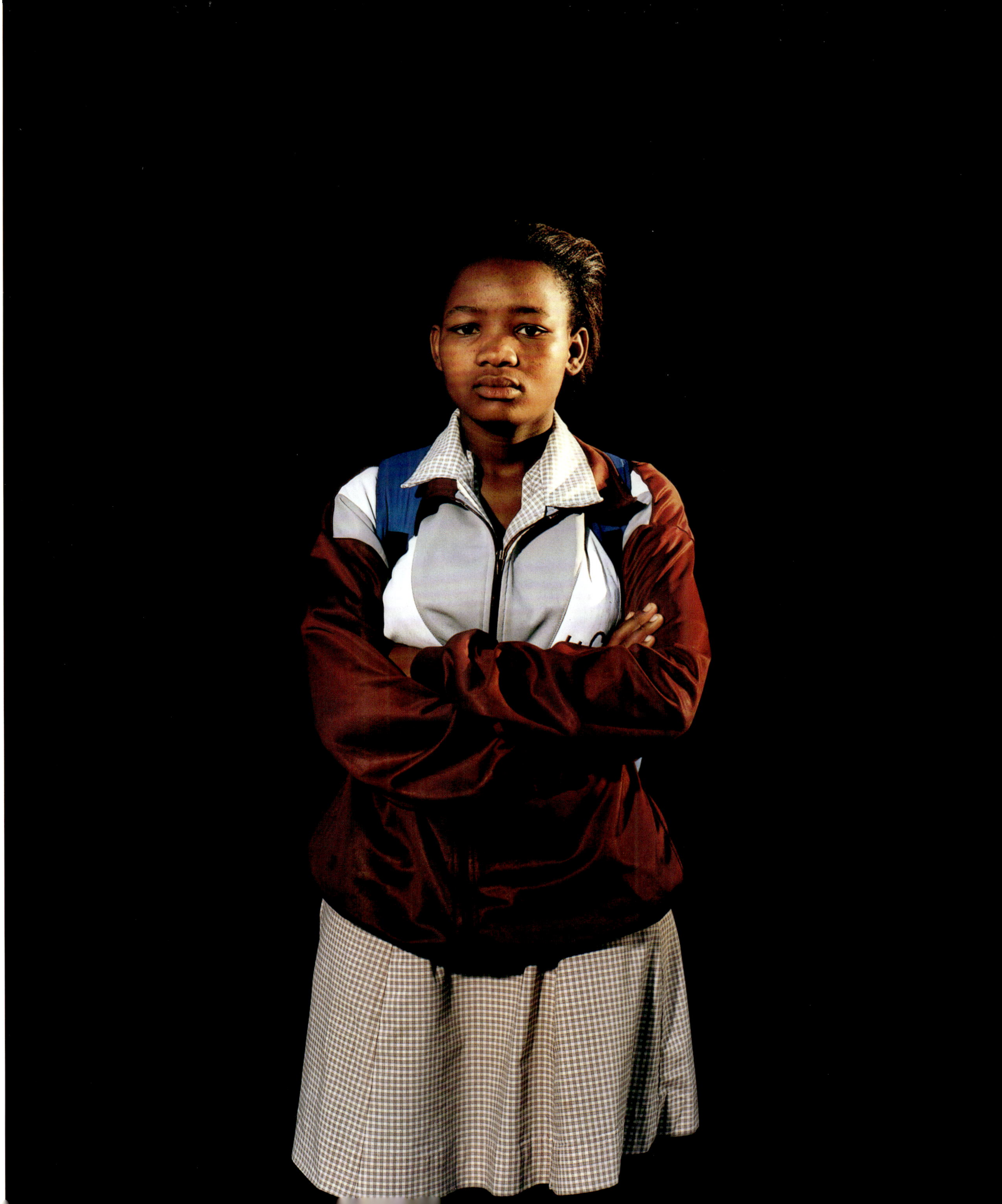

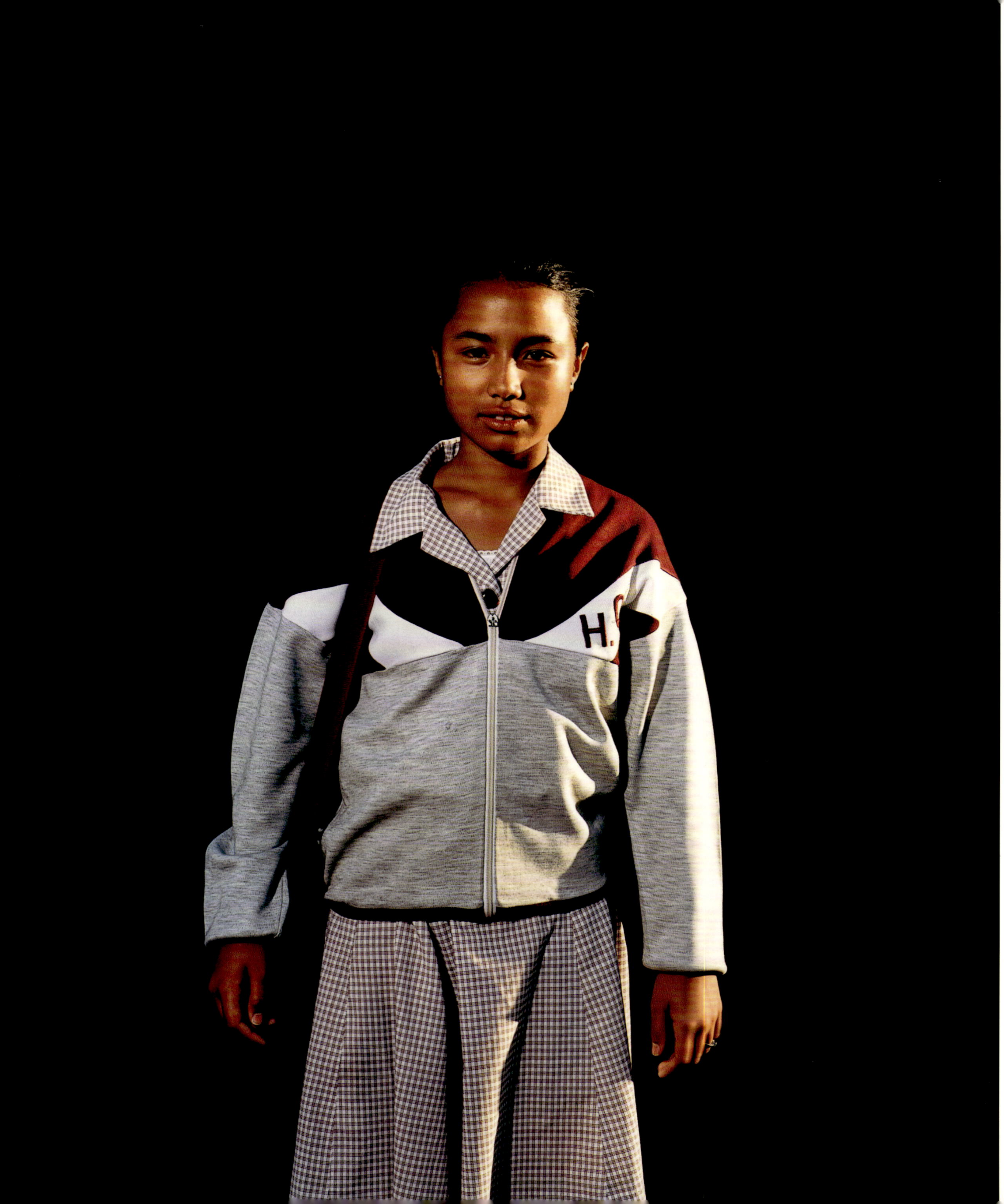

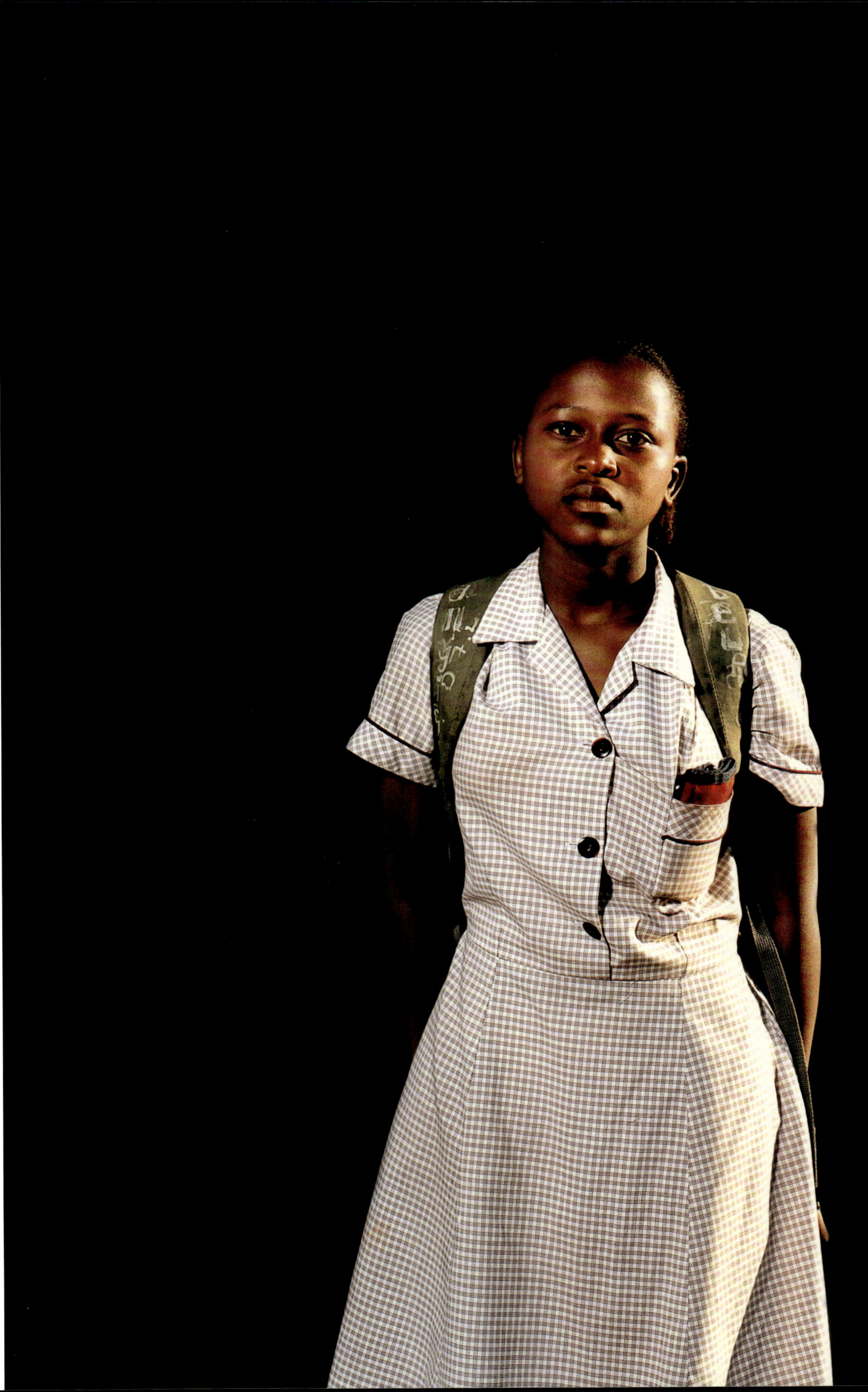

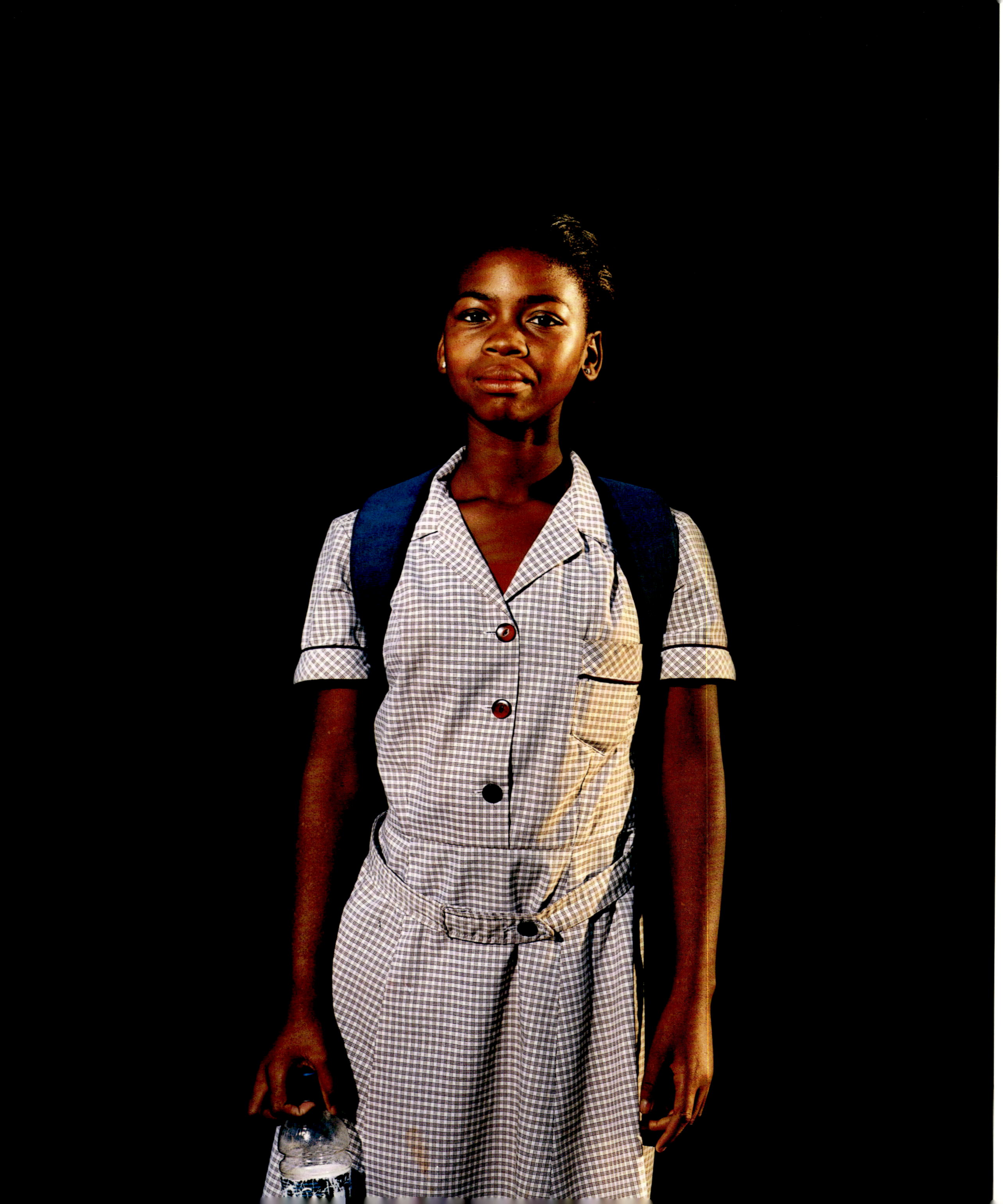

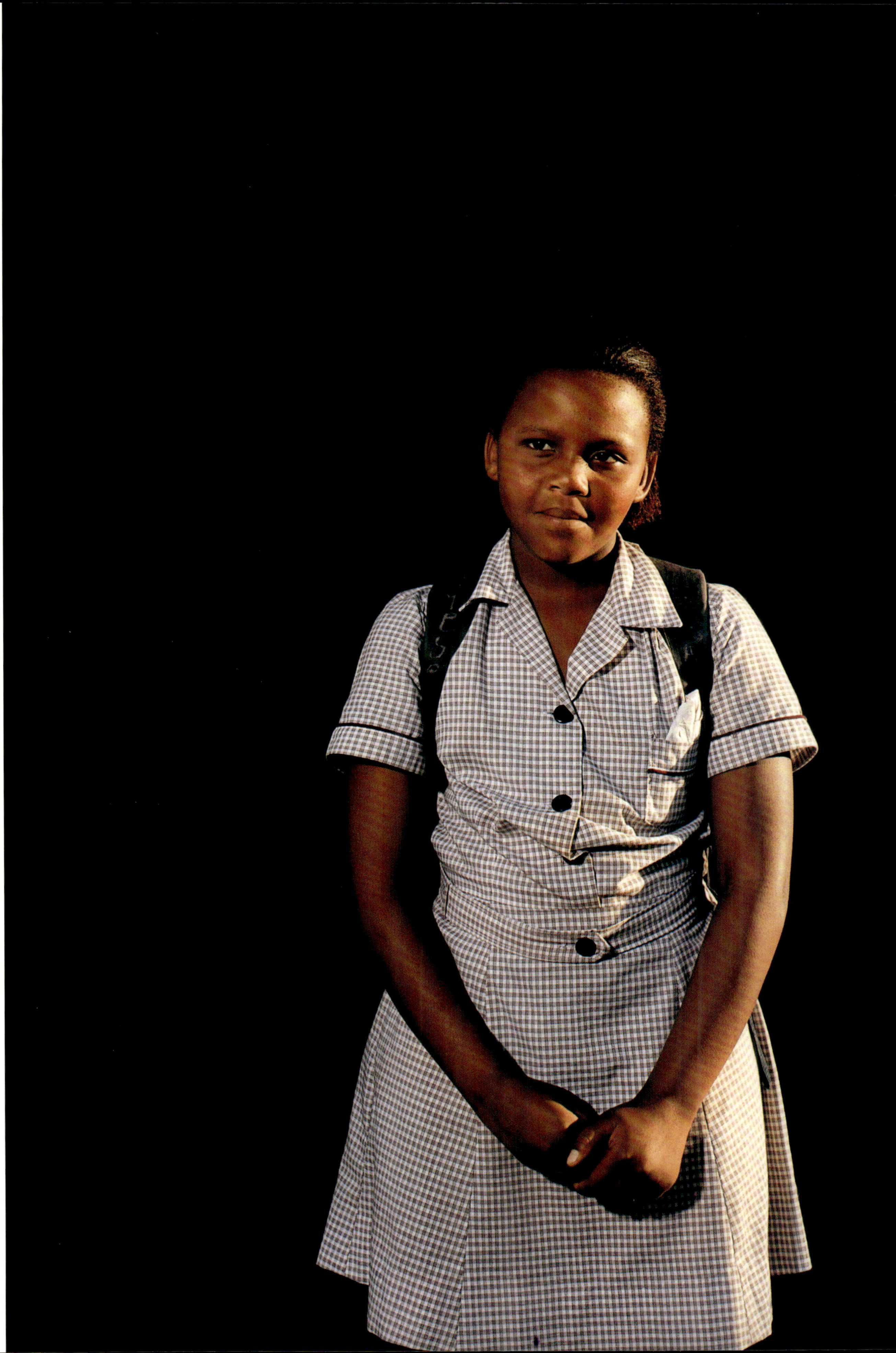

16

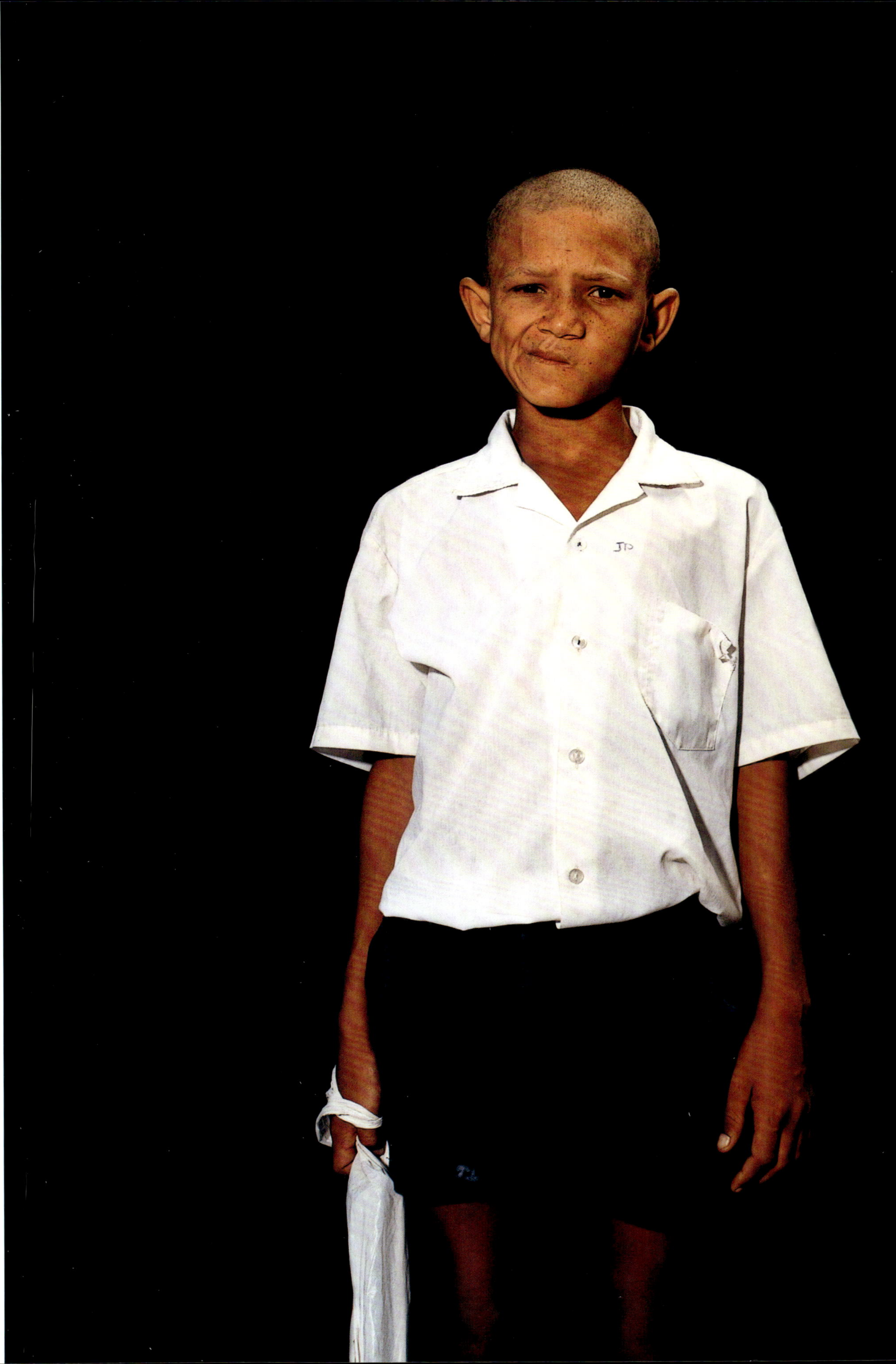

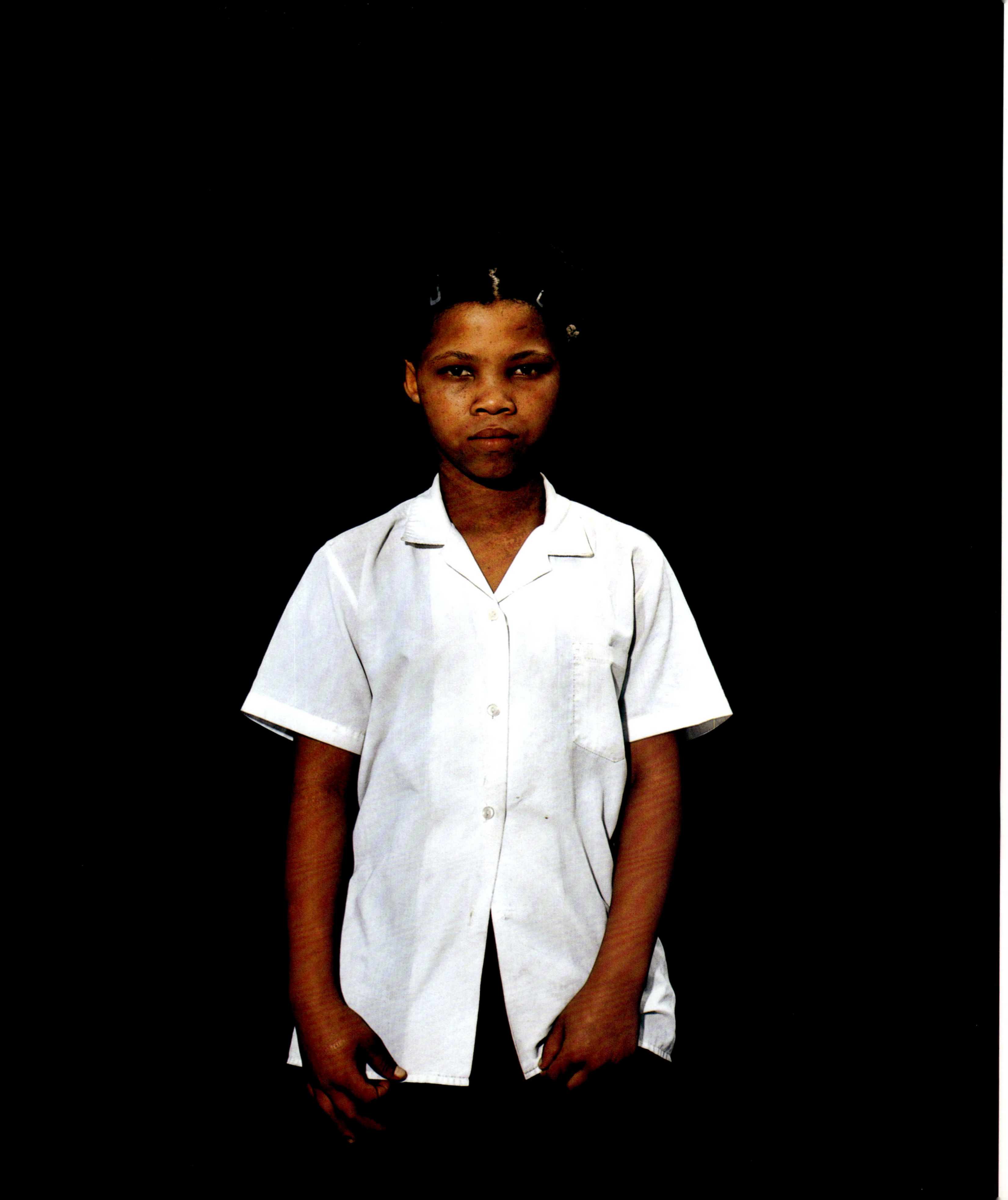

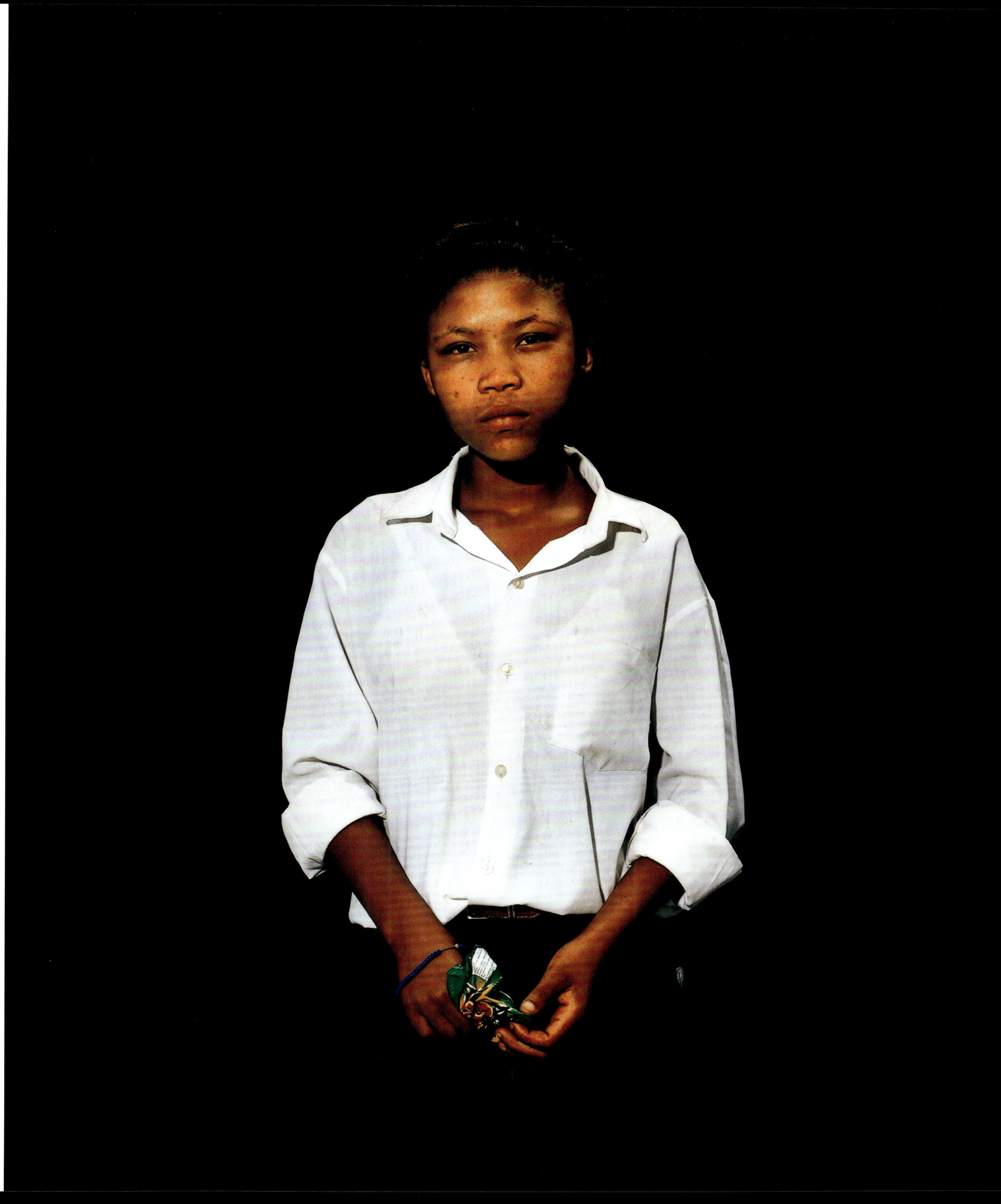

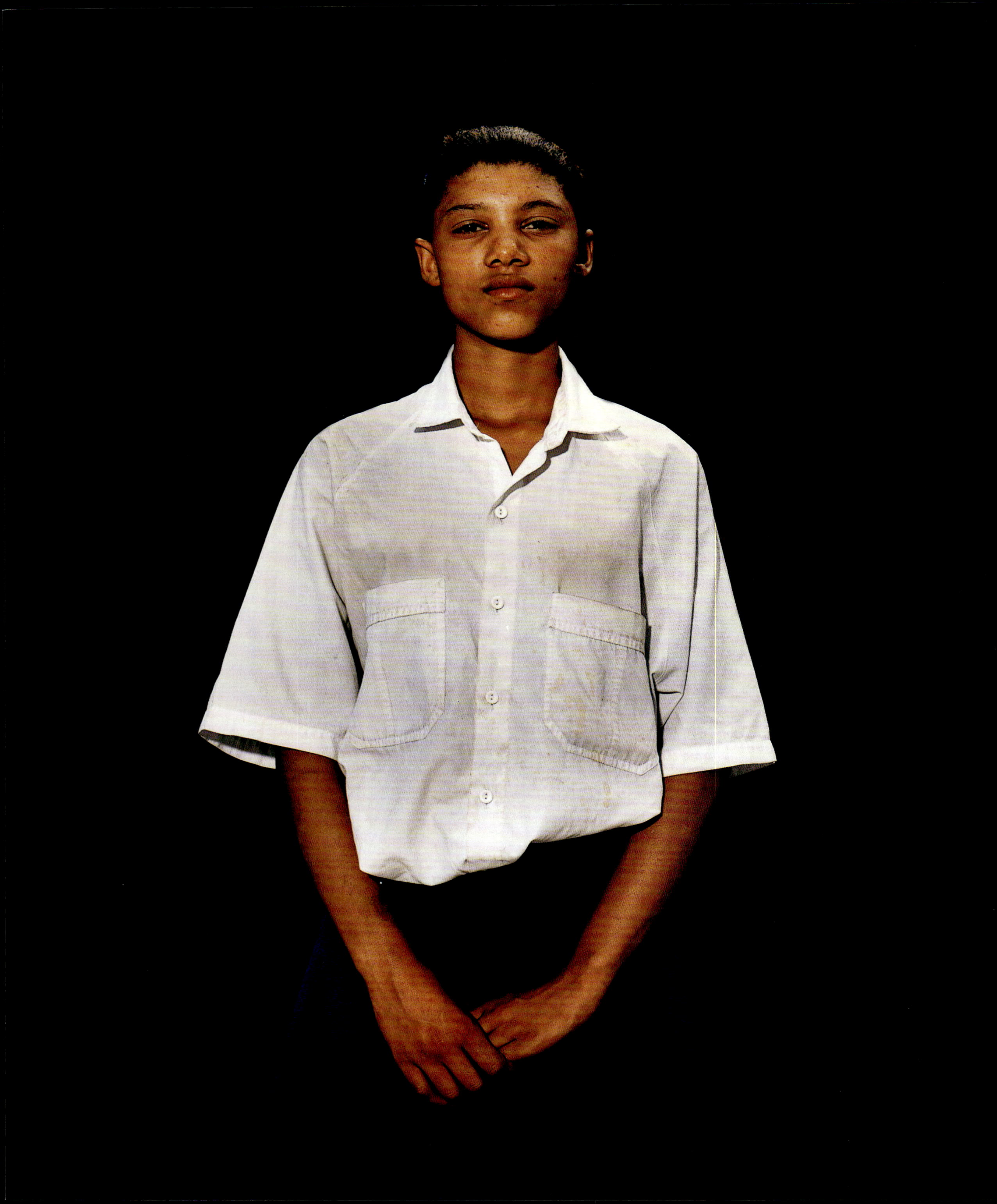

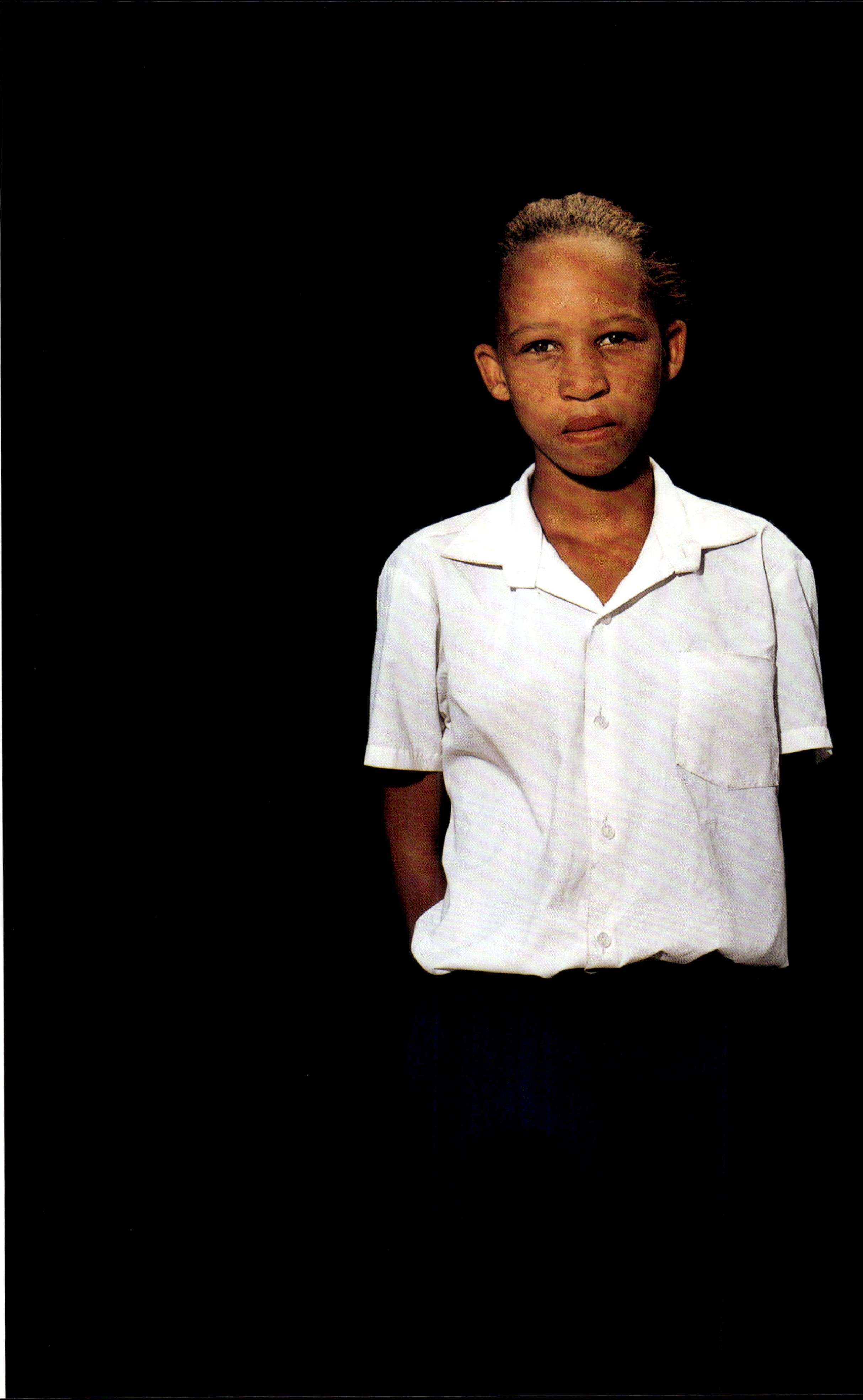

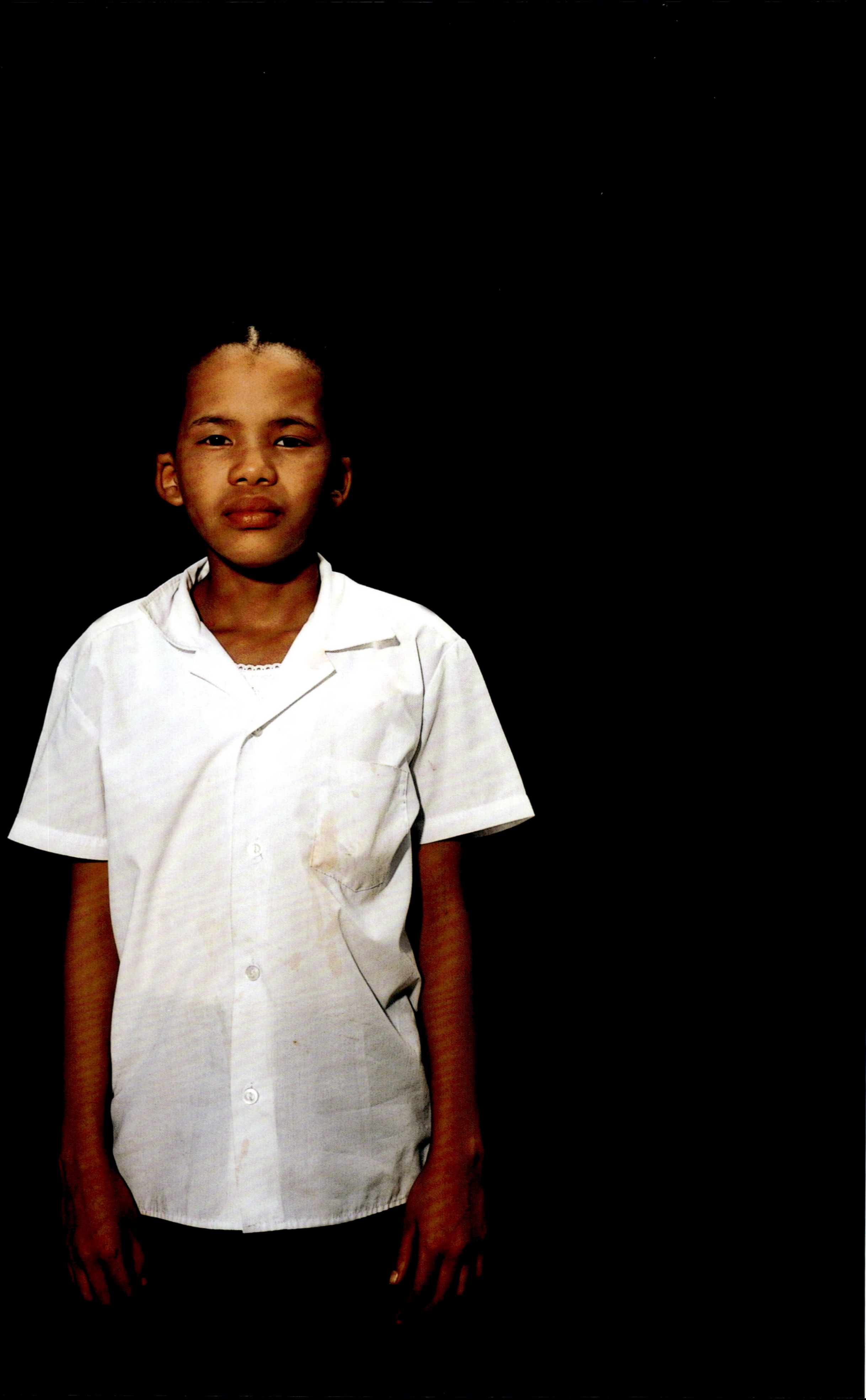

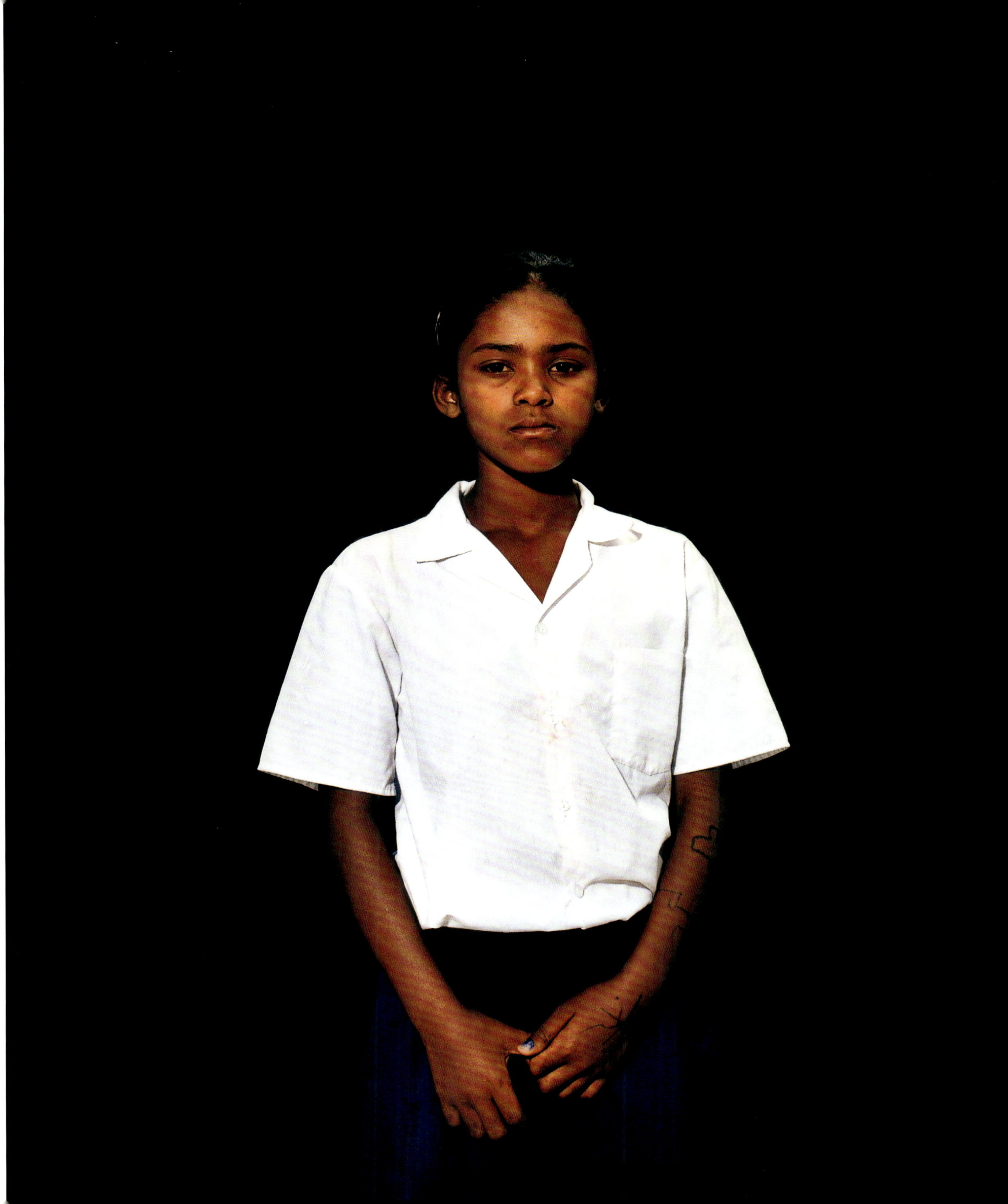

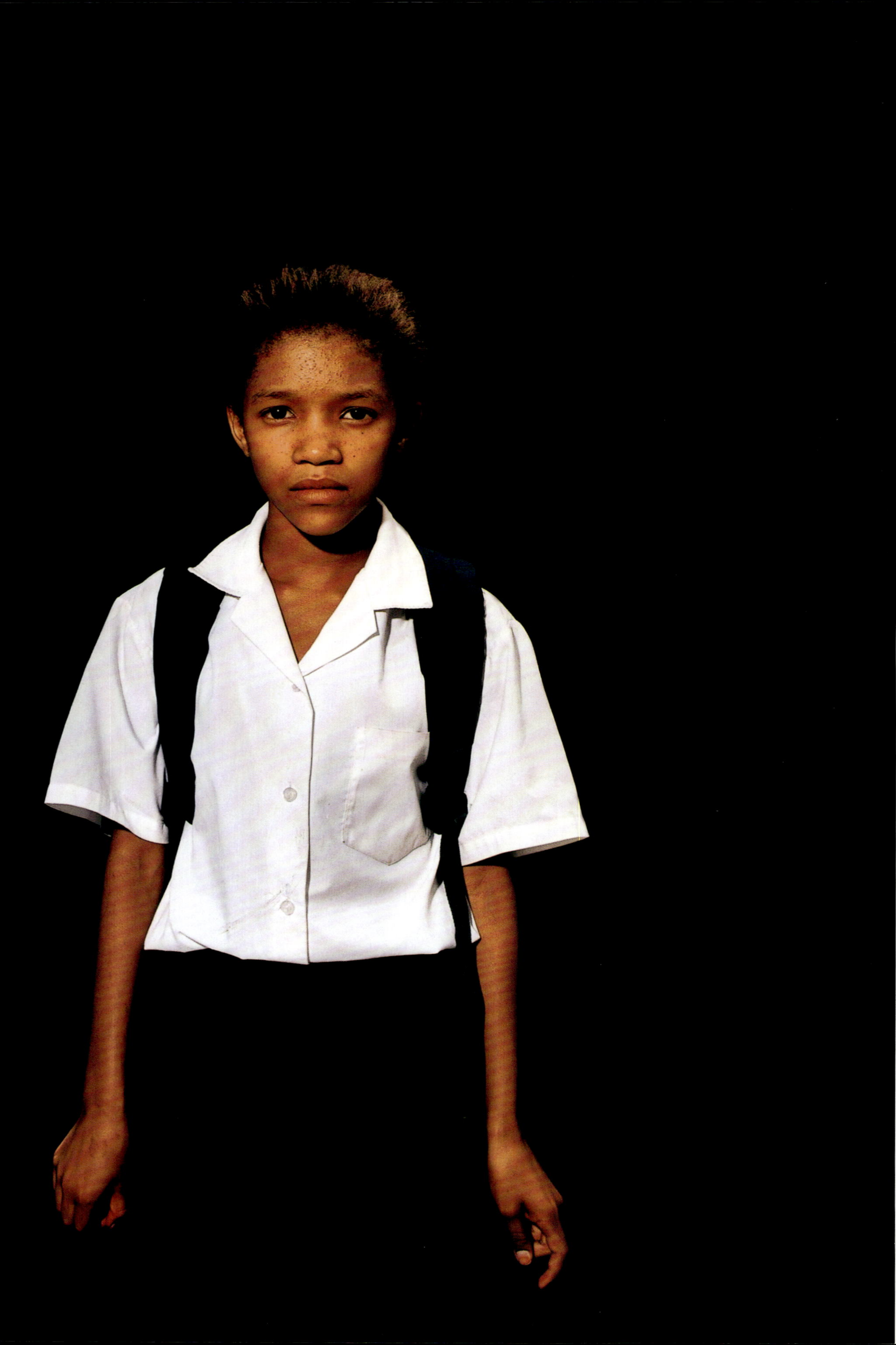

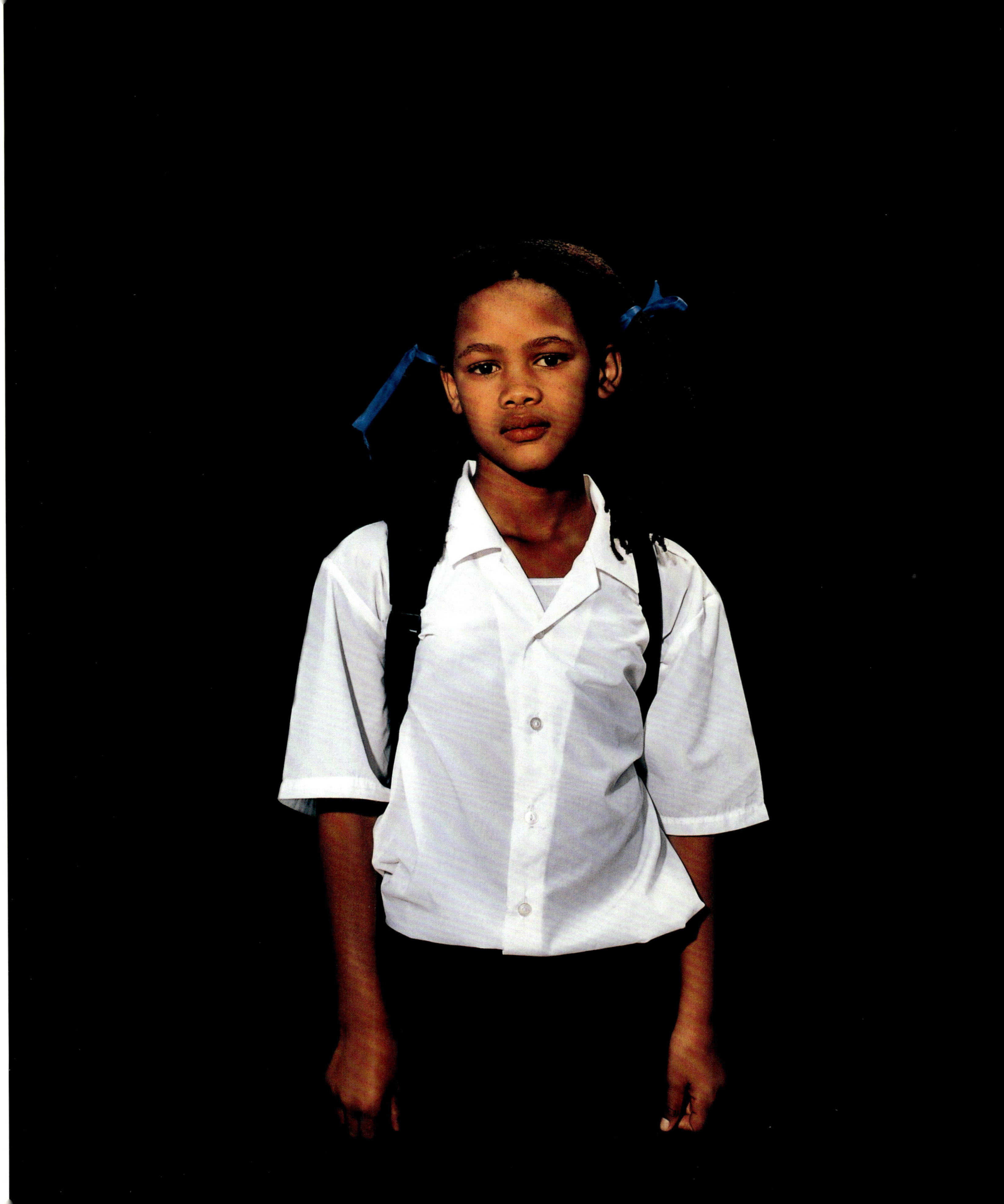

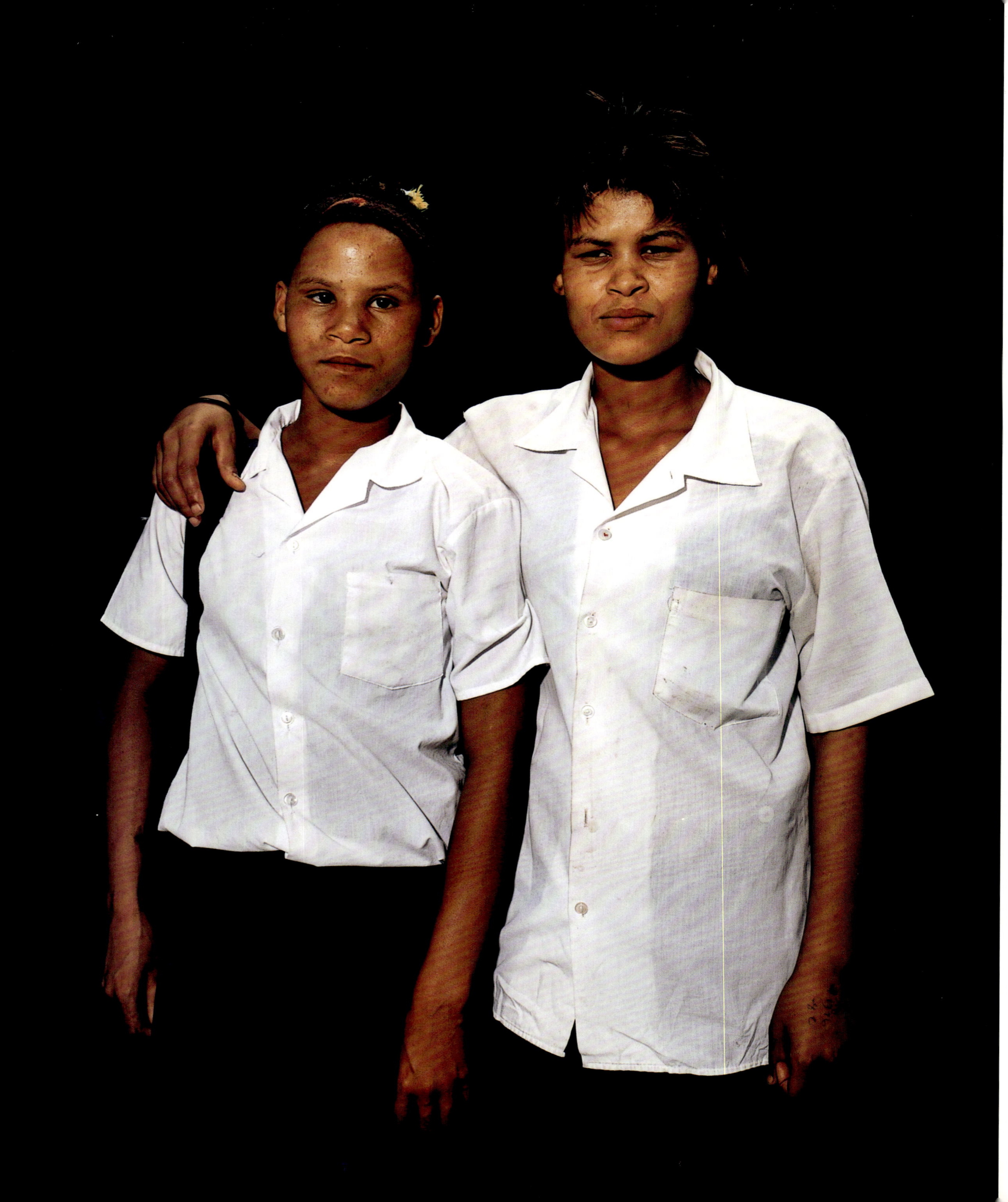

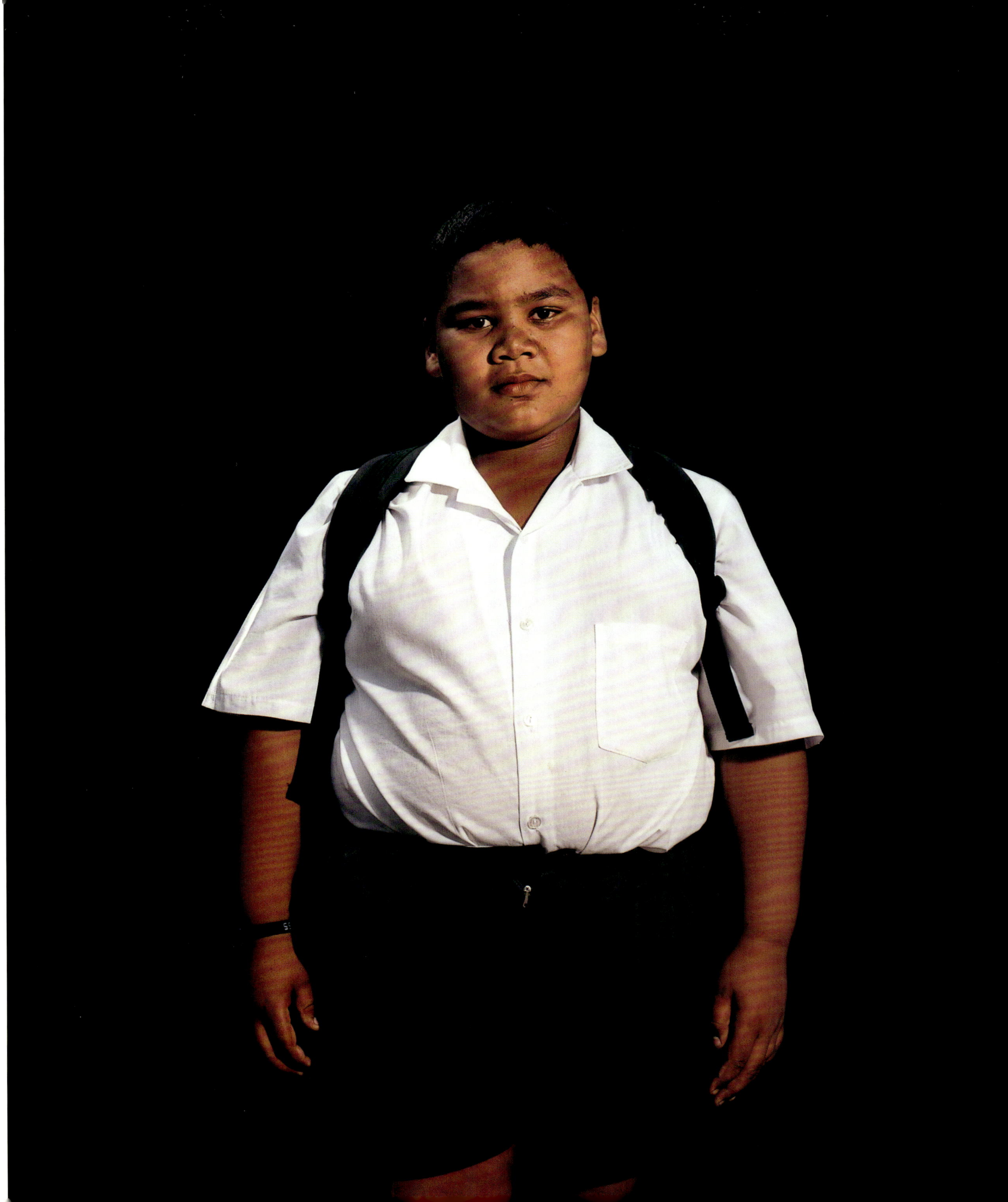

1

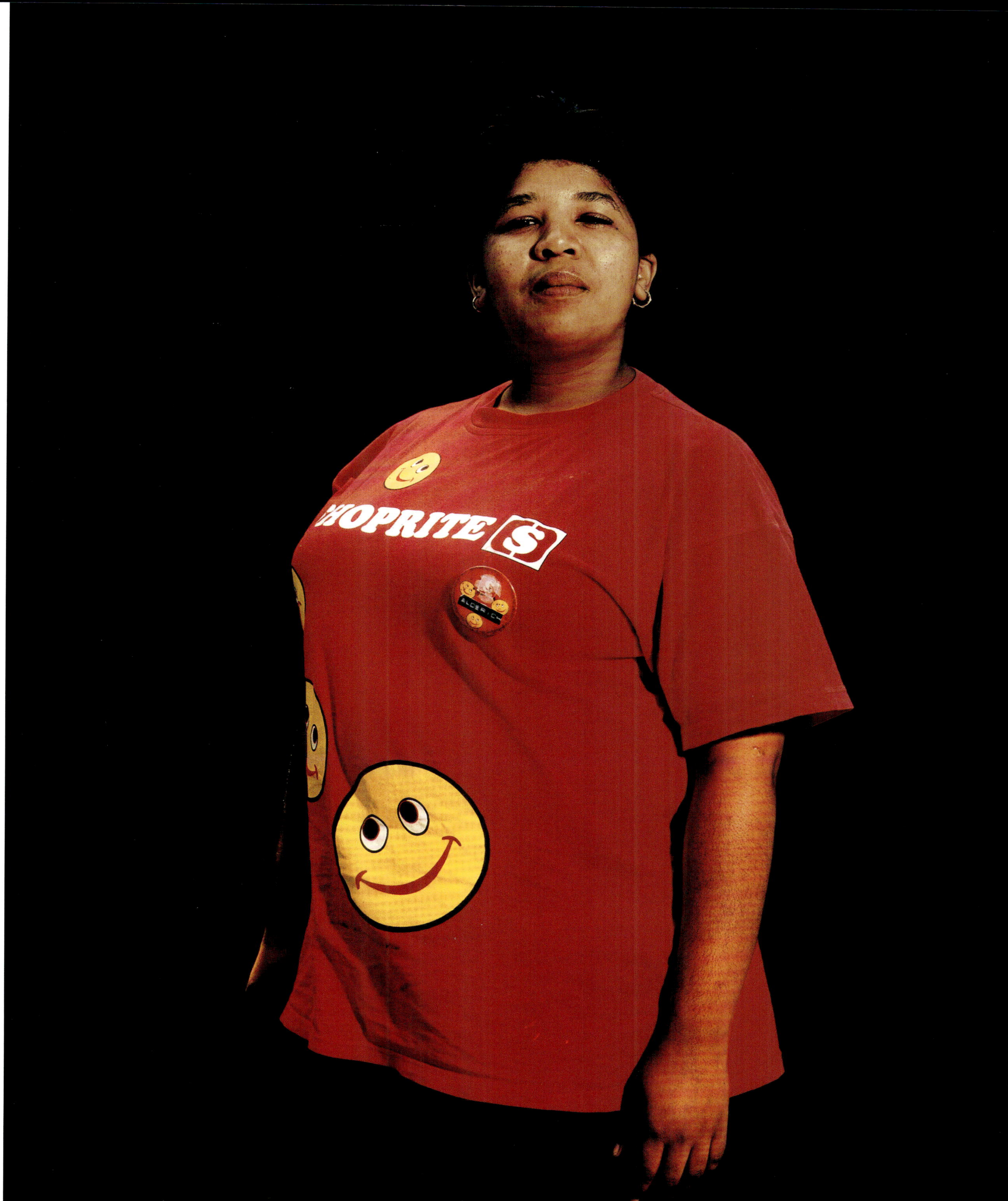
HOPRITE

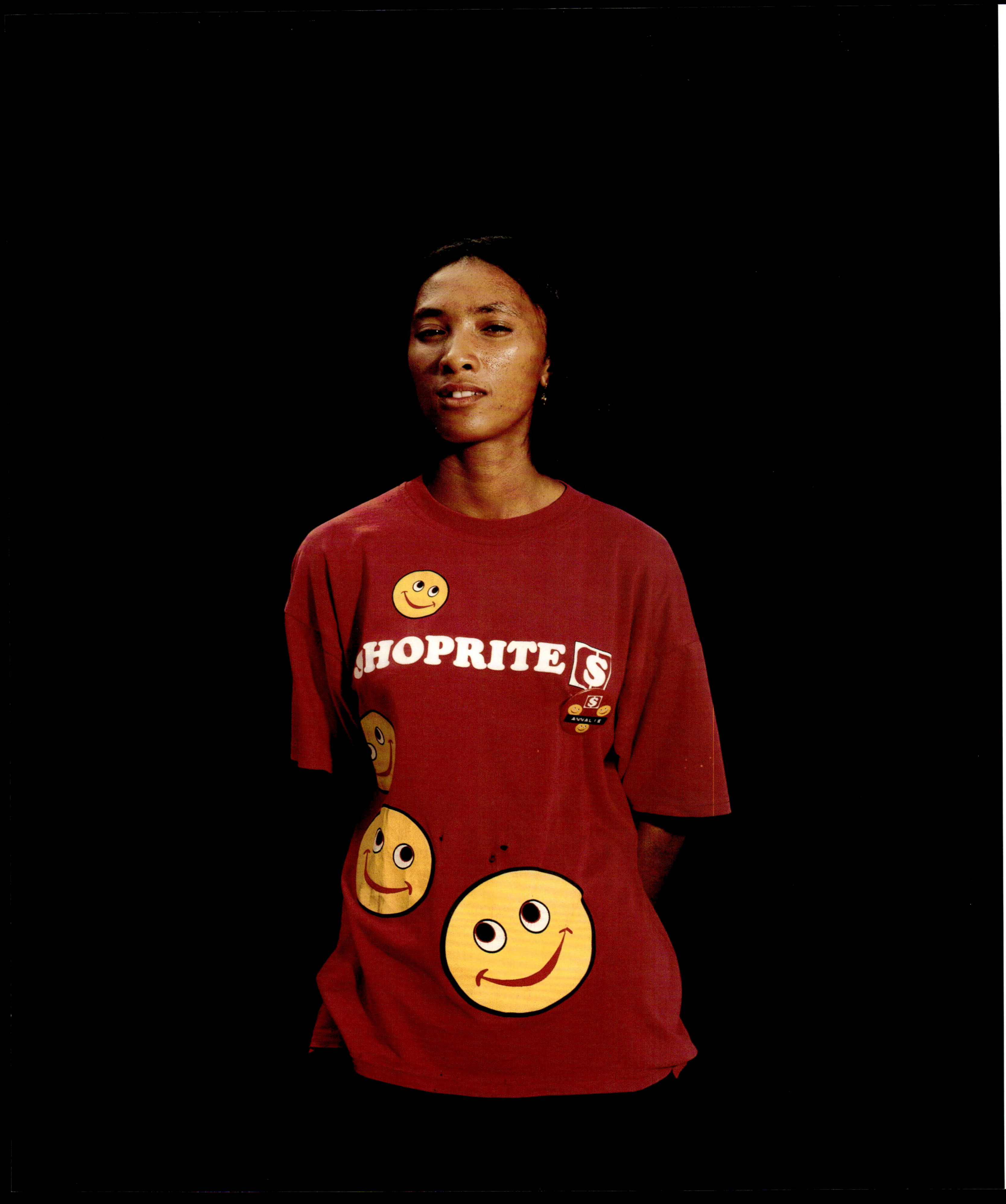
SHOPRITE

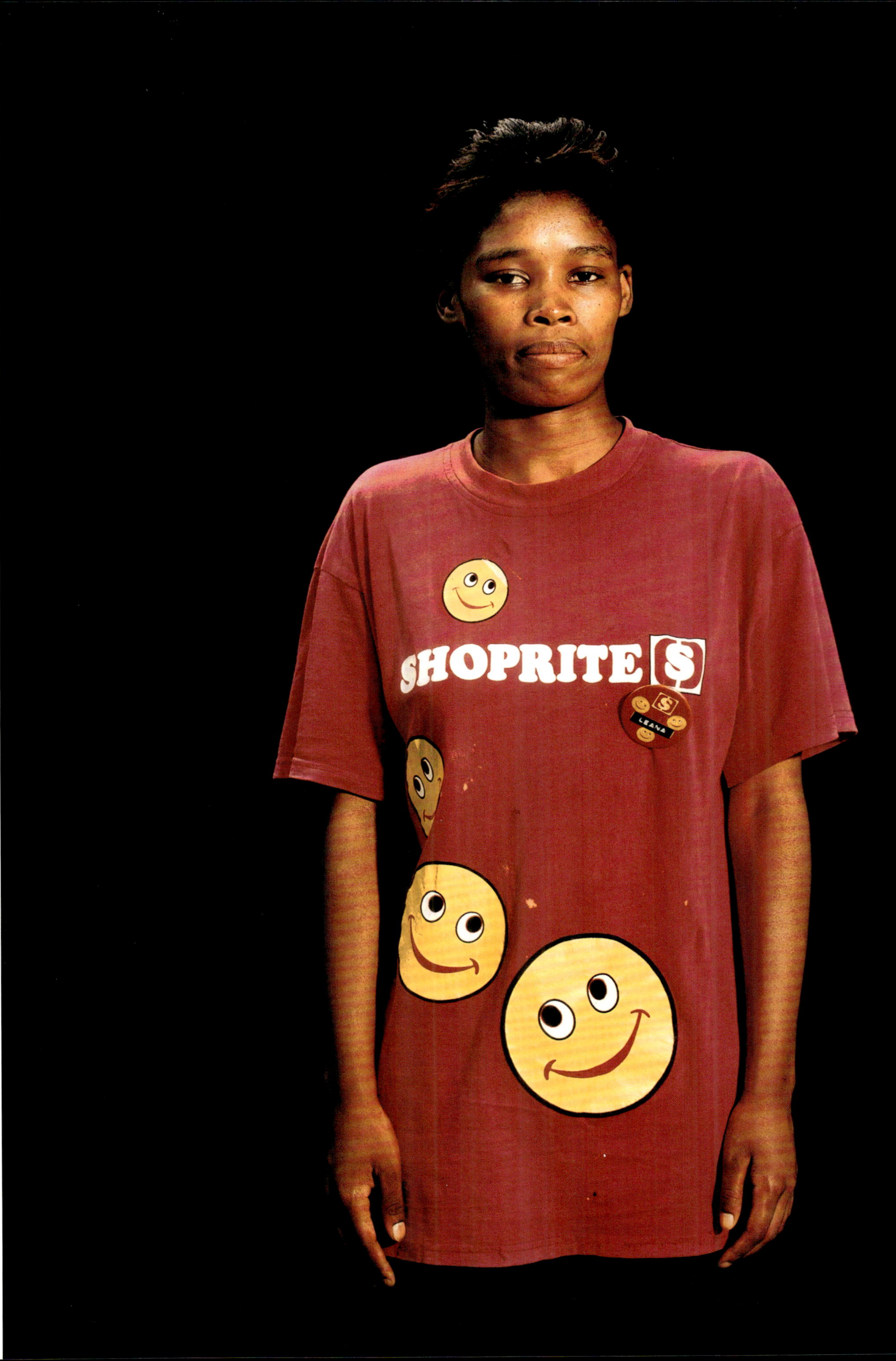
SHOPRITE
LEANA

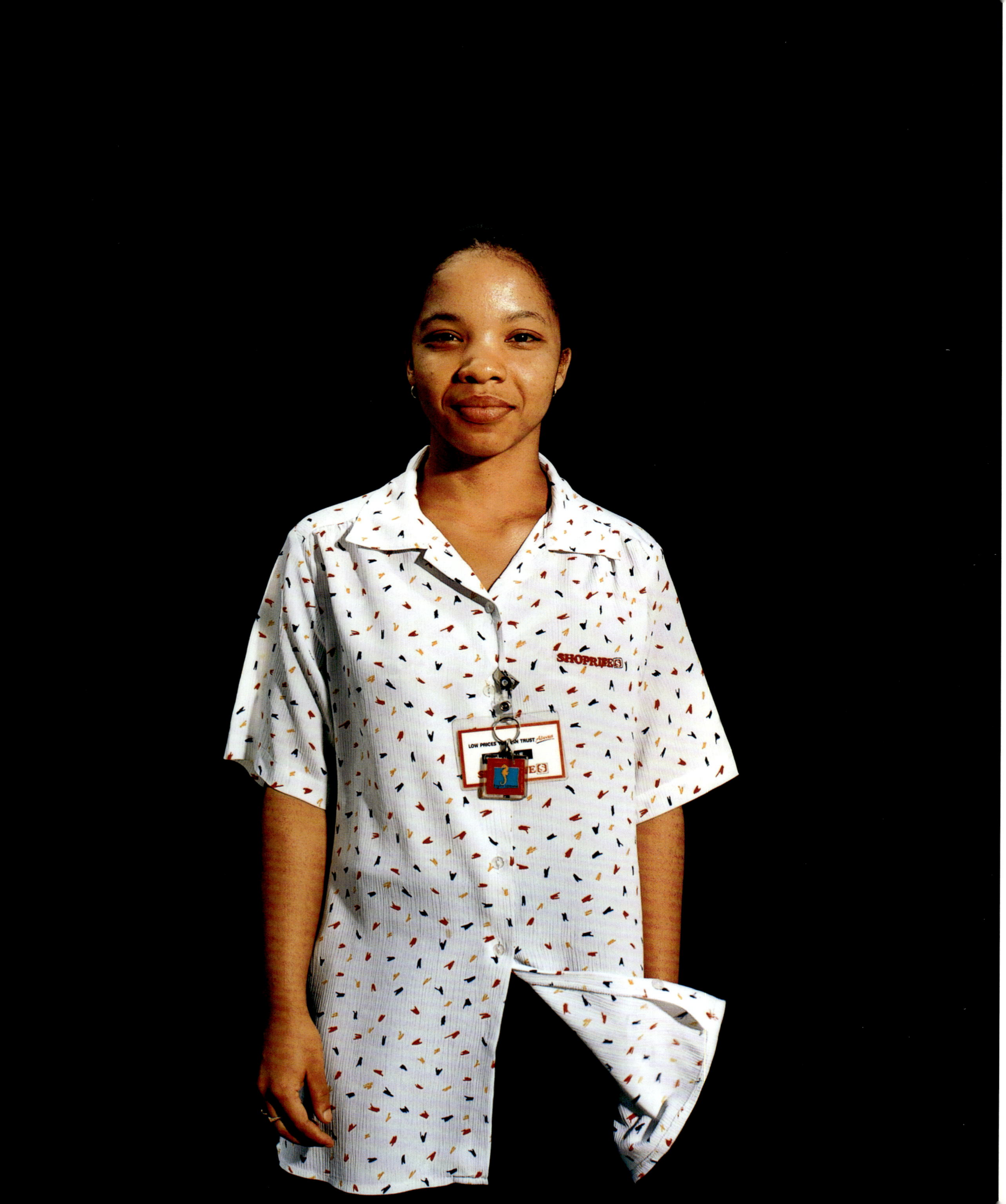

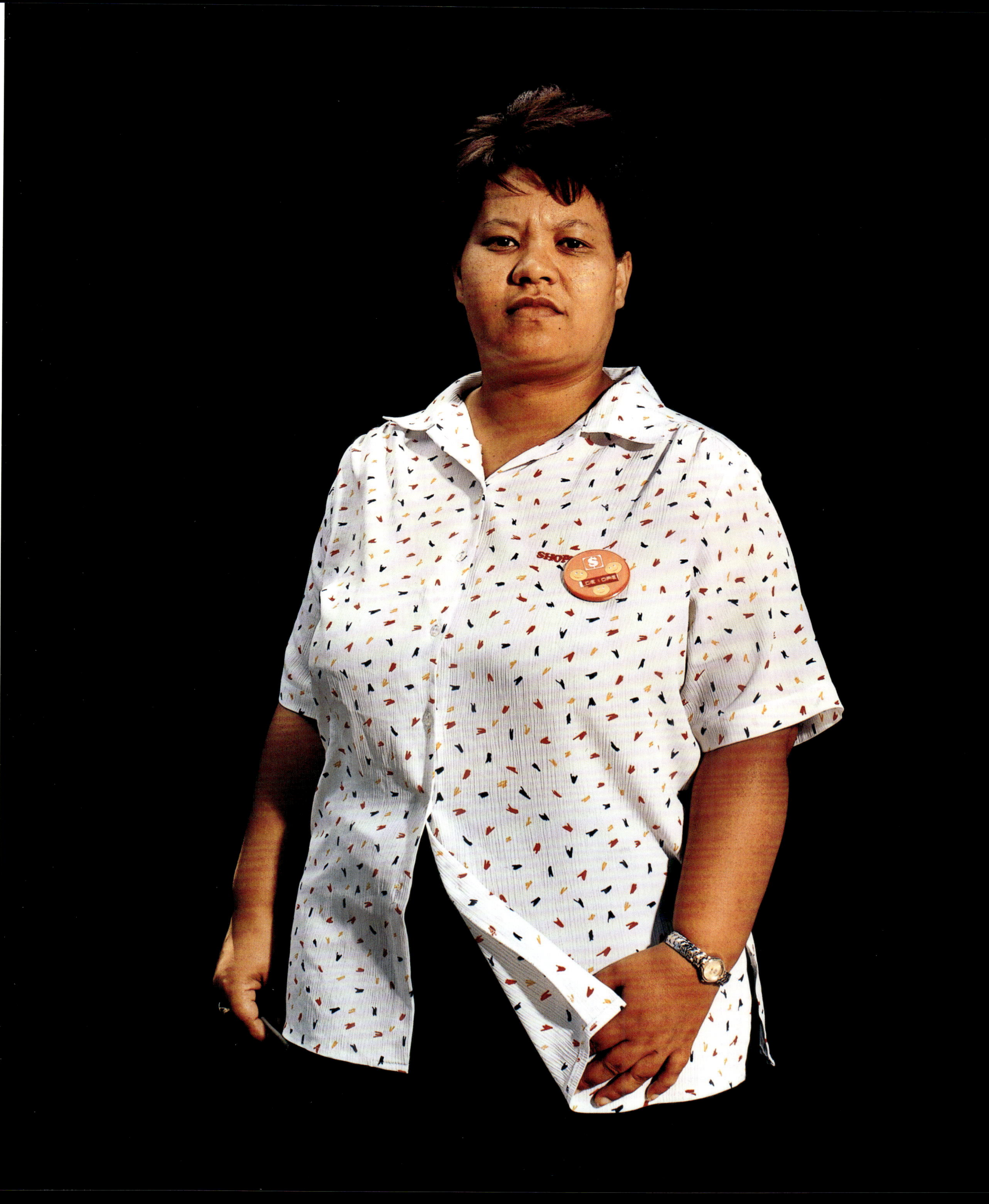

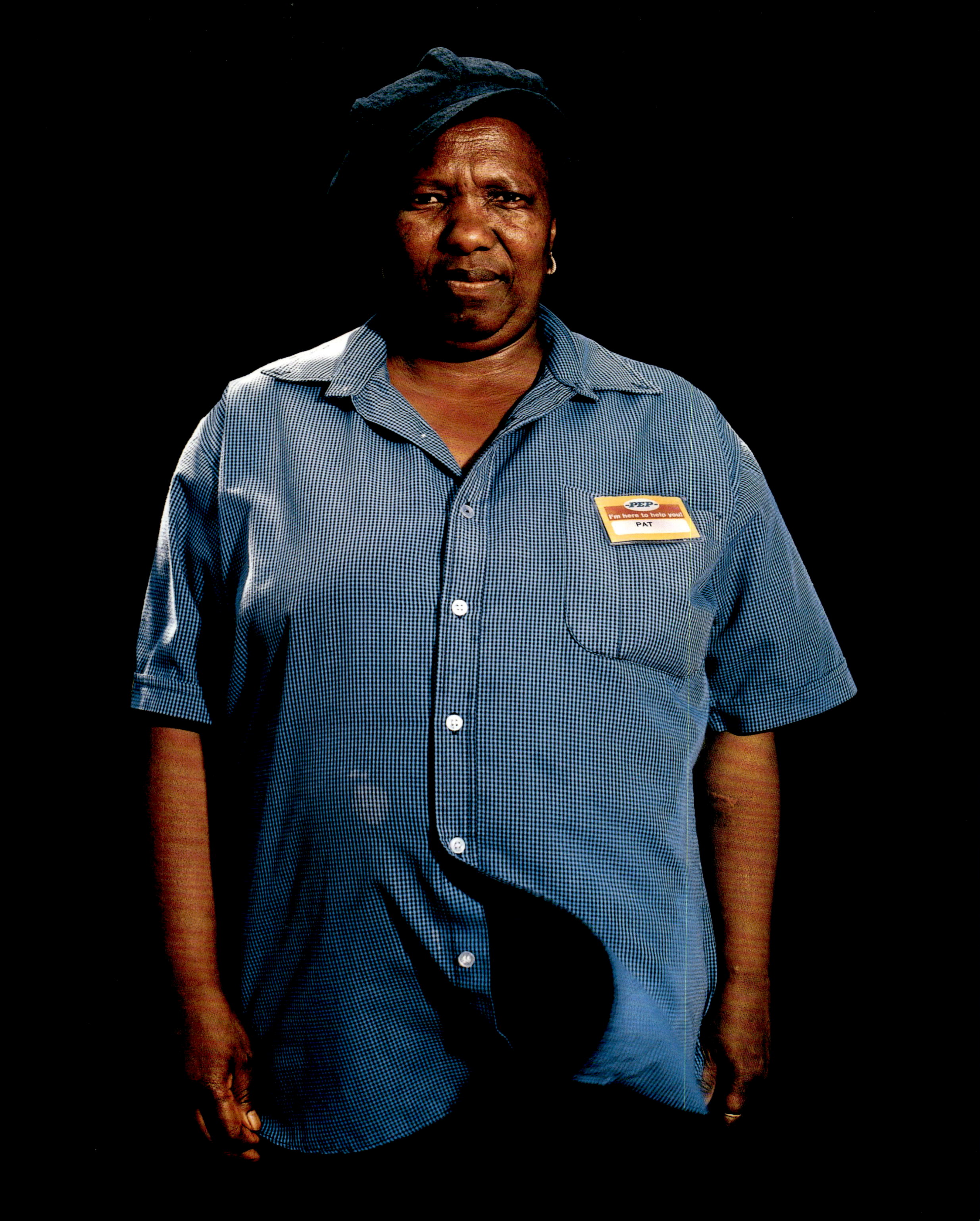
PEP
I'm here to help you!
PAT

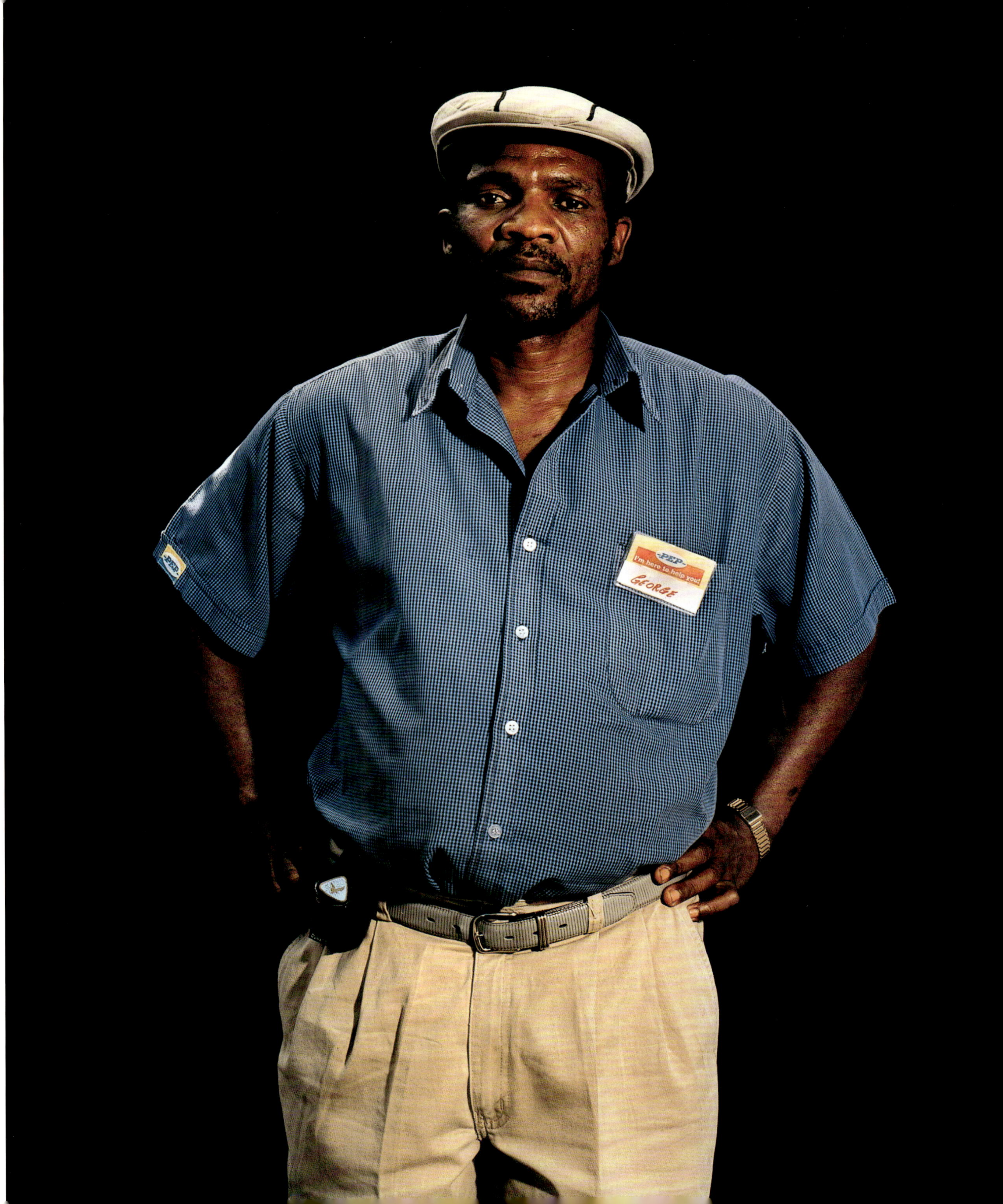
PEP
I'm here to help you!
GEORGE

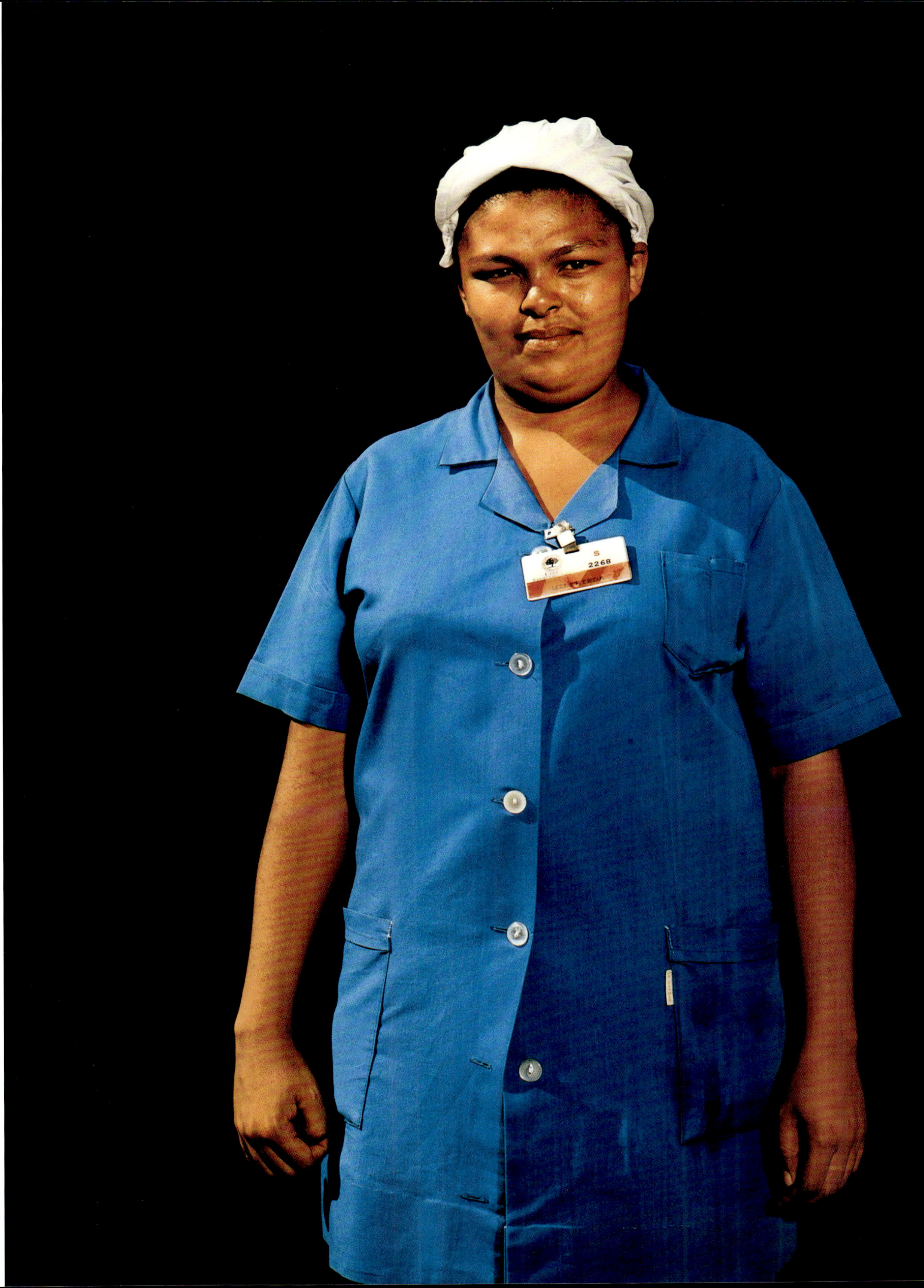
S
2268

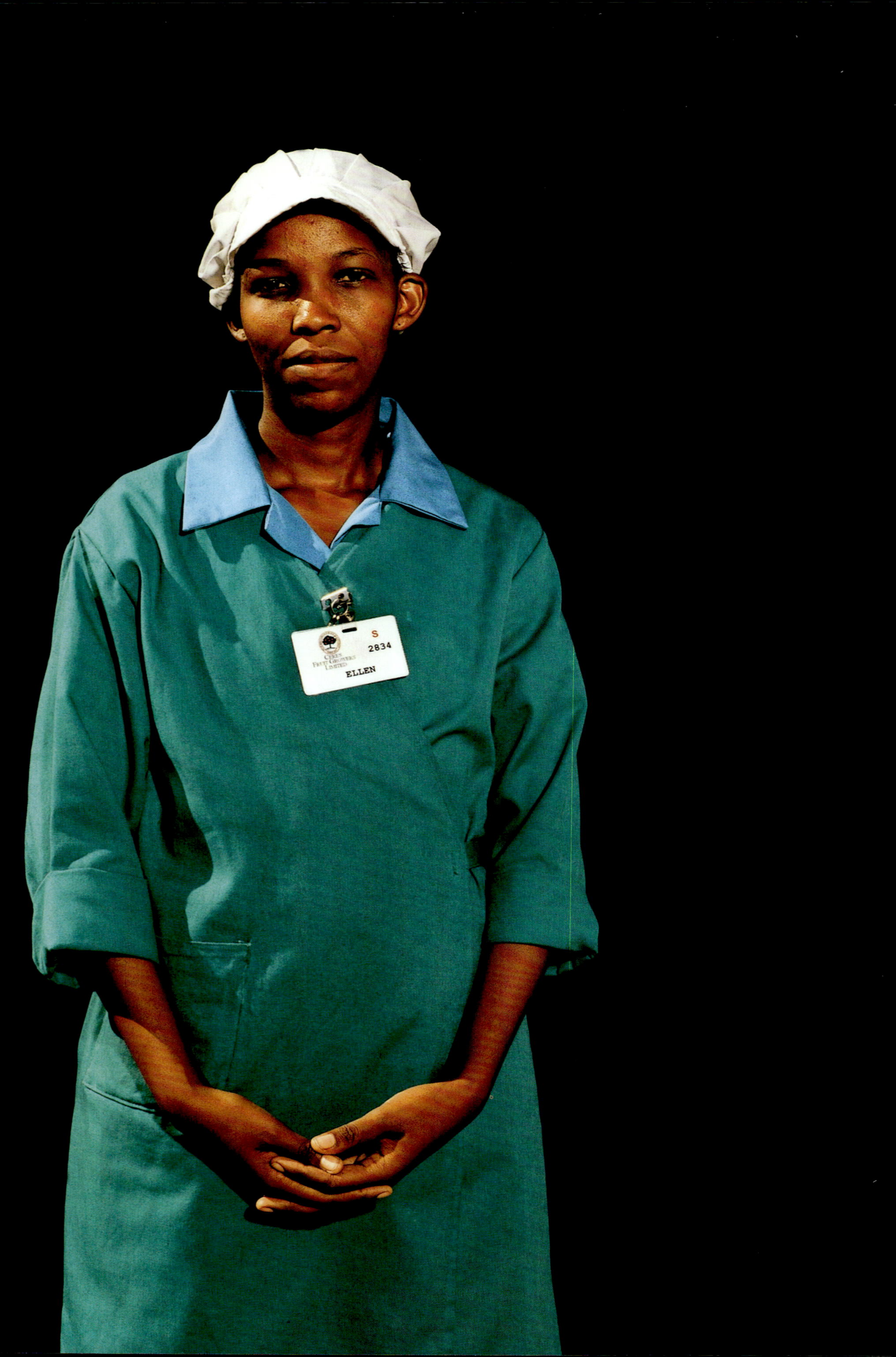
S
2834
CERES FRUIT GROWERS LIMITED
ELLEN

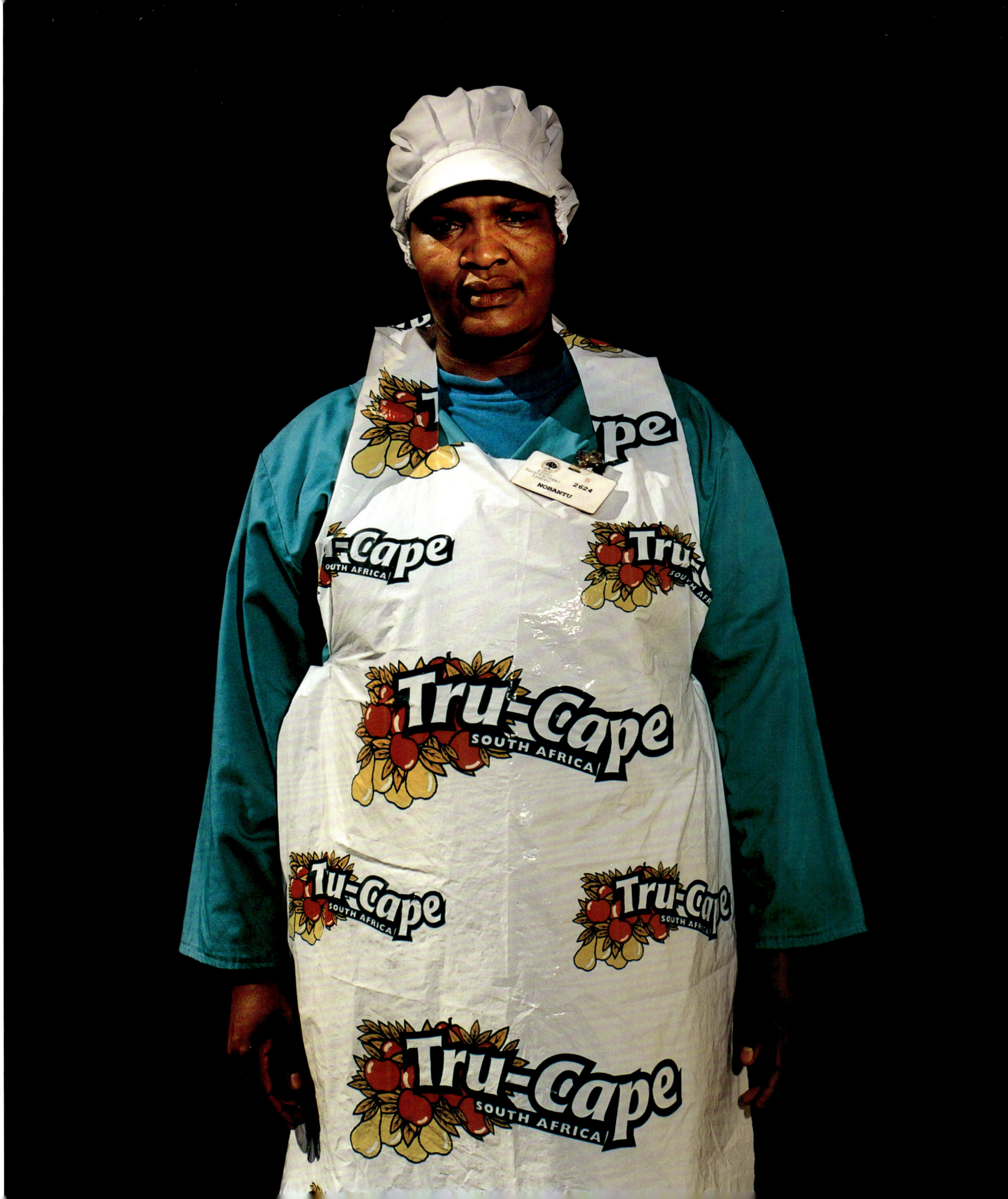
Tru-Cape
SOUTH AFRICA
2624
NOBANTU

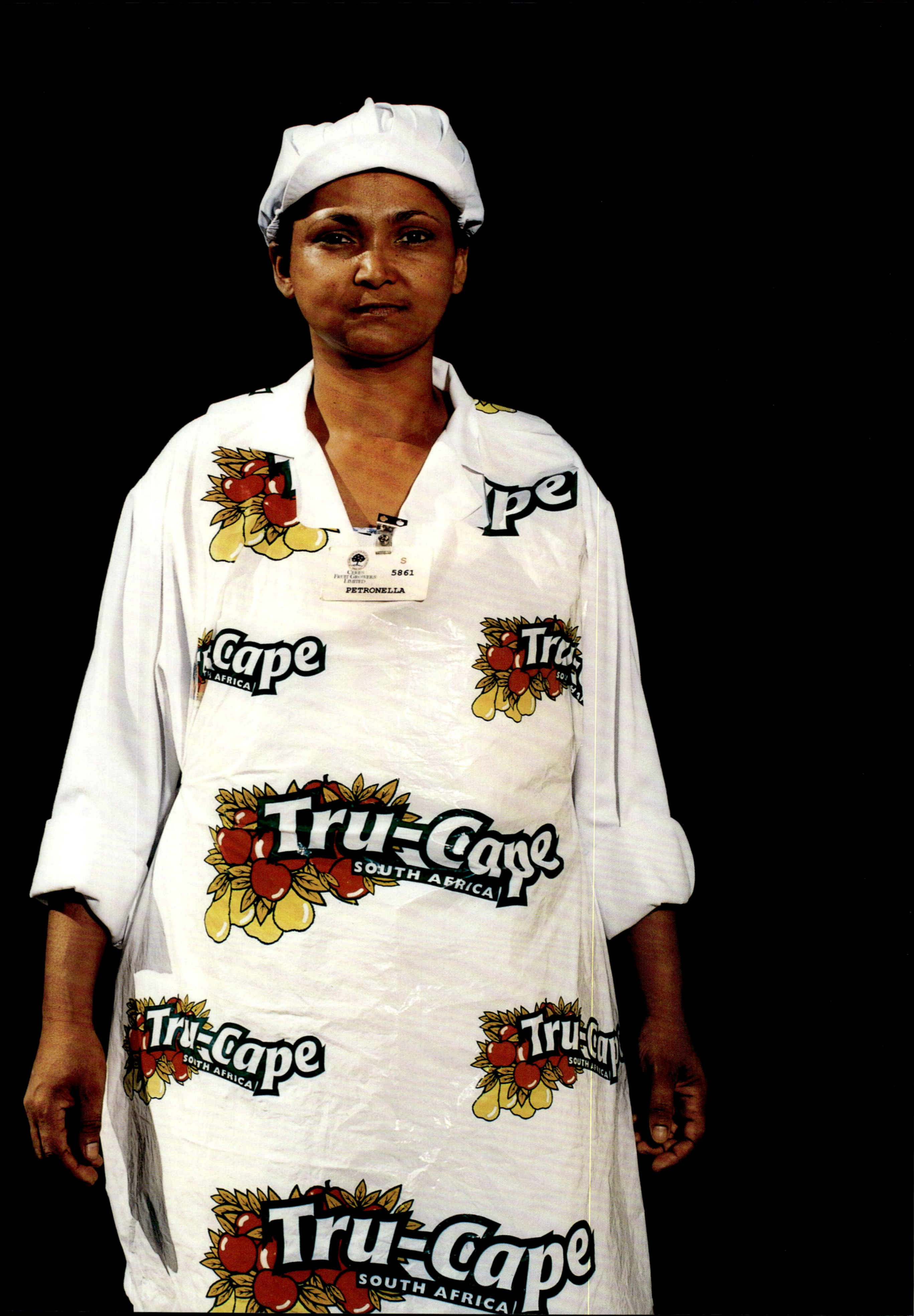
S
5861
PETRONELLA
Tru-Cape
SOUTH AFRICA

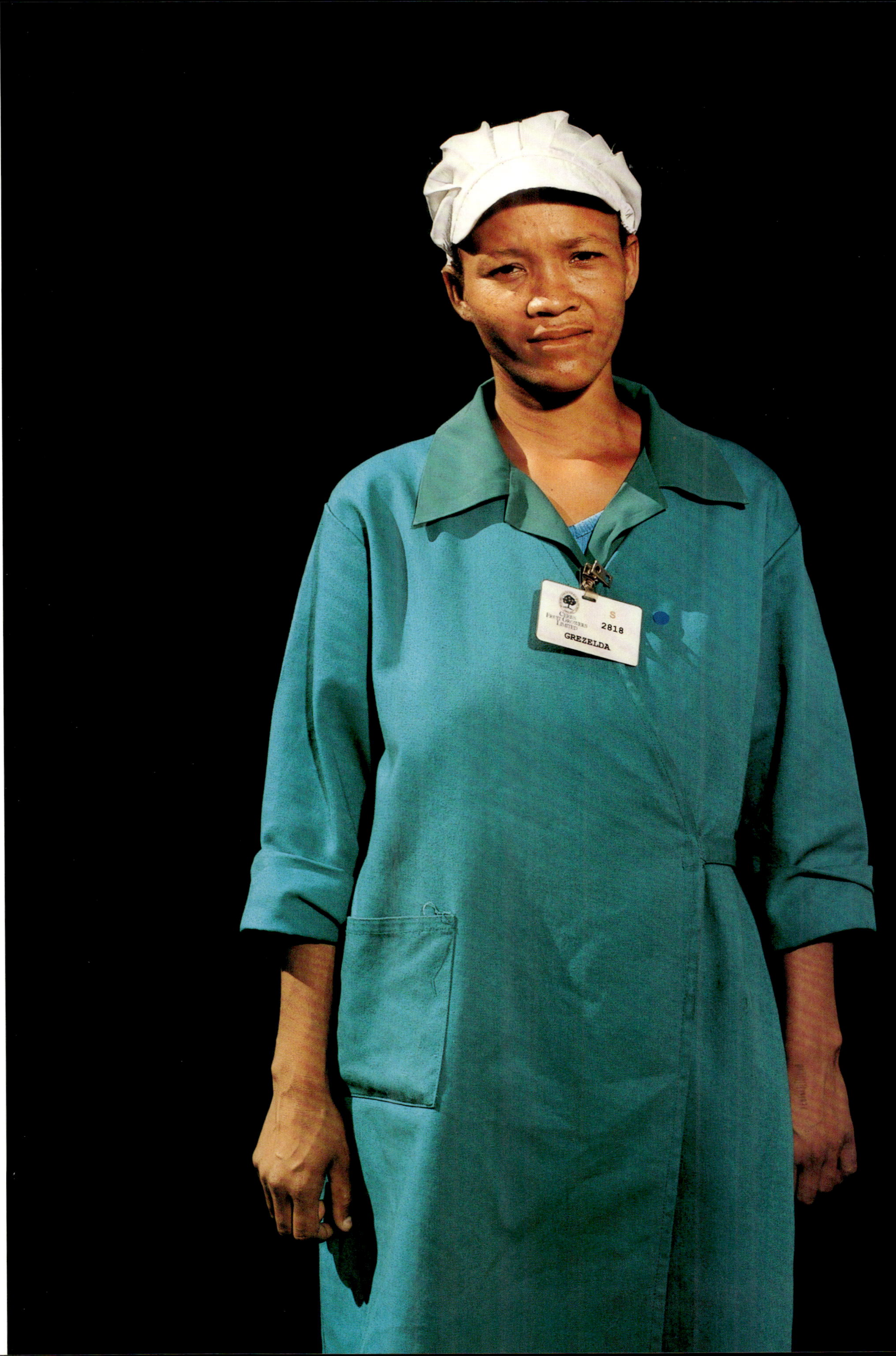

89

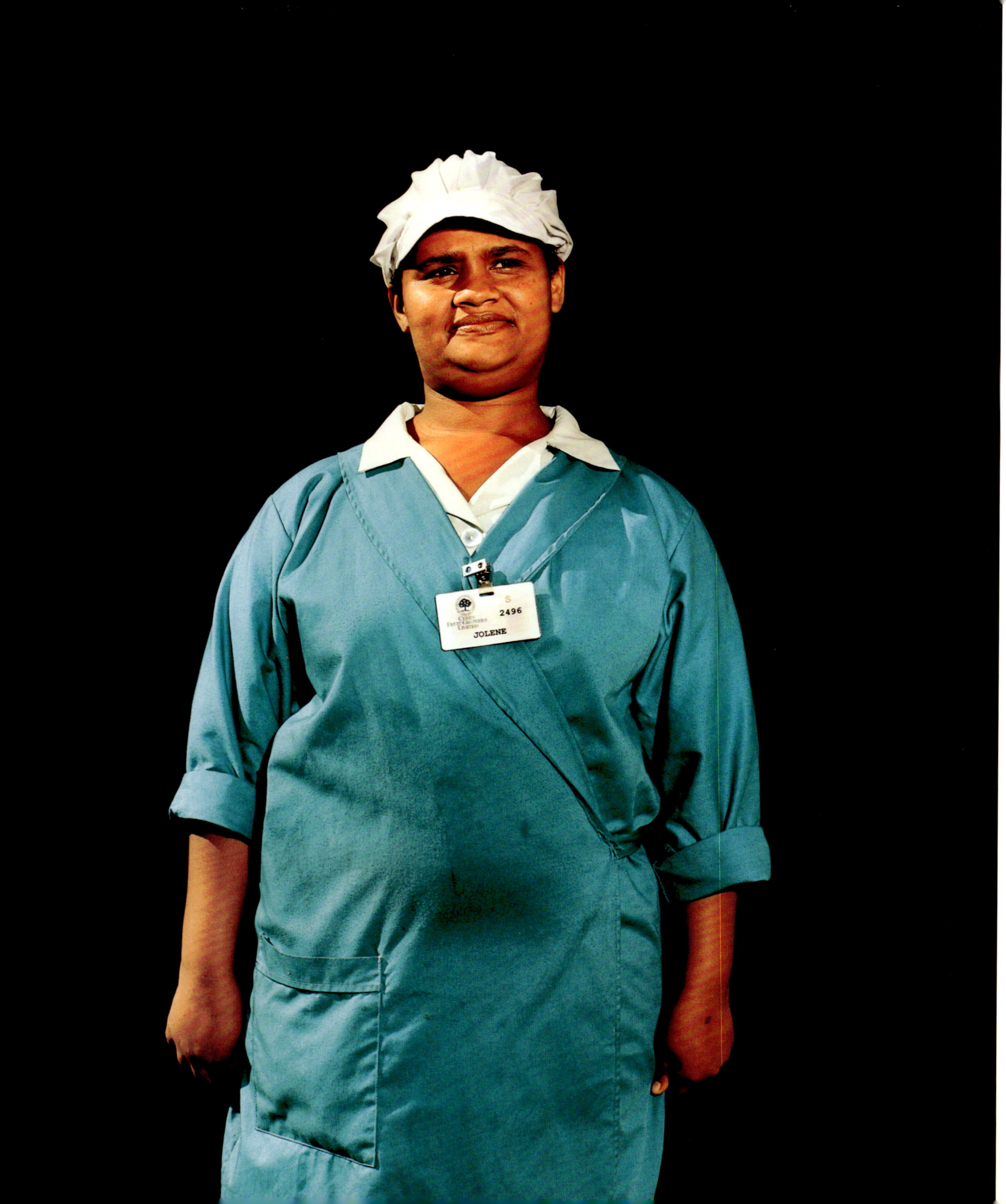
S
2496
JOLENE

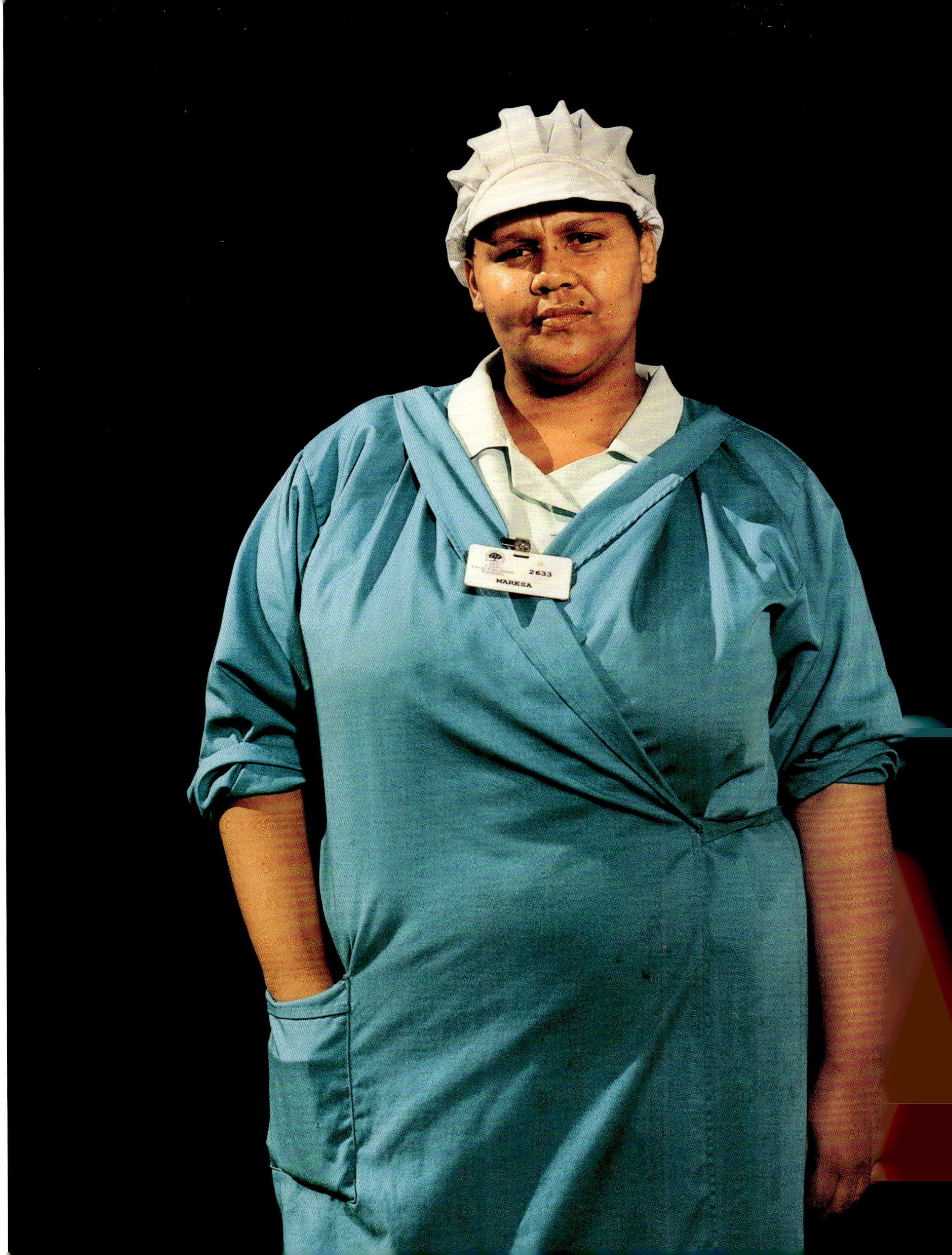
2633
MARESA

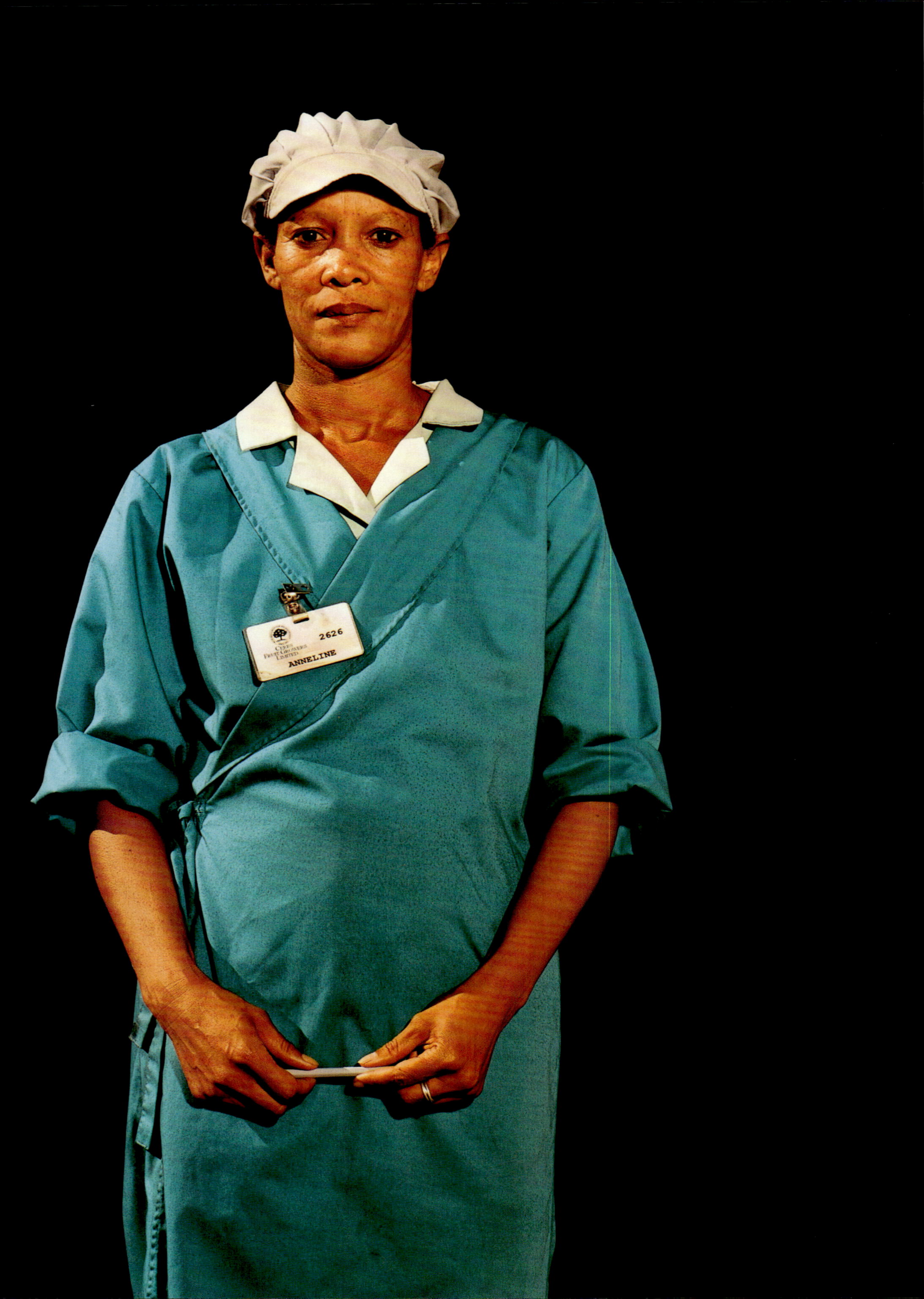
2626
CERES
FRUIT GROWERS
LIMITED
ANNELINE

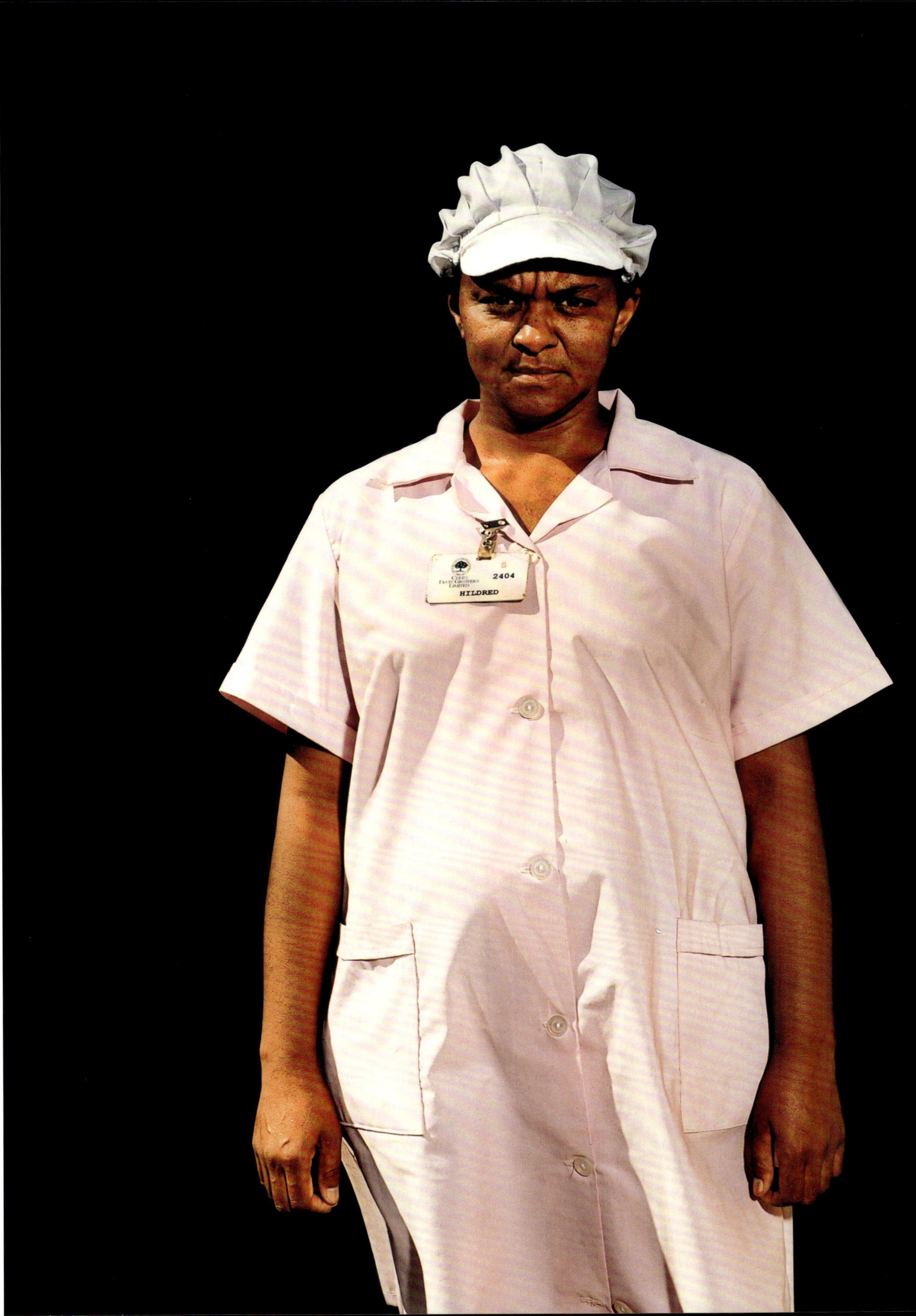
S
2404
HILDRED

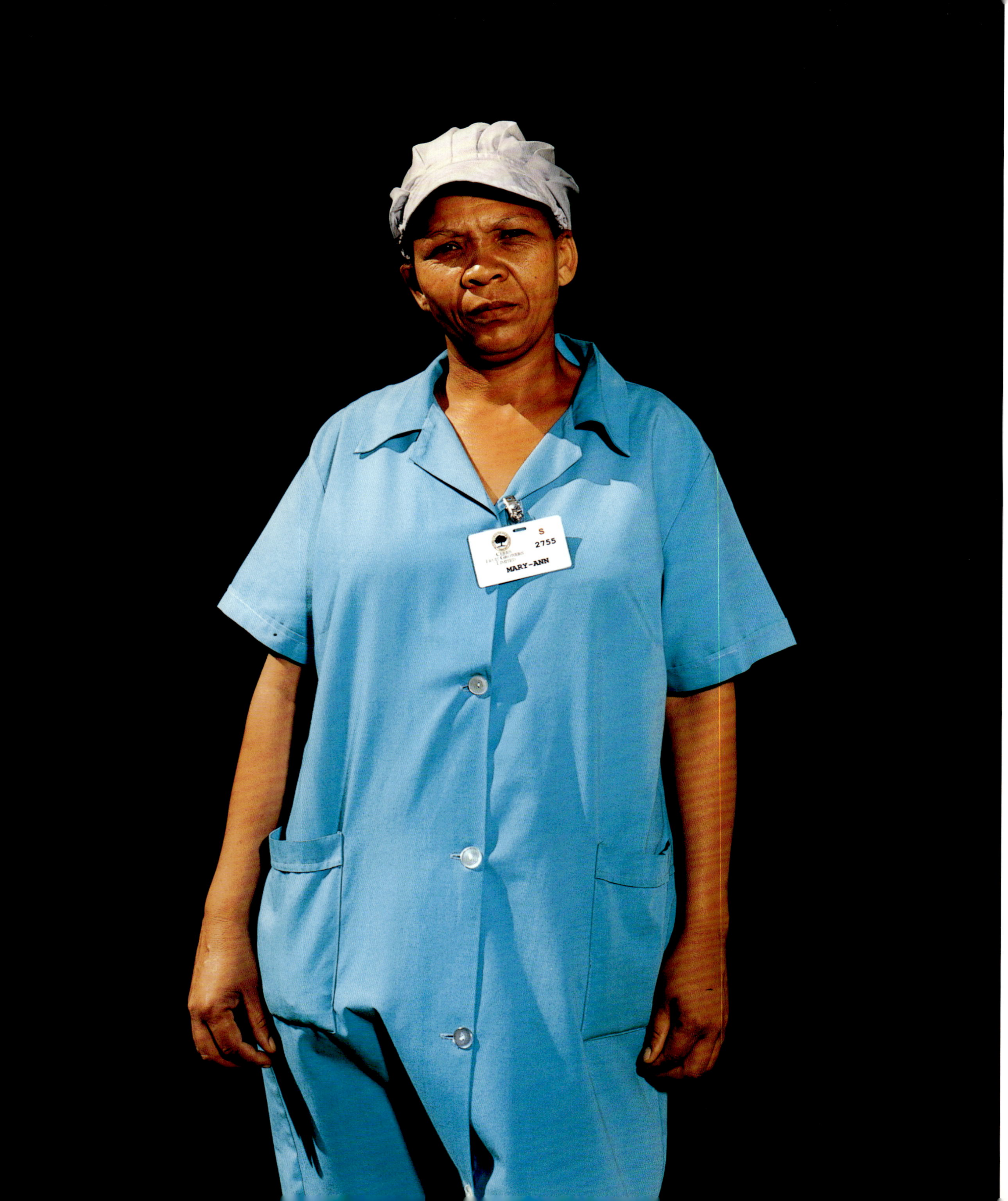
S
2755
MARY-ANN

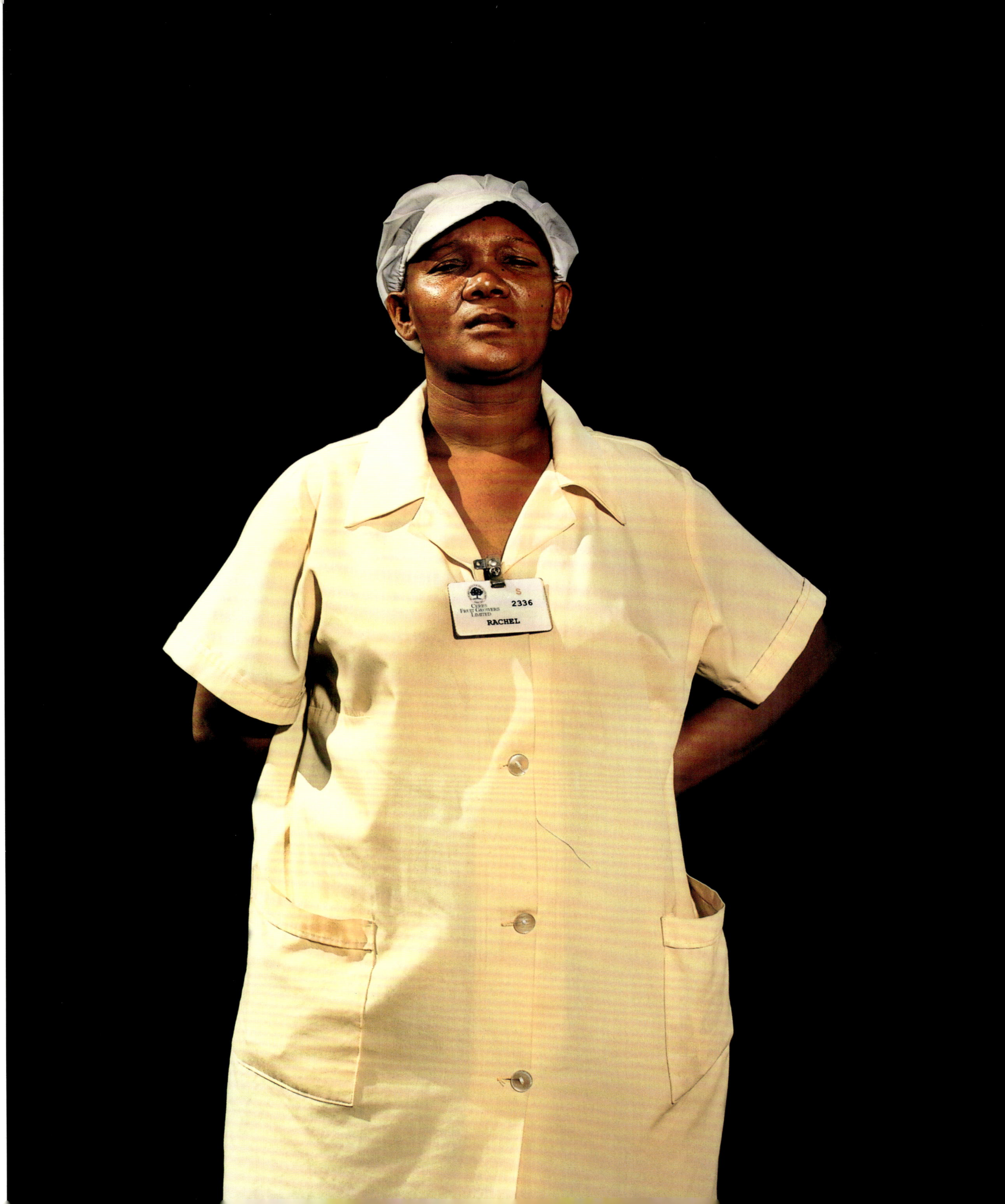

5

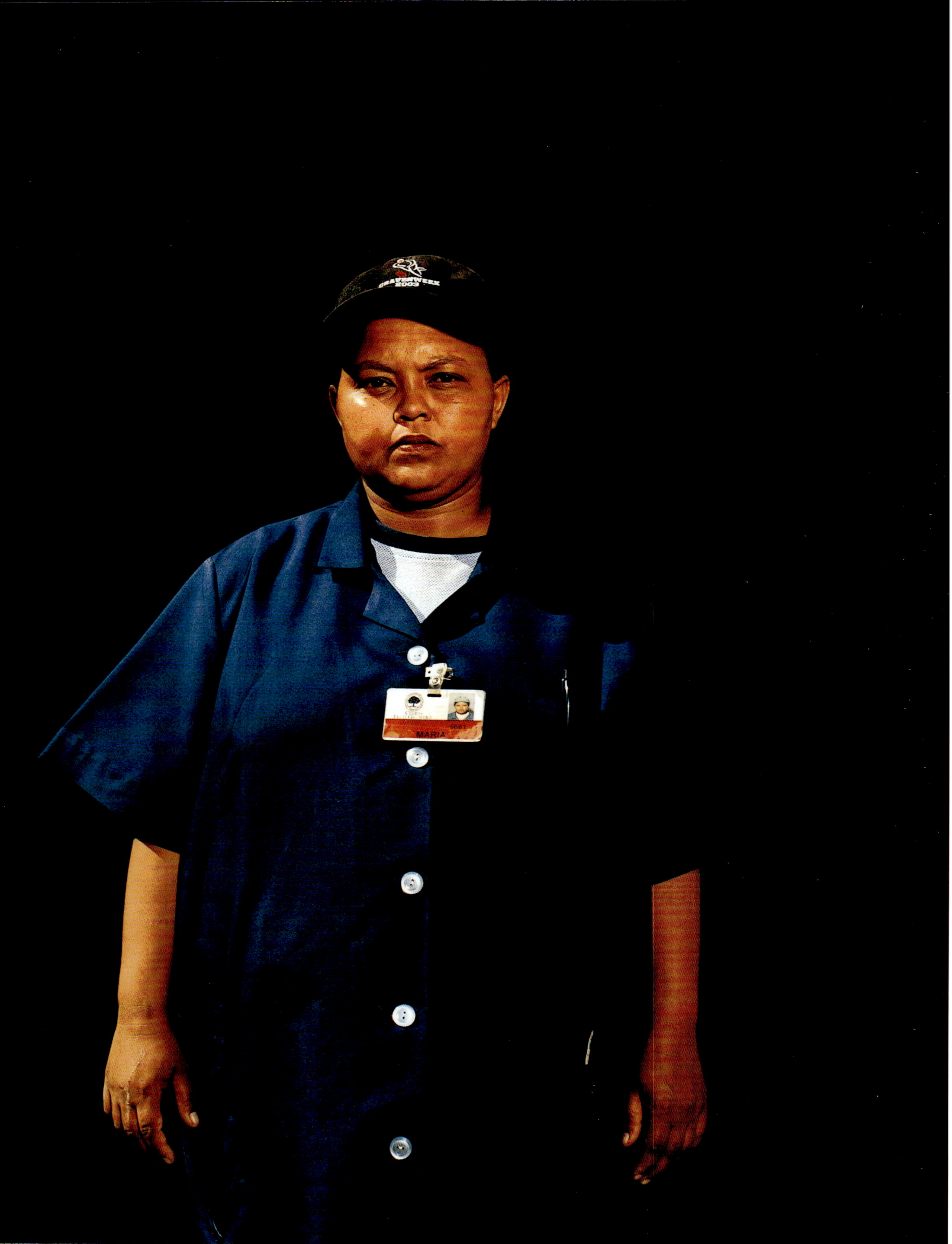
CRAVENWEEK
2003
5661
MARIA

7

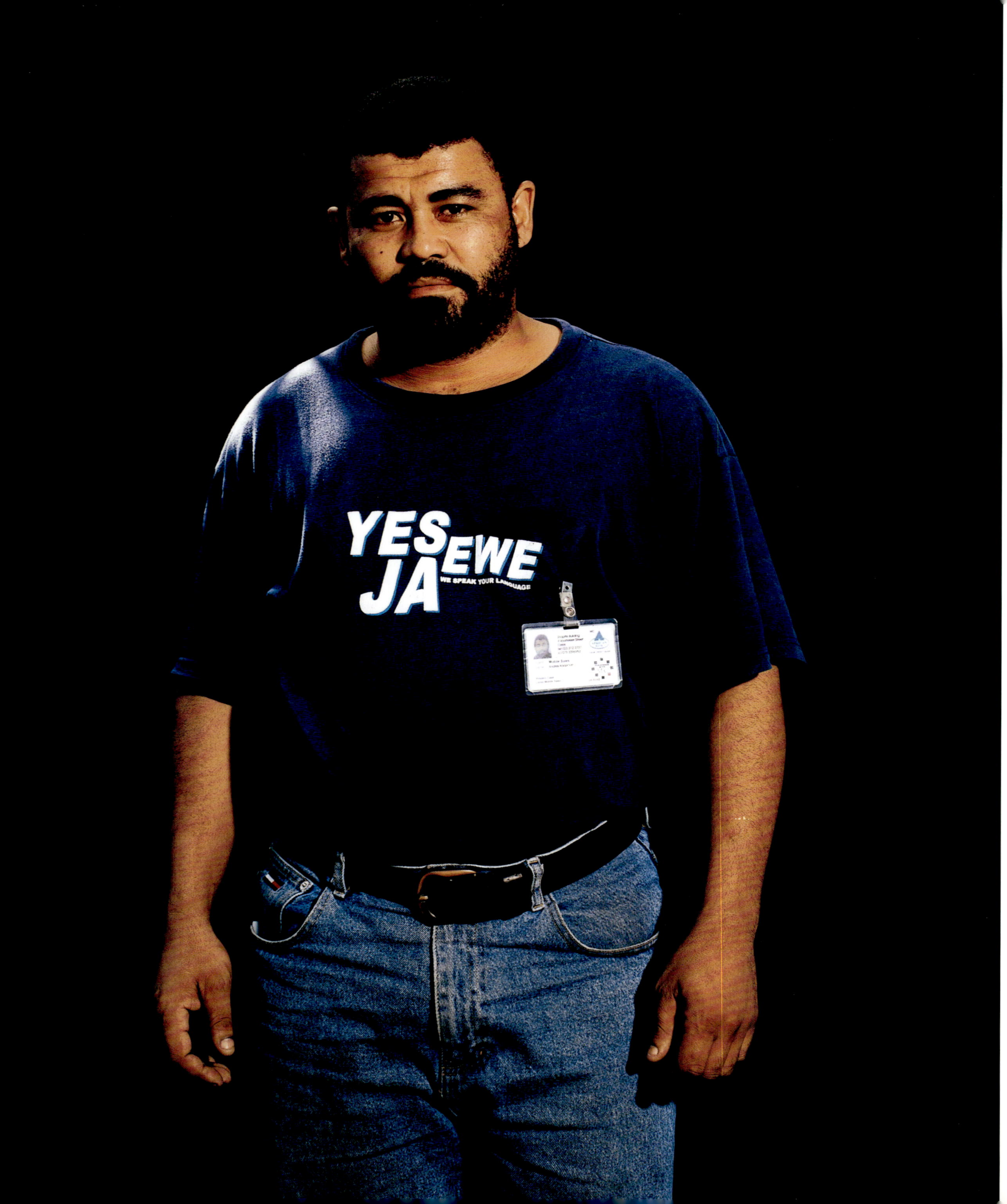
YES
EWE
JA
WE SPEAK YOUR LANGUAGE

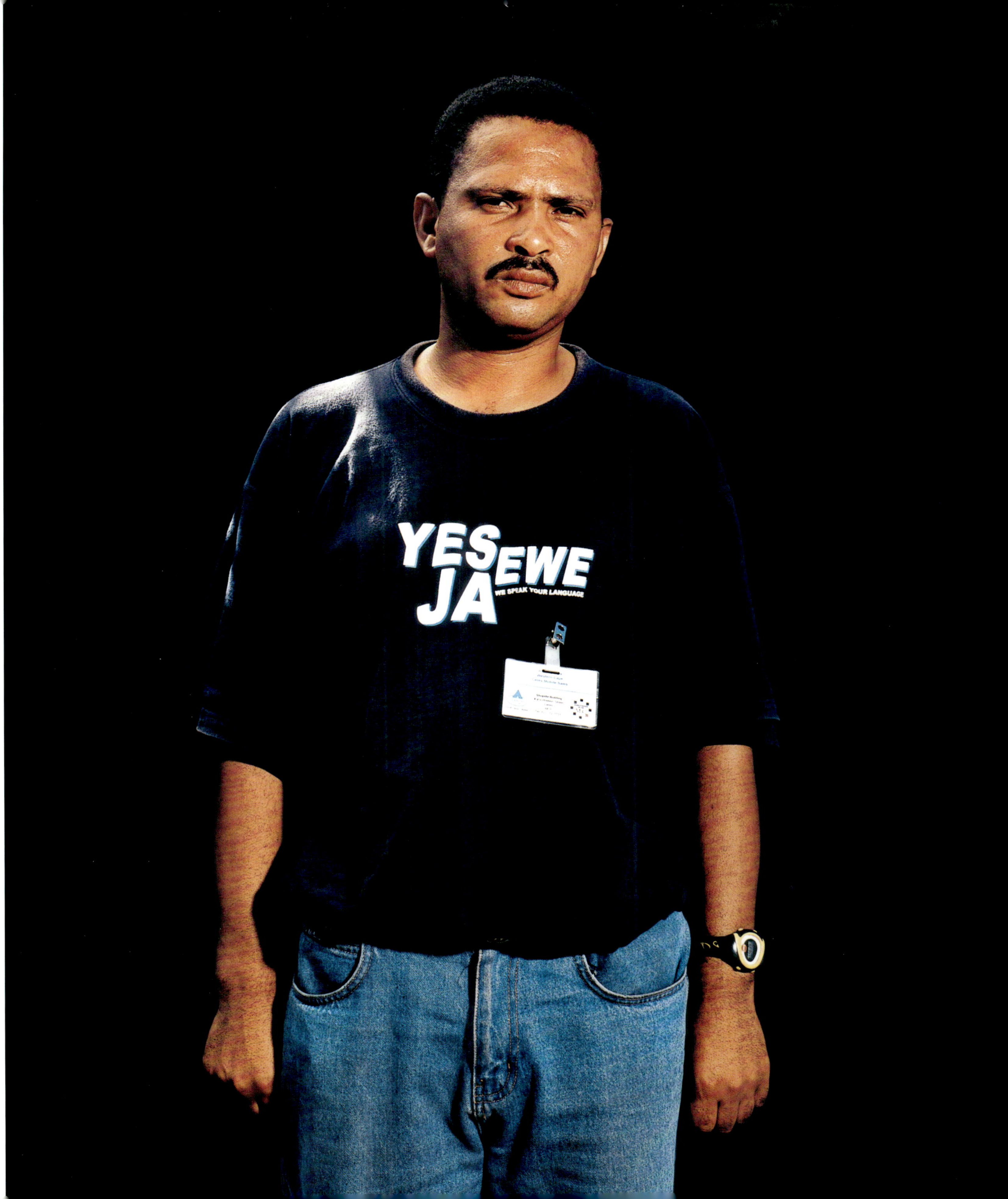
YES
EWE
JA
WE SPEAK YOUR LANGUAGE

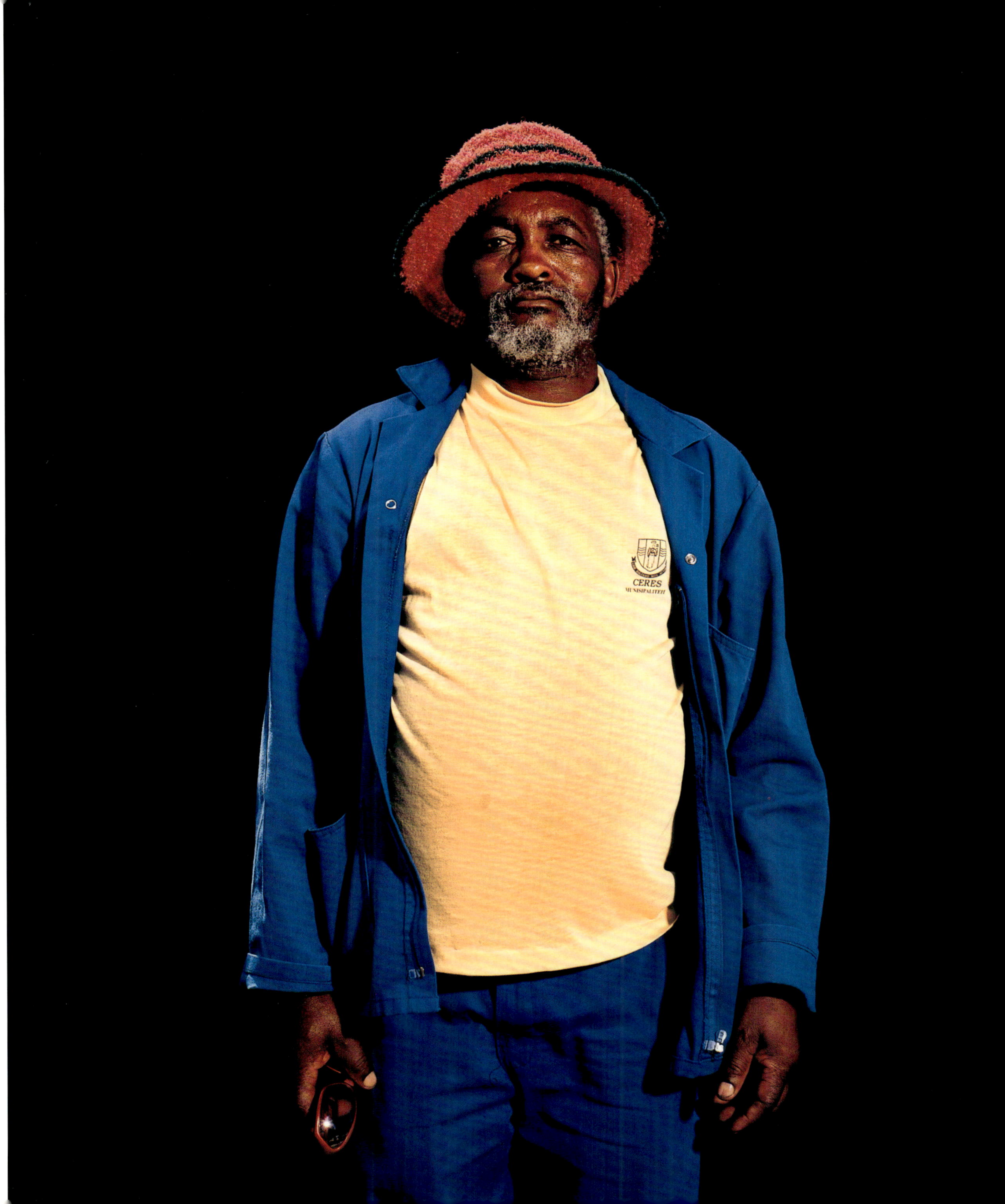

1

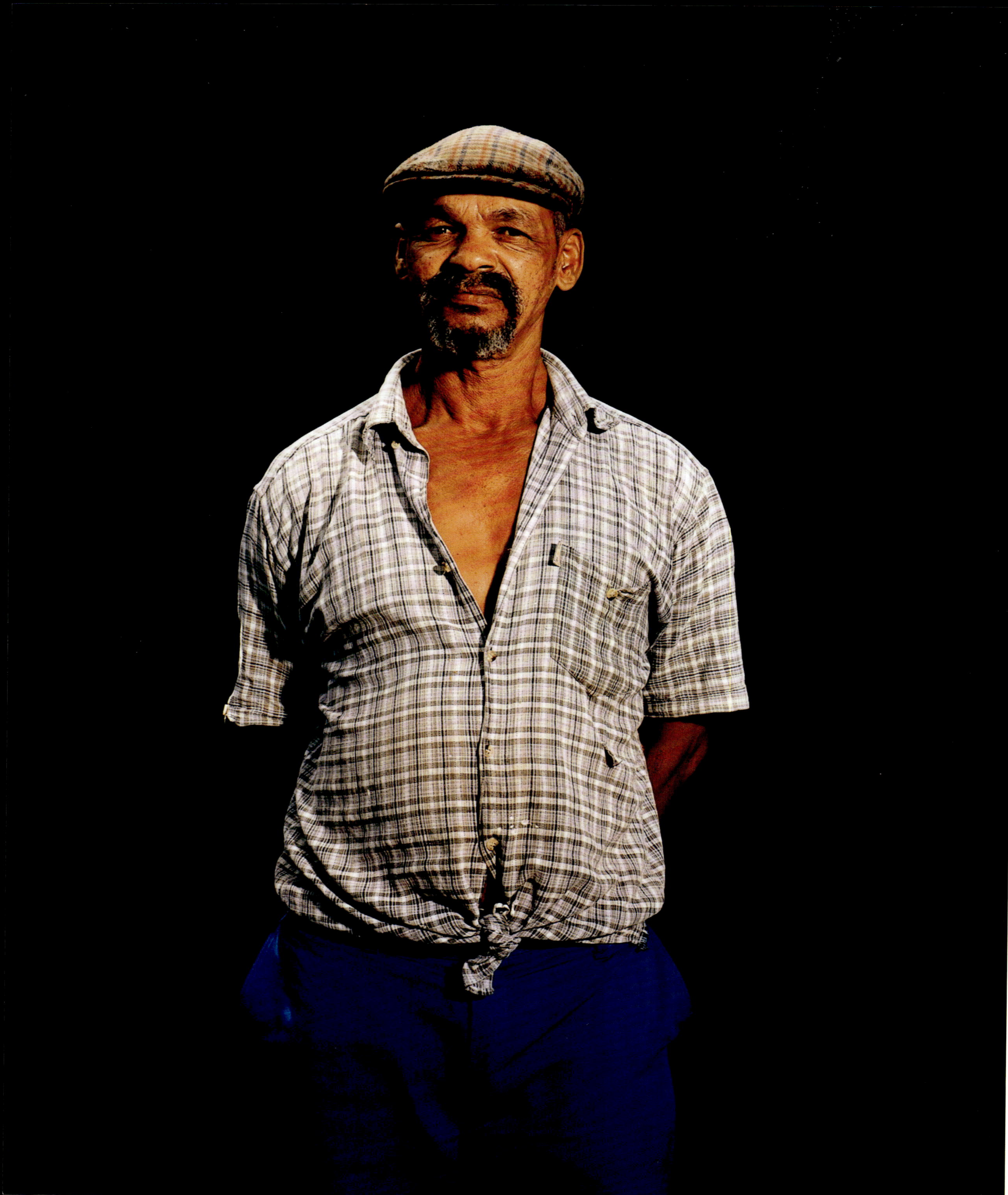

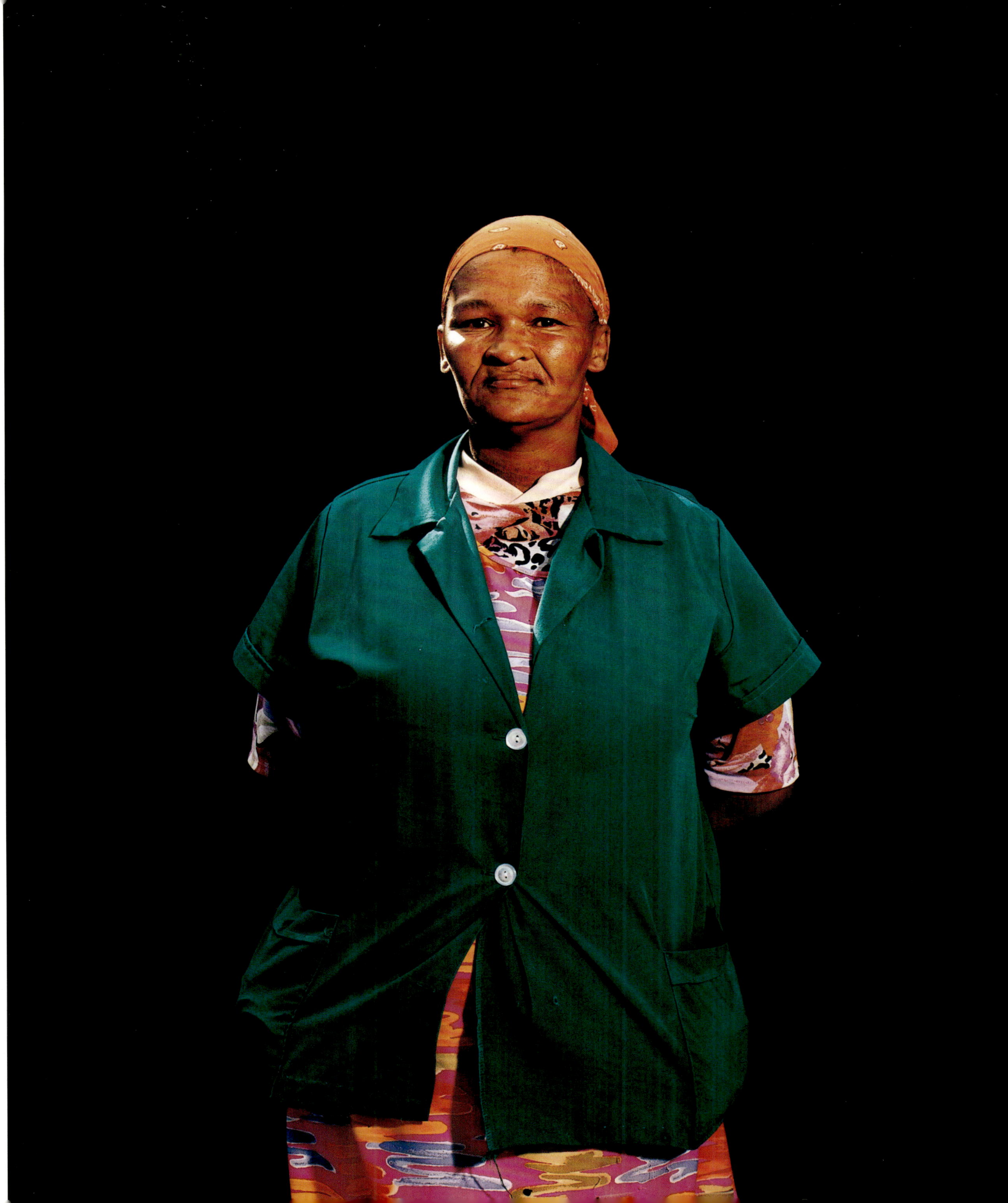

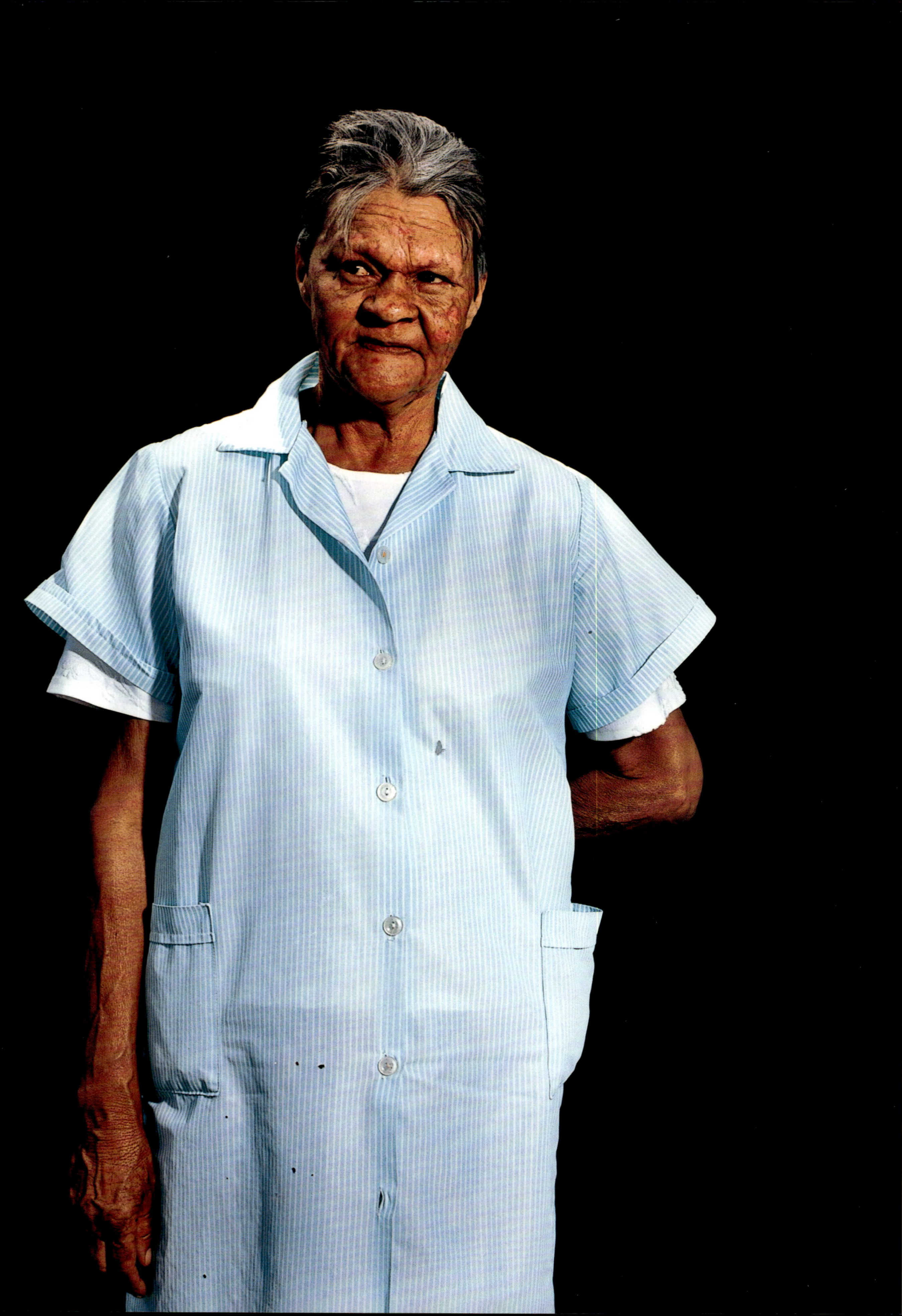

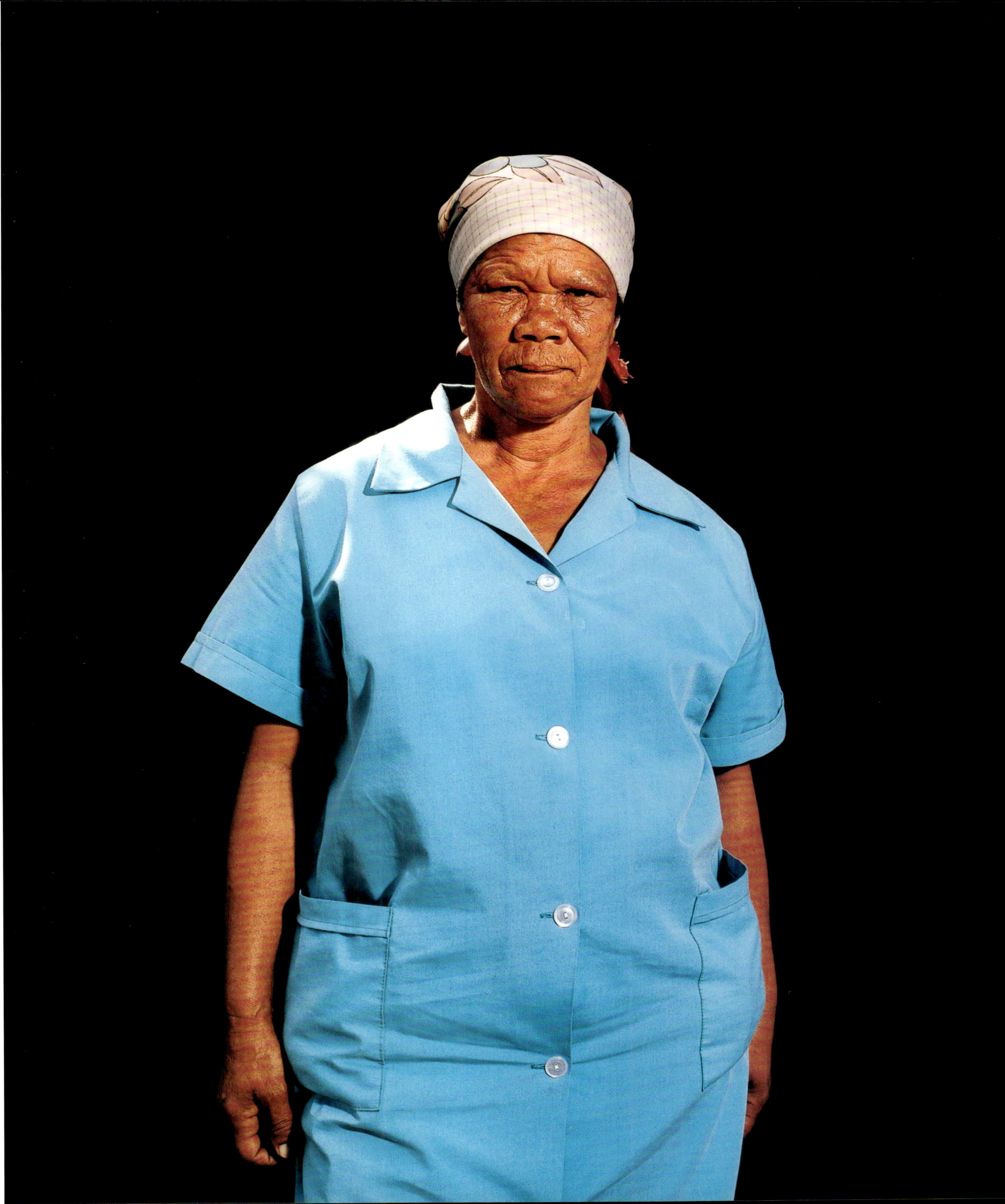

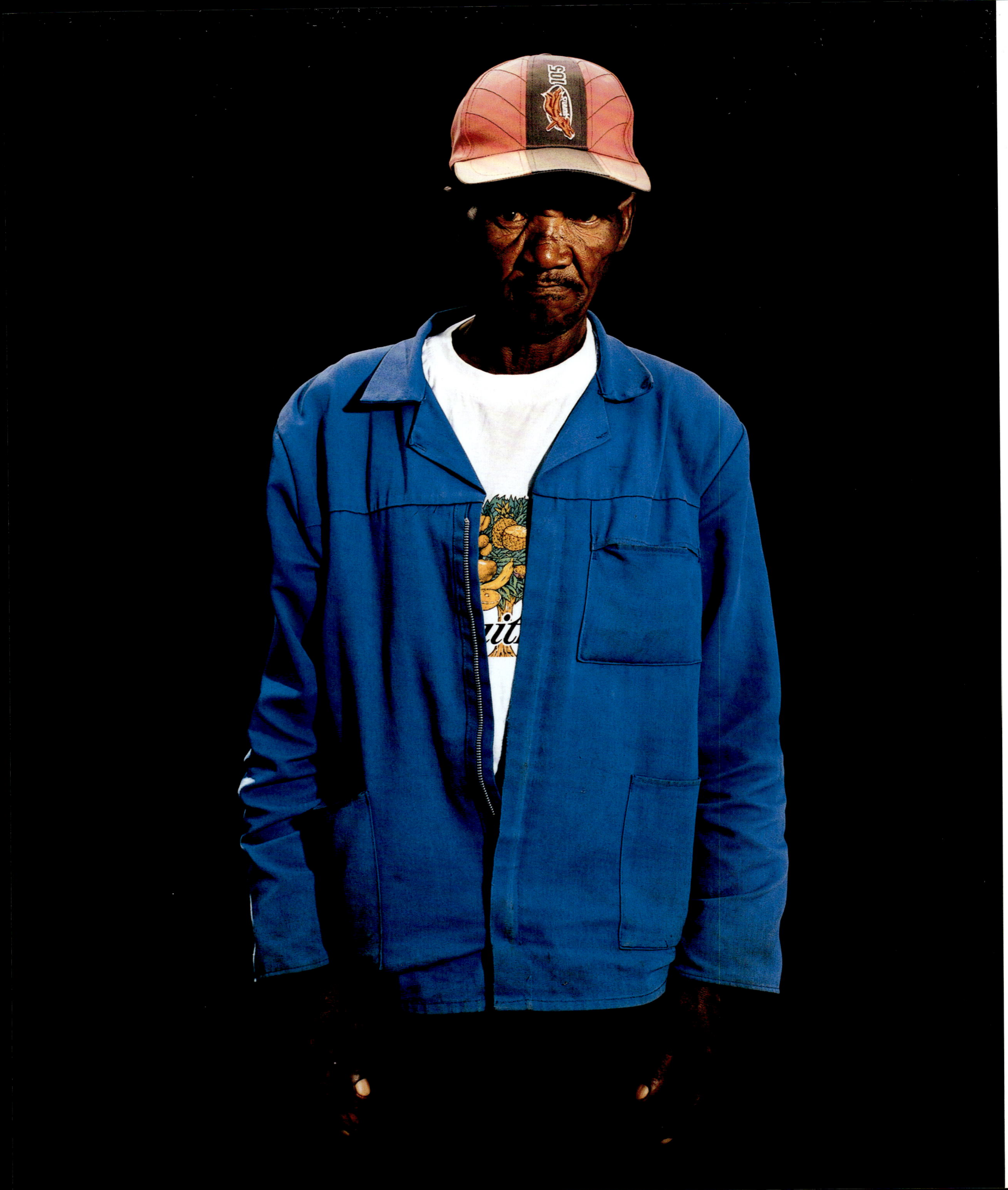
105

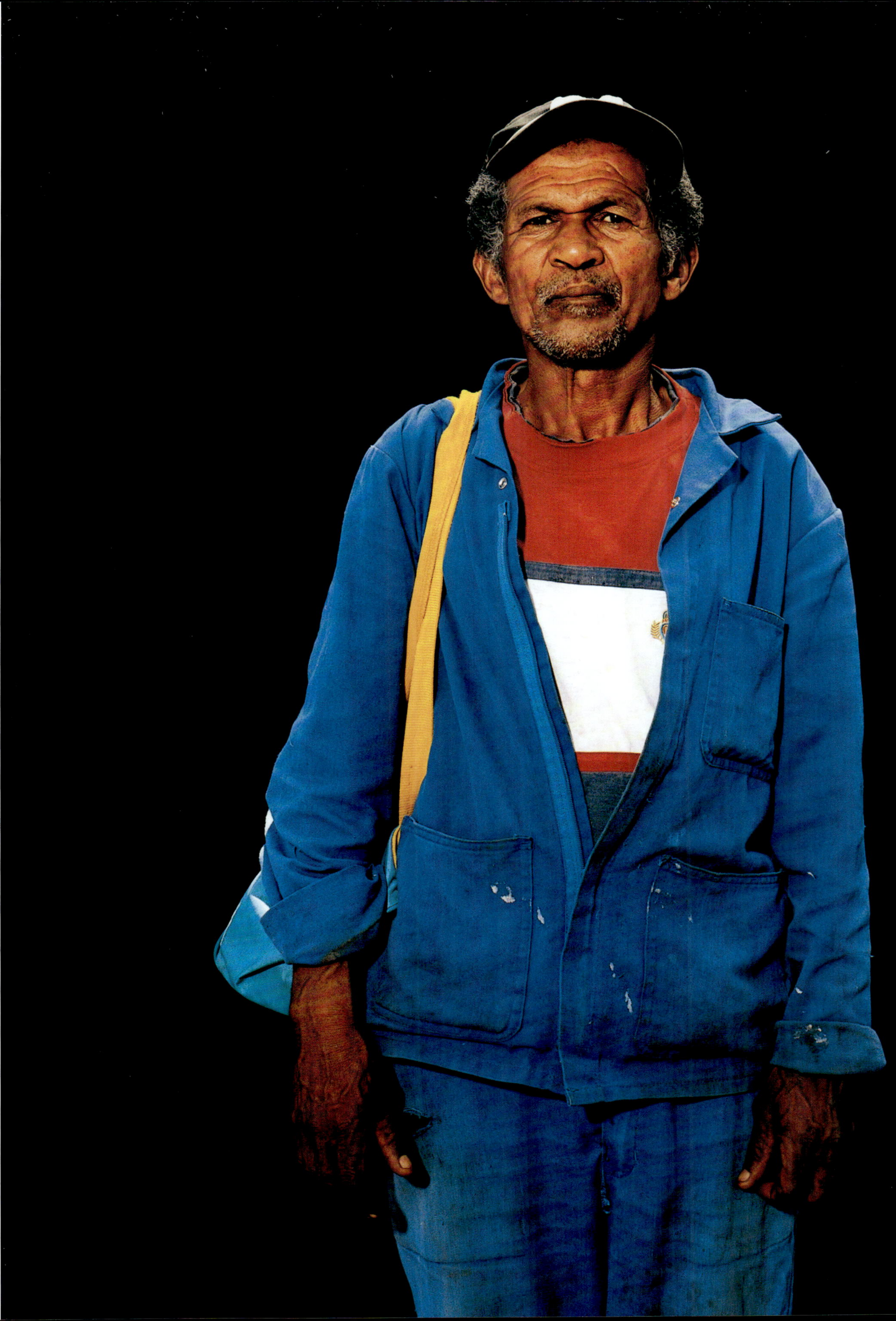

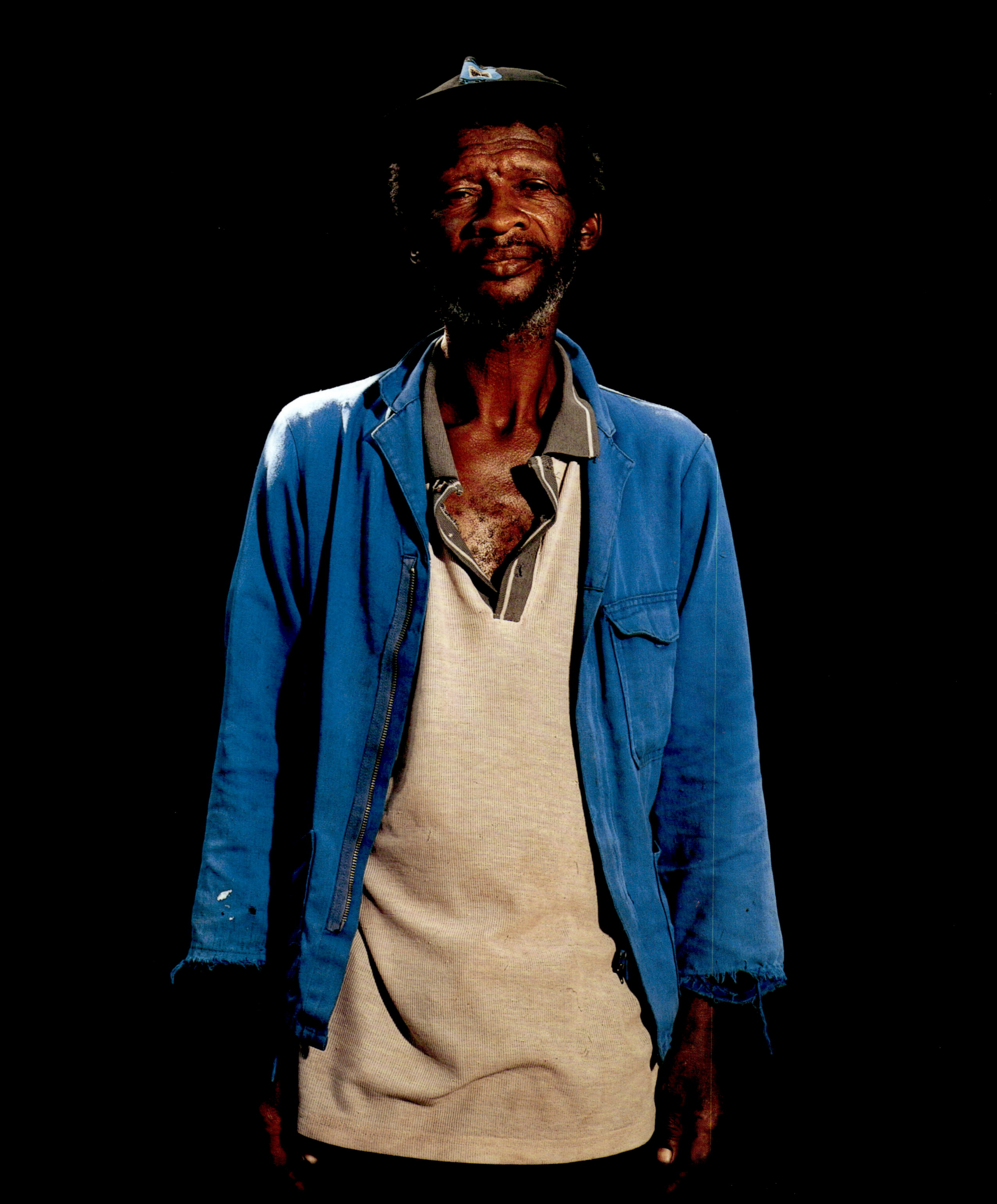

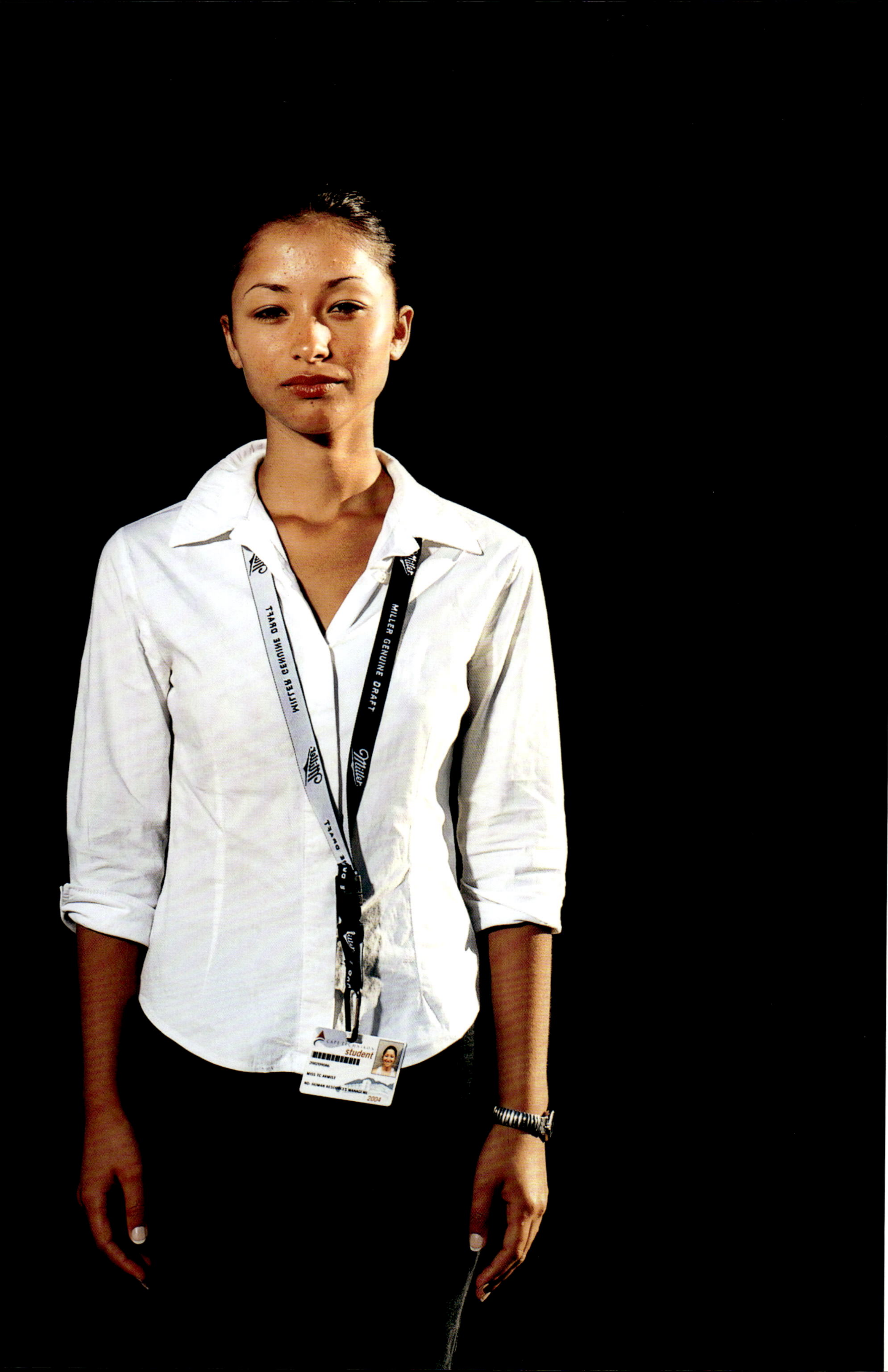
MILLER GENUINE DRAFT
Miller
student
2004

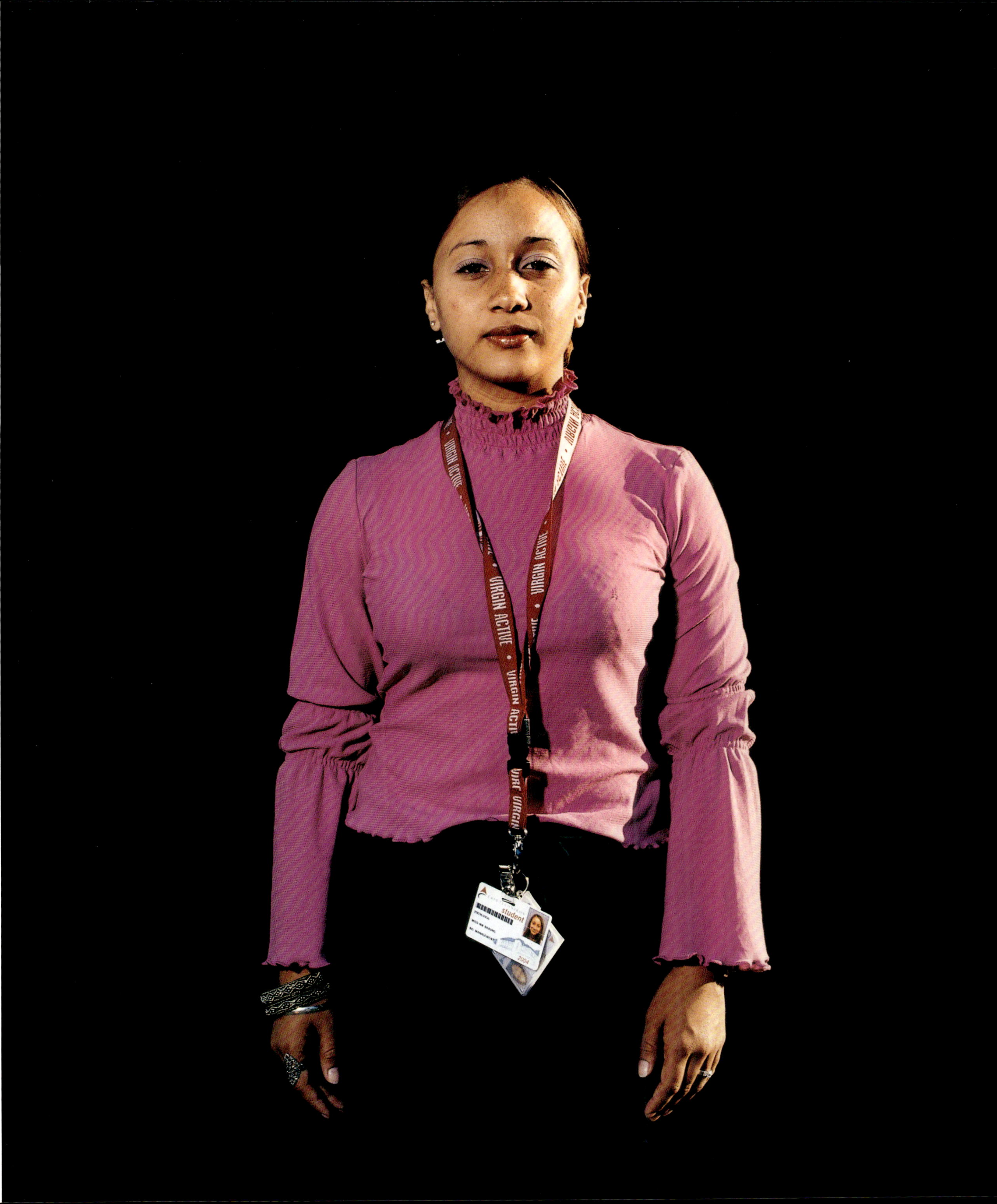

1

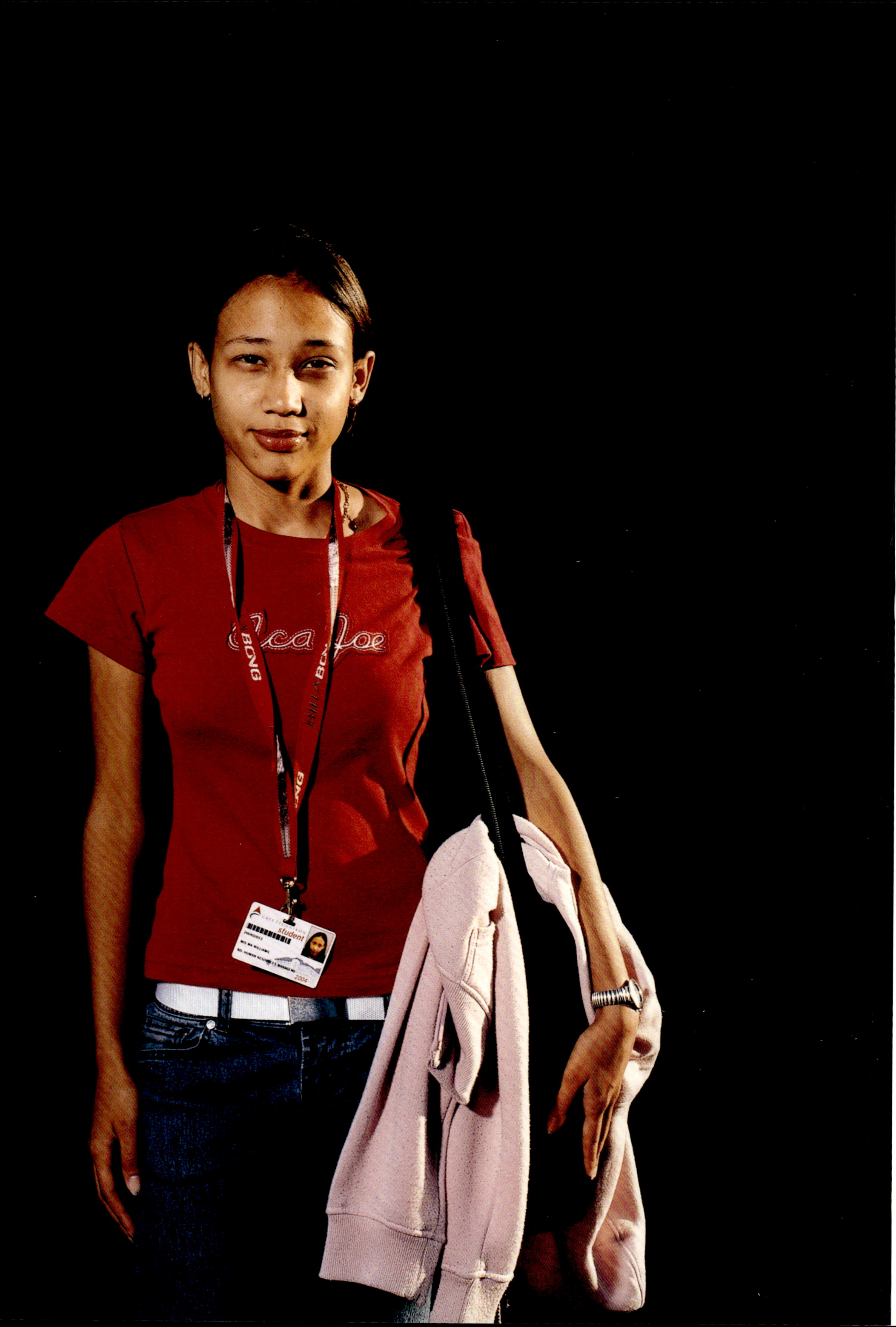
student
2004

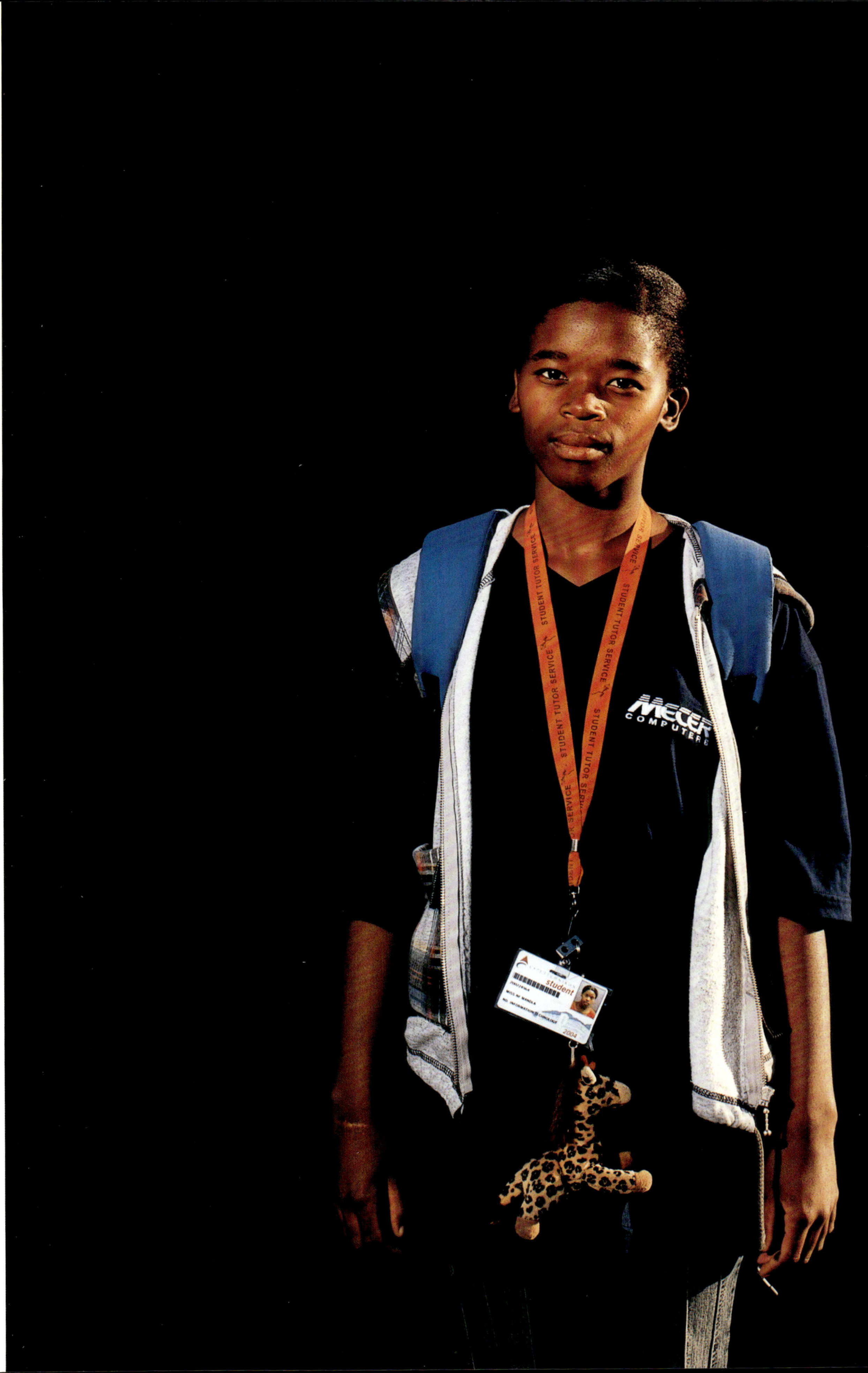
STUDENT TUTOR SERVICE
MECER
COMPUTERS
student
2004

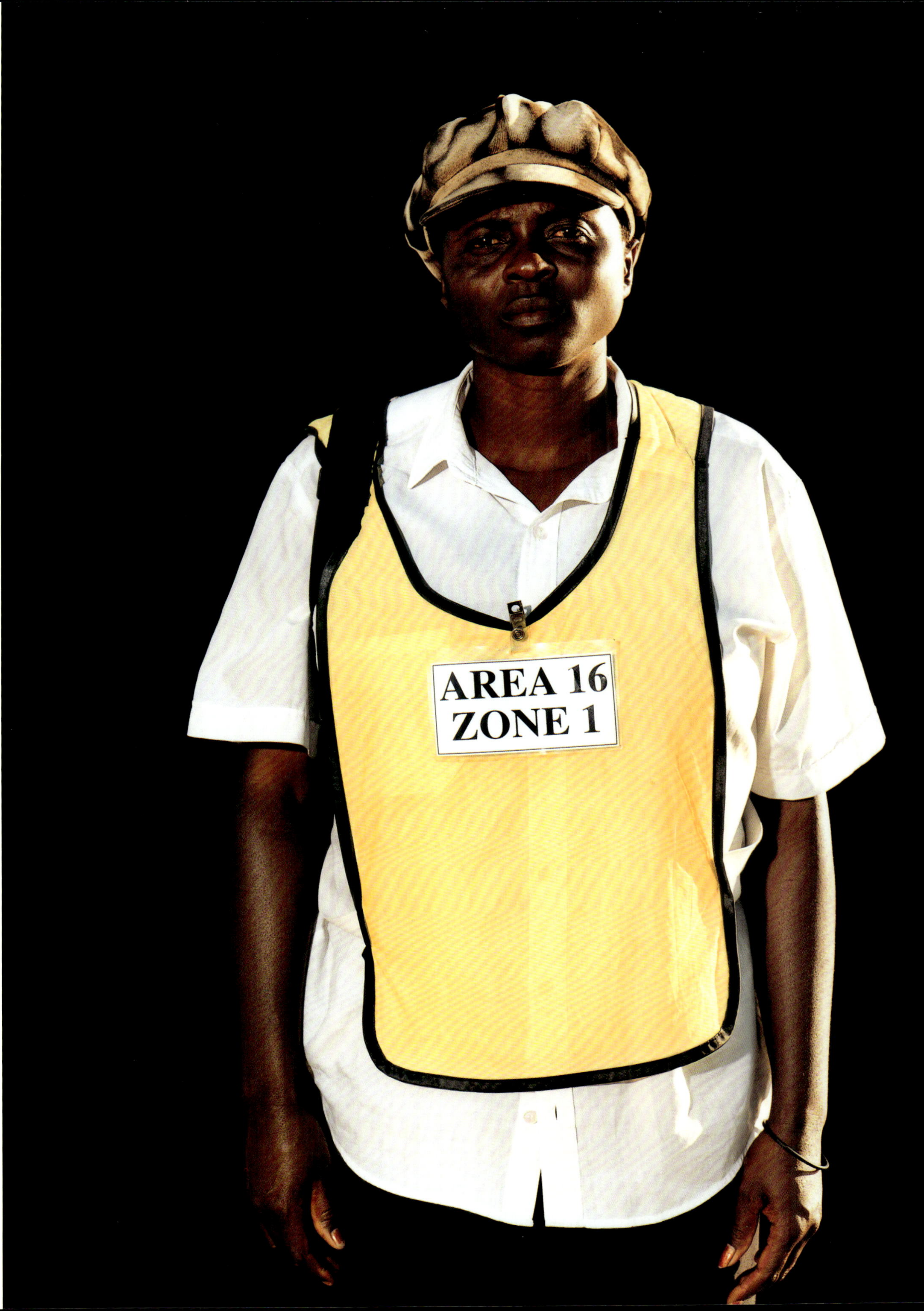
AREA 16
ZONE 1

2.

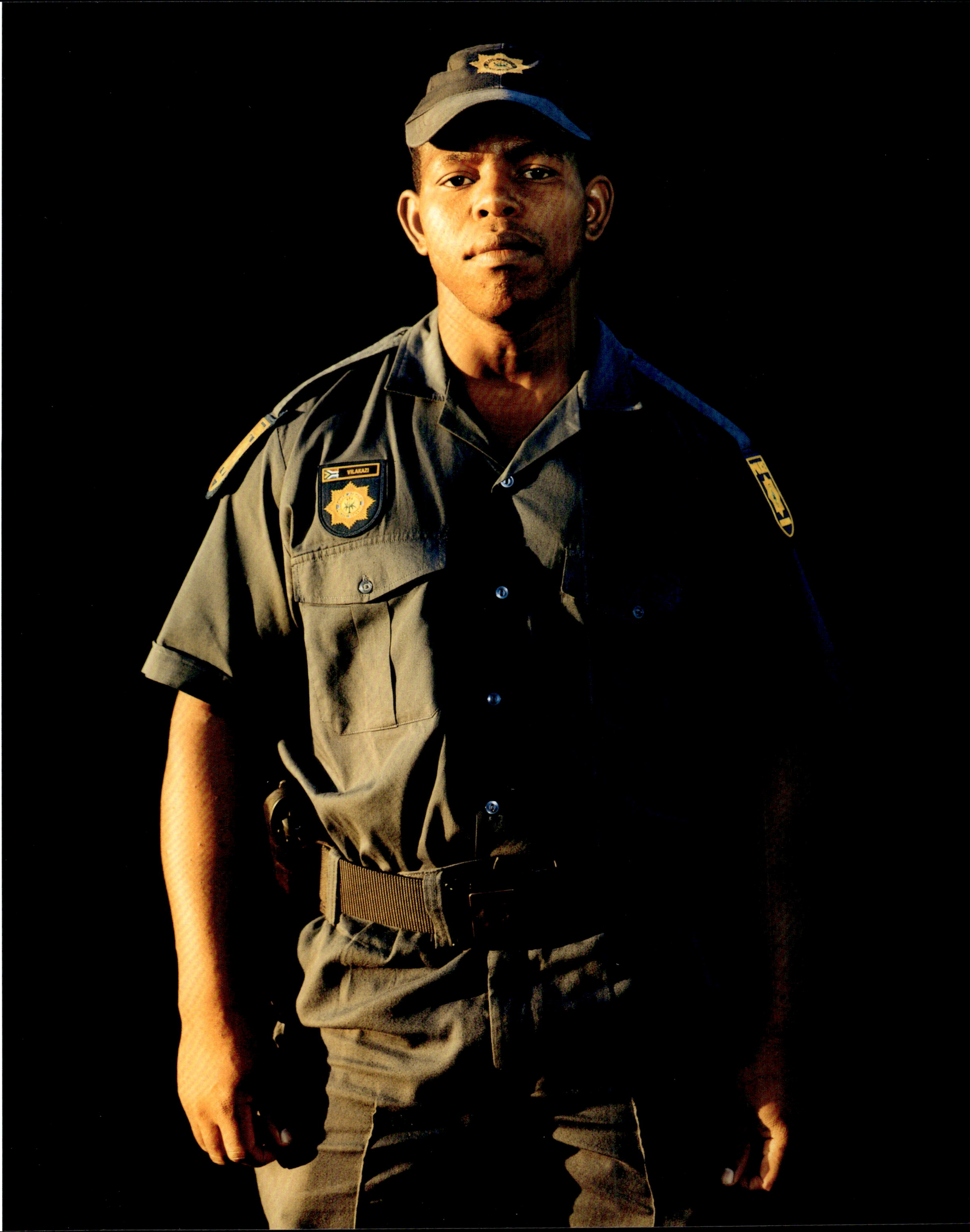
VILAKAZI

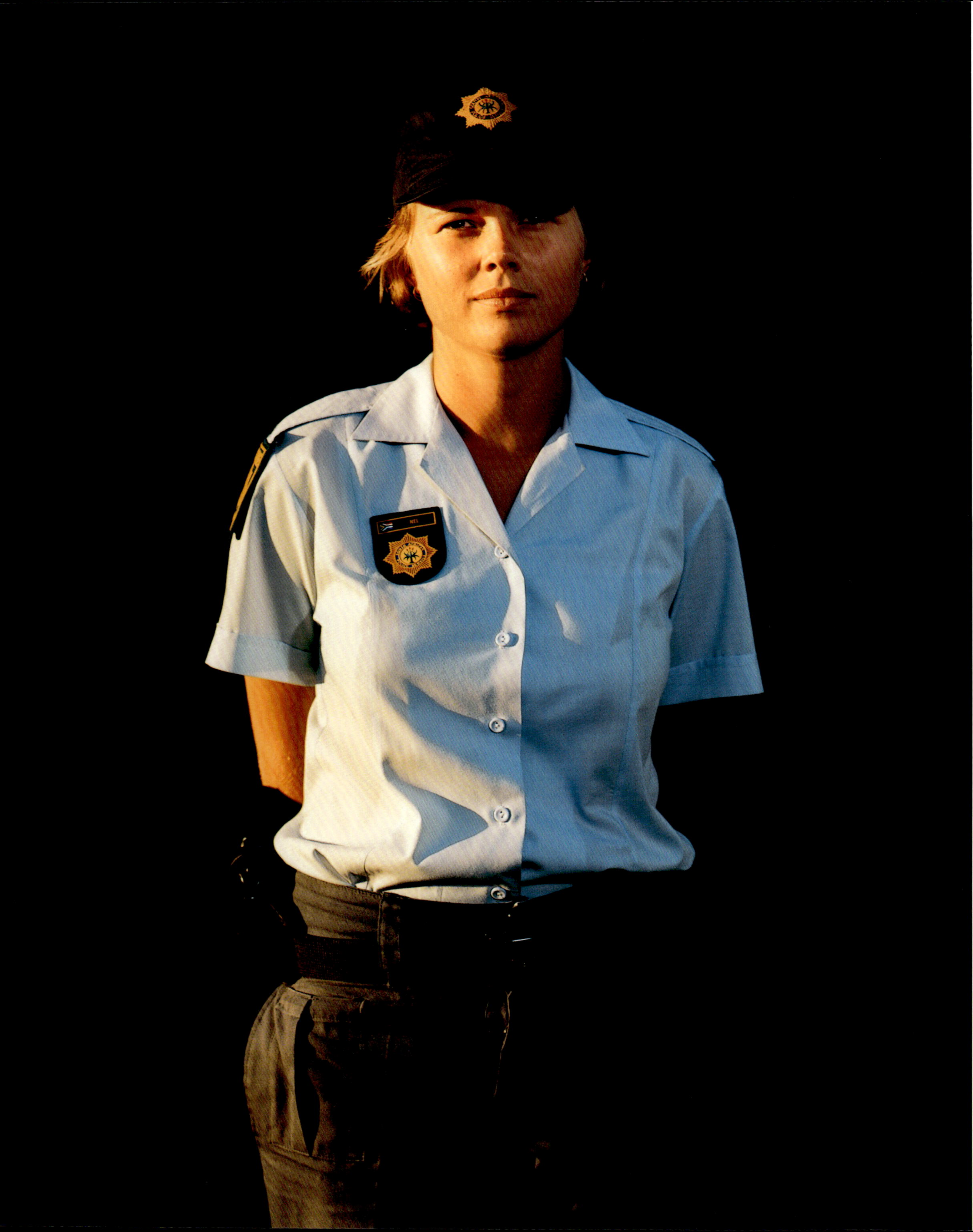
NEL

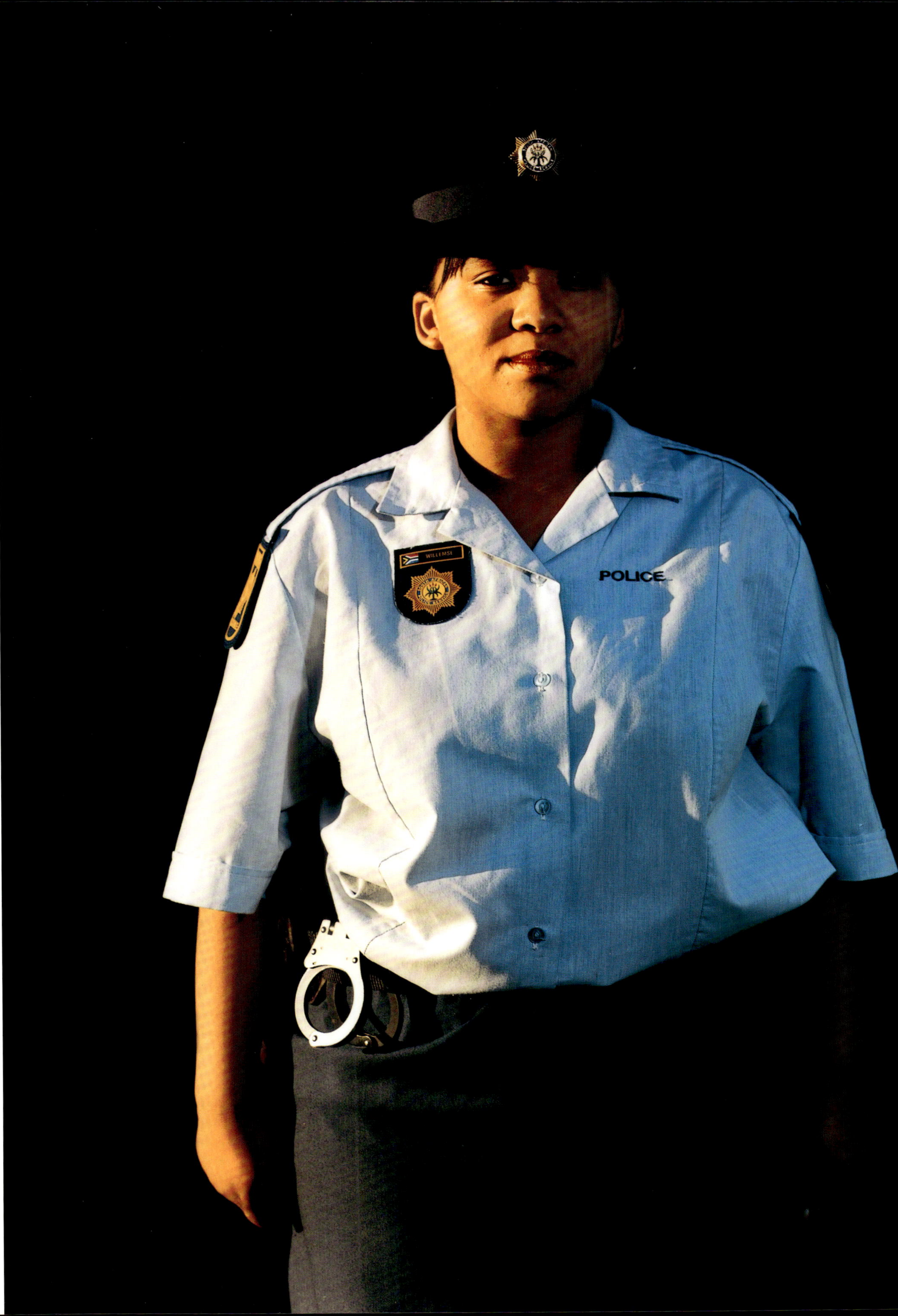
WILLEMSE
POLICE

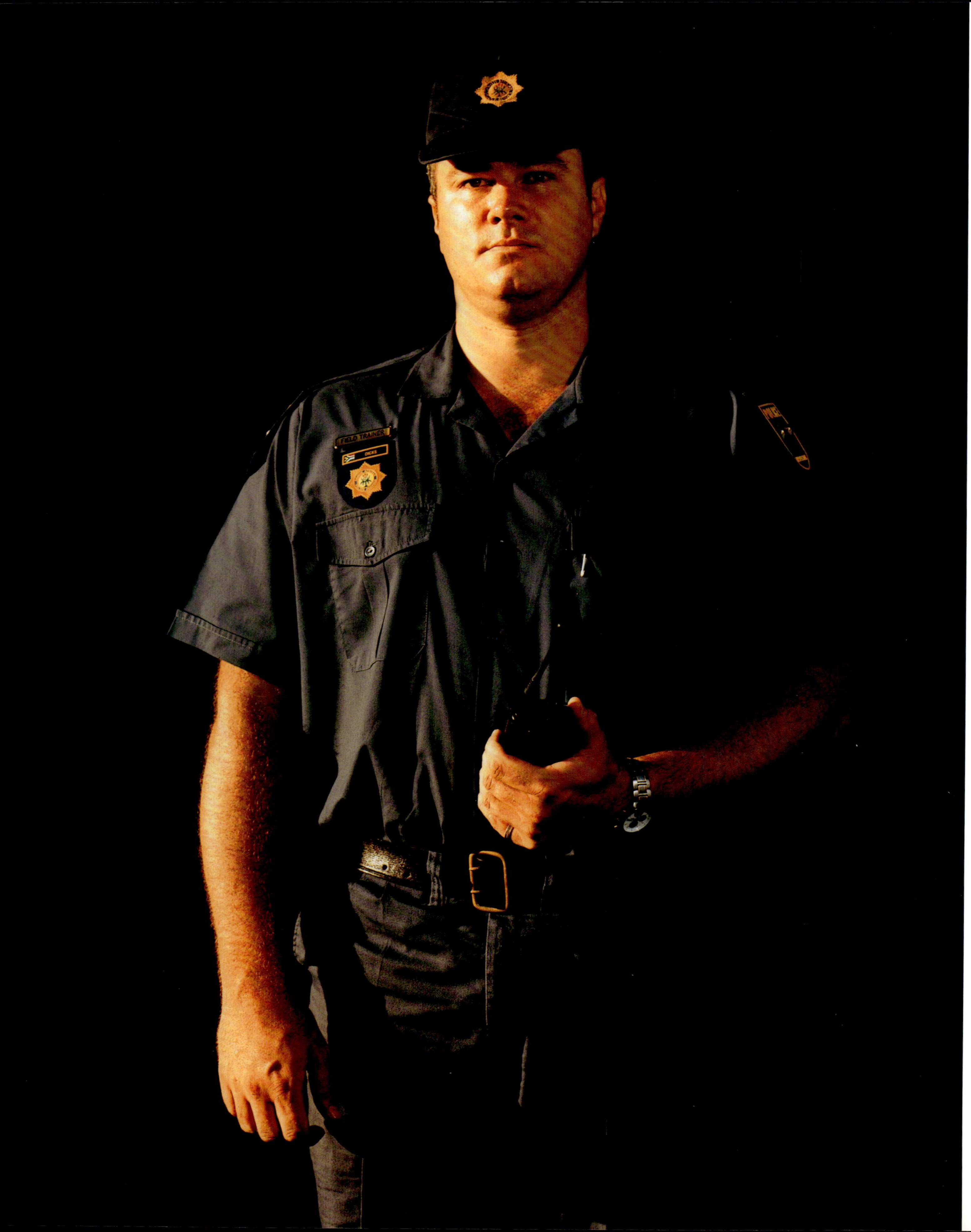
FIELD TRAINER
DICKS

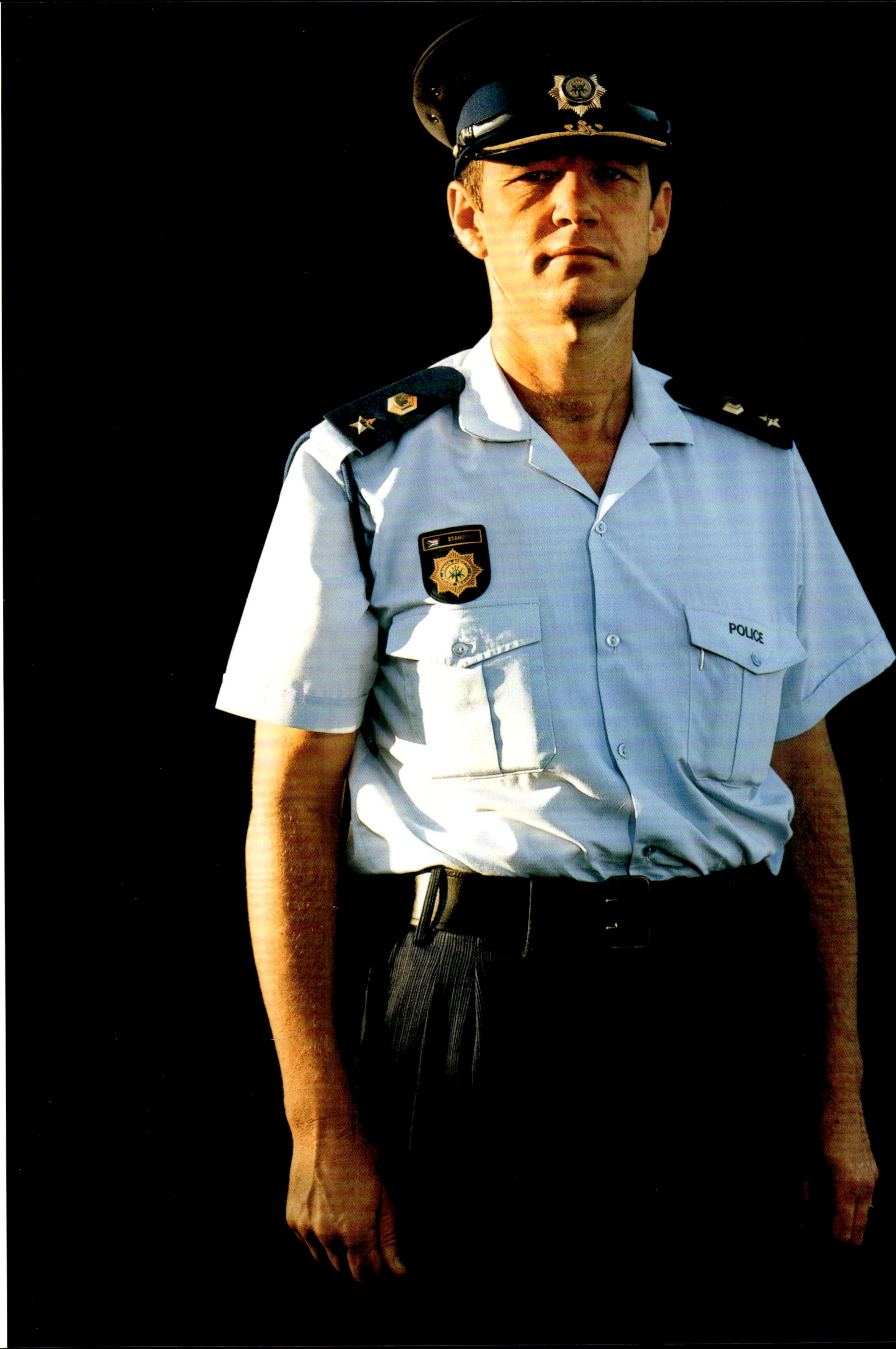
POLICE

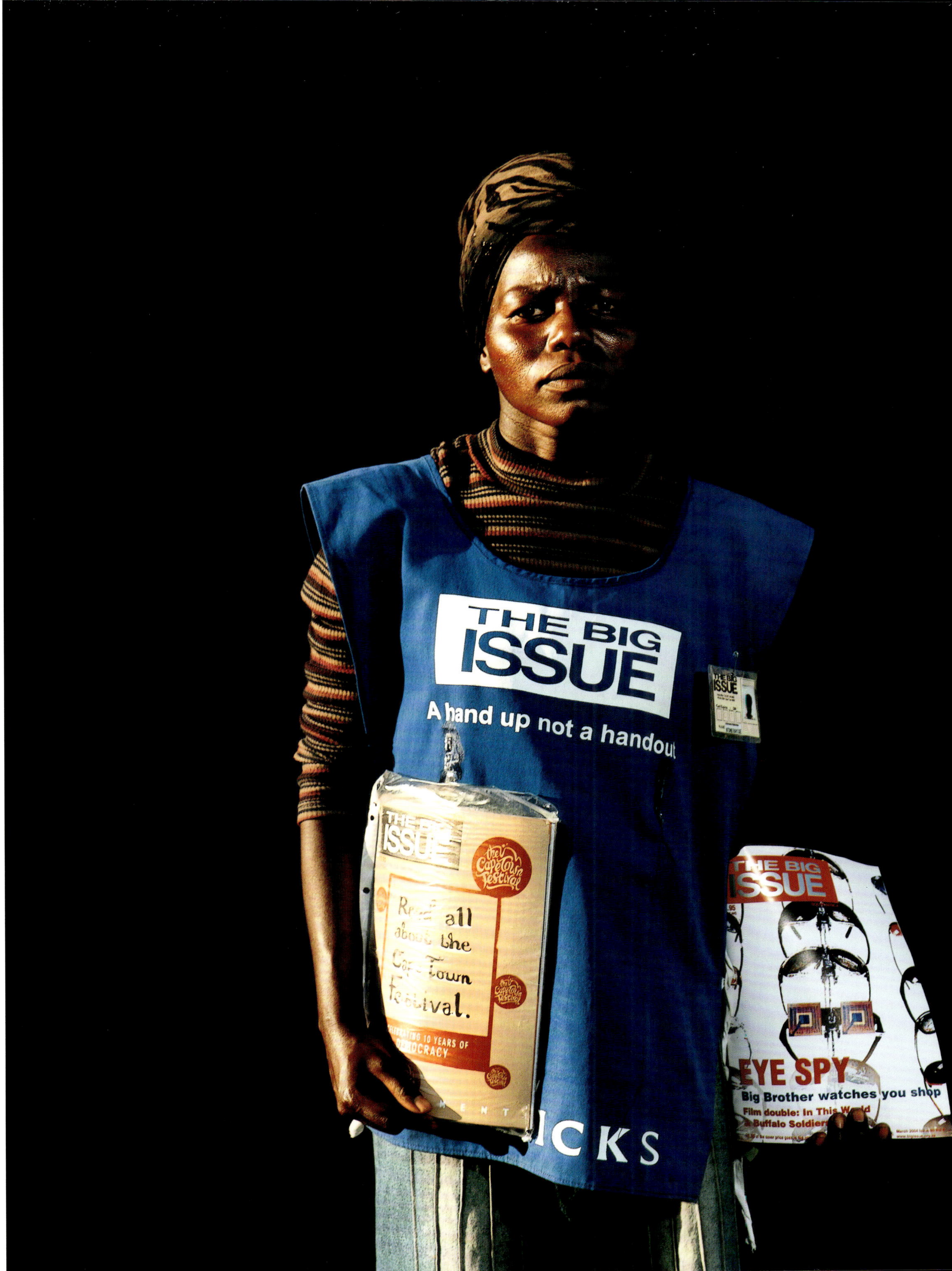
THE BIG ISSUE
A hand up not a handout
THE BIG ISSUE
Read all about the Cape Town Festival.
THE BIG ISSUE
EYE SPY
Big Brother watches you shop
Film double: In This World
Buffalo Soldiers

FREE GROUND
LIST OF WORKS

2

The idea behind these works—which were also made using a large-format camera—was to photograph City Bowl street kids in their informal family-type groups.

The street kids generally band into groups for basic survival purposes. There are few social services available in South Africa, and often to escape appalling domestic living conditions children find themselves on the street in even more precarious situations.

Saunders is a small and little-known beach in Bantry Bay—an affluent suburb on the western edge of Sea Point—and another location offering protection against the South-Easter. It is frequented predominantly by locals, a diverse mix of Capetonians who include coloureds, Sea Point Jews and 'Bergies'.

101	2004	*Jeremy Cranston*	Green Point
103	"	*Alfred Mngxuma*	Cape Town Docks
105	"	*Steven Modise*	Saunders
107	"	*Edwin Roenganger*	Green Point
109	"	*Anton Claasen*	"
111	"	*Angelo Brooks*	"
113	"	*'Papsak'*	Saunders
115	"	*'Papsak'*	"
117	"	*James Manese*	Cape Town Docks

Among these eight disparate portraits are two of street kids, two of out-of-uniform shipbuilders, one of a male prostitute and three of 'Bergies'—two of the same man.

UNIFORMS
CAPE TOWN AND CERES, SOUTH AFRICA

The same working process was adopted with *Uniforms* as with *Beaches*. This is not a representative study of South Africans in uniform as such, but rather a random edit of the 'people in uniform' revealed by travels around the streets of Cape Town and Ceres. The subject matter was determined by who was on the street and accessible at the time.

121	2004	*C.J. Saal, Foreman*	Cape Town Docks	Shipbuilders
122	"	*Xola Ntelezi*	"	"
123	"	*Isaac Manzani*	"	"
124	"	*Dalasile Noxheki*	"	"
125	"	*Nezaan Daniels*	"	"
126	"	*Shane Peterson*	"	"
127	"	*Alfred Mnqxuma*	"	"
128	"	*Sidwel Ndintelo*	"	"
129	"	*Stanley Mtshobile*	"	"
130	"	*Xhobo Getyegetye*	"	"
131	"	*Michael Mbantsa*	"	"
132	"	*Vusi Mzimane*	"	"
133	"	*Zet Phakati*	"	"
134	"	*Rodney Josephs*	"	"

These images provide an example of the spontaneous nature of the working process—of the studio acting as a conductor. Having set up at dawn—in this case at the Cape Town Docks—a troop of 40 shipbuilders appeared and 'hijacked' the studio.

In such a context, each member of a group is equally interesting, and it was decided to represent as many of them as possible.

The uniforms unite the shipbuilders, creating a logical reference point from which to perceive the group as a whole. The studio can be a door through which it is possible to access people in a very short space of time. It is a rare privilege to be able to arrive in an arbitrary space and leave it again a short while later, having obtained in the interim a unique and intimate insight into a different world.

136	2004	*Wellington Mbolompo*	Waterfont	Fisherman
137	"	*James Africa*	Kalk Bay Harbour	"

139	"	*Sali Sulelo*	Grand Parade	Security guards
140	"	*Joseph Modiko*	Sea Point Promenade	"
141	"	*Welington Msebe*	Grand Parade	"

South Africa is a country with a massively under-resourced police force, which has led to a proliferation of private security companies. Different companies base their liveries on familiar military, traffic and police uniforms.

143	2004	*Aron Ngqumergque*	Green Point	Builder

145	2004	*Roshana Carr*	Green Point	School athletes
146	"	*Megan Johnson*	"	"
147	"	*Candice Conradie*	"	"
148	"	*Fadwa Ryclieff*	"	"
149	"	*Malikah Davids*	"	"
150	"	*Ryan Kriedemann*	"	"
151	"	*Zandhule Tshangana*	"	"

The studio was erected near an athletics stadium a mile inland in order to escape another prevailing south-easterly wind. In a manner similar to the shipbuilders portraits, the studio was 'seized' upon by this group of high-school kids as they returned home after an athletics meeting.

153	2004	*Wendy Kalimashe*	Grand Parade	School kids
154	"	*Khanyiswa Mateza*	"	"
155	"	*Ncumisa Vephile*	"	"
156	"	*Ntombomzi Makele*	"	"
157	"	*Nomhle Bara*	"	"
158	"	*Busisiwe Mbhatahi*	"	"
159	"	*Nokubonge Sizenu*	"	"
160	"	*Sisanda Martin*	"	"
161	"	*Xoliswa Mbulawa*	"	"
162	"	*Faith Mandla*	"	"
163	"	*Nankosi Vikilahle*	"	"

The studio was located at the Grand Parade, a large car park in front of the Town Hall in central Cape Town. The edit is derived from different groups of schoolgirls who were walking past the studio on their way to school.

As this process took place over the course of a sunrise, the works have been presented chronologically. The changing intensity of the light in each image offers a way of watching the sunrise unfold. Ordering the works in this way also reflects the finite process of working during a sunrise or sunset. There is a small window of suitable light available, which creates a tension akin to that of a performance.

165	2004	*Dextar Du Toit*	Ceres	School kids
166	"	*Anesia Wildskit*	"	"
167	"	*Shaleen Hardneck*	"	"
168	"	*Esmeralda Jansen*	"	"
169	"	*Eldine Okhuis*	"	"
170	"	*Melony Ancoia*	"	"
171	"	*Davene Reitz*	"	"
172	"	*Brumilda Hardnek*	"	"
173	"	*Desere Farvier*	"	"

174	2004	*Beula van Wyk and Zany Minaar*	Ceres	School kids
175	"	*Jonathan Sekels*	"	"

177	2004	*Alderich Minaar*	Ceres	Supermarket workers
178	"	*Annalie Bosman*	"	"
179	"	*Leana Geduld*	"	"
180	"	*Deidre van Wyk*	"	"
181	"	*Lizette Robinson*	"	"
182	"	*Patricia Maksiko*	"	"
183	"	*George Mackenzie*	"	"

A more flexible working approach was adopted in Ceres, a small town located in a fruit-producing region of the Western Cape. It was necessary to deviate from the fixed rhythm of working only during sunrise or sunset, due to the distance that had to be travelled to reach the town.

Once the studio was erected, various groups would intermittently show an interest in having their portraits taken and approach. It was difficult to control the selection process at times due to the nature of working in a small country town, unaccustomed to such novelties.

185	2004	*Wilfrieda Ockhuis 2268*	Ceres	Fruit packers
186	"	*Ellen Jacobs 2834*	"	"
187	"	*Nobantu Hinana 2624*	"	"
188	"	*Petronella Vergotine 5861*	"	"
189	"	*Grezelda Engelbrecht 2818*	"	"
190	"	*Jolene Nasson 2496*	"	"
191	"	*Maresa Titus 2633*	"	"
192	"	*Anneline Muller 2626*	"	"
193	"	*Mildred Minaar 2404*	"	"
194	"	*Mary Ann Wildskutt 2755*	"	"
195	"	*Rachel Marsch 2336*	"	"
196	"	*Maria Widskut 6835*	"	"

Although these women were first encountered on the street during their lunch break, it was only possible to photograph them after obtaining permission. It was interesting to identify the same family names previously encountered when photographing the school kids, and to recognise that some of these women were probably their parents. The uniforms seem designed to blend everyone into homogeneity; the workers are numbered and colour-coded.

198	2004	*Andries Koopman*	Ceres	Bank workers
199	"	*Brandon Mentor*	"	"

These men work for a private bank that provides loans at inflated interest rates to impoverished people with little or no collateral. They seemed to possess a self-imposed separateness from the other people who approached the studio, a sense that is reflected in their stance.

201	2004	*Baza Beki*	Ceres	Out-of-work workers
202	"	*Frederick Segels*	"	"
203	"	*Katriena Claasen*	"	"
204	"	*Lena Sampson*	"	"
205	"	*Anna-Marie Jonas*	"	"
206	"	*Richard Jonkers*	"	"
207	"	*Anthony Wildochutt*	"	"
208	"	*Simon Ntleki*	"	"

In a country with an official unemployment rate exceeding 40%, it is common for people dressed in 'patched-up' uniforms to locate themselves in strategic areas in the hope of procuring some temporary work. The neutral environment of the studio seems to reflect something truthful about people when they present themselves to the camera. There is an ambiguity and vulnerability lurking here.

210	2004	*Miss T. C. Armist*	Grand Parade	University students
211	"	*Miss N. W. Brauns*	"	"
212	"	*Miss M. A. Williams*	"	"
213	"	*Miss N. Mandla*	"	"

Photographed individually, these girls are still united by their identity tags.

215	2004	*Euphonia Nyesi*	Camps Bay	Parking attendant

Euphonia was a migrant labourer from the DRC (Democratic Republic of Congo).

217	2004	*Constable Vilakazi*	Green Point	Police
218	"	*Constable Nel*	"	"
219	"	*Constable Willemse*	"	"
220	"	*Field Trainer Dicks*	"	"
221	"	*Superintendent Standler*	"	"

As with the fruit packers, official permission was required to photograph members of the South African Police (SAP). A limited number of police force members were pre-selected and presented two at time. These works were made using the larger 5x4 format camera.

223	2004	*Maude Taute*	Sea Point Promenade	*Big Issue* seller

SOUTH AFRICAN TERMS FROM
A DICTIONARY OF SOUTH AFRICAN ENGLISH ON HISTORICAL PRINCIPLES

Bergie/'bargi,bergxi/ n. colloq. Also with initial capital. [BERG + Eng. Suffix –ie, denoting an inhabitant of a place; or formed in Afk., *berg* mountain + IE.]
1. (*obs.*) berg canary
2. In the Western Cape: a vagrant living on the mountain slopes above Cape Town.; any vagrant. Cf. OUTIE.
1952 *Drum* Feb. 8 The 'Bergies' who live on the slopes of Devil's Peak .. are in a class by themselves. **1959** J. Packer *High Roof* 59 Sometimes he had camped out in a mountain cave with the bergies, who stood high in nobody's esteem and were always being chivvied by the foresters because they were vagrants and likely to set the bush on fire. **1964** M. Murray *Under Lions Head* 3 Some of these people [sc. Hottentots] probably, had hide-outs along the bush land of the Green and Sea-Point coast, or, like our *bergies* of today, behind the boulders of the Lion's Head. **1972** *Argus* 10 Aug Sea Point is a Riviera for most of the won't-works. Even the Bergies come down to do their shopping … Bergie woman smelling of drink frequently come to the door begging. **1973** *E.Prov.* Herald 9 May The police immediately suspected that someone other than a Coloured mountain-dweller (a 'Bergie') had committed the crime. **1982** *Cape Times* 15 Apr. Cape Town's vagrants or bergies are not confined to the mountainside areas but are living in large number in the elite suburbs of Rondebosch and Claremont. **1987** [see DRONK] **1990** *Weekend Post* 3 Feb. (Leisure) 4 Bergies of all colours .. zigzag across the road.

Cape Doctor *n. phr.* [Cape + Eng. *doctor*, see quot. 1890.] ***The Cape Doctor:*** A nickname given in the Western Cape to the prevailing south-east wind which blows strongly esp. during the summer months; *the Doctor*, see DOCTOR sense 2. Cf. BLACK SOUTH-EASTER.

1861 Lady Duff-Gordon *Lett. From Cape* (1925) 31 It portends a 'south-easter', i.e. a hurricane, and Cape Town disappears in impenetrable clouds of dust. But this wind .. is the Cape Doctor, and keeps away cholera, fever of every sort, and all malignant or infectious diseases. **1882** C. Du Val *With Snow through Sn Afr.* I. 50 The 'Cape Doctor' .. does for Cape Town what its Town Council and Urban Authorities appear unwilling or unable to do—viz., drives out the contagion, low fever etc., generated by the insufficient drainage and want of care .. in .. its sanitary requirements. **1890** A. Martin *Home Life* 15 That rough but benevolent south-east wind, which, owing to its kindly property of sweeping away the germs of disease, is called 'the Cape Doctor'. **1913** H. Tucker *Our Beautiful Peninsula* 2 Even the worst enemy of our comfort, the impetuous south-east wind, bears 'healing on its wings', as its proper title 'the Cape Doctor' signifies. **1948** H.V. Norton *In Search of S. Afr.* 46 The 'Cape Doctor' is the name of Cape Town's private and personal monsoon, the South-Easter .. because it always blows seaward and is said to carry away all the germs with it. **1966** *Listener* (U.K.) 18 Aug. 237 The Cape south-easter was blowing—the wind they call the Cape Doctor because it blows the rubbish from the streets. **1973** *Cape Times* 27 Jan. (Weekend Mag.) 10 It is a little like the air pollution question in Cape Town .. Just when the .. media make the public aware of the extent of the problem .. the old Cape Doctor comes along and the problem seems to have solved itself. **1976** W. Hefer in *Optima* Vol. 26 No.2, 46 It used to be said that this wind, known as the Cape Doctor, helped the fruit farmer by blowing away various diseases. **1983** *Sunday Times* 14 Aug. The 'miracle Cape Doctor'—the south-easterly wind—has saved the rich, beautiful West Coast from oil pollution. **1987** Kirby & Houwing in *Weekend Argus* 26 Sept. 1 The eight sailing ships of the Australian Bicentenial First Fleet were pinned down in Table Bay Harbour by a raging south-easterly gale … The Cape Doctor, gusting to more than 50 knots, prevented the fleet from leaving Table Bay. **1993** A.Jardine in *Ibid.* 9 Jan. 18 The Cape Doctor took centre stage .. as the [golf] tournament entered .. 'championship round'. An uncharitable south-easter played havoc with the pack yesterday and swept hats, golf balls and aspirations away.

Cape Flats *n. phr.* [Calqued on S. Afr. Du. *Kaapsche Vlakte* 'Cape Plains'; perh. influenced by Eng. *flat* 'piece of level ground'.] ***The Cape Flats:*** The stretch of flat, sandy country lying between Cape Town and Somerset West and linking the Cape Peninsula to the hinterland; *the flats*, see FLATS sense a. Also *attrib.*
1822 W.J. Burchell *Trav.* I. 58 The Dutch denominate one part, the *Kaapsche Duinen* (Cape Downs), and another, the *Kaapsche Vlakte* (Cape Flats). **1835** G. Champion *Jrnl* (1968) 8 We crossed what are styled the 'Cape Flats' being the perfect level ground which lies between Table & False Bays … Nothing but Sand, Sand, Sand. **1836** A.F. Gardiner *Journey to Zoolu Country* 397 Having ridden eighty-four miles, the latter part of which, over the Cape Flats, being loose sand, is the most tedious. **1841** B. Shaw *Memorials* 220 Reached the house of *Diana*, a woman of colour, who resides upon the Cape Flats, a little after sunset. **1881** *Cape Monthly Mag.* IV. Mar. 137 At Captain Kuiper's Kraal across the Cape Flats they found one of Gonnema's people, whom they compelled under threat of death to act as guide. **1913** H.Tucker *Our Beautiful Peninsula* 70 The designation of the 'Cape Flats' is given to all the low-lying plain which extends beyond the succession of suburban townships strung on the thread of the railway line. **1949** J. Mockford *Golden Land* 34 From these town ships on the Cape Flats fast and frequent trains transport the Coloureds to their places of work in and around Cape Town. **1953** *Drum* Oct. 45 The proposals of the Land Tenure Advisory Board .. envisage the non-Europeans in small pockets in the Cape Flats while the best and the most desirable areas are reserved for European ownership and occupation. **1973** *Sunday Times* 9 Dec., Many Coloureds .. trekked to .. the Cape Flats, but unlike other trekkers before them there was no promised land. **1986** *Weekly Mail* 18 April.4 The rents boycott in the Cape Flats townships, already entering its sixth month, took a new turn this week. **1990** R. Gool *Cape Town Coolie* 147 The entire population of District Six would be evacuated to the Cape Flats … The Cape Flats could be turned into a Coloured and Malay dormitory. **1991** [see GHOMMA sense 2].

Capey /'kerpi/ *n. colloq.* Also **Ca(a)pie, Cape-jie.** [Prob. Formed on Afr. *Kaapie*, *Kaap* Cape + -IE.]
1.a. CAPE COLOURED *n. phr.* Also *attrib.*
1940 V. Pohl *Bushveld Adventures* 188 Our oarsman, a 'Capie' named Willem, a short but extremely powerfully built fellow, placed a shotgun in the boat as we were about to depart. **1949** O. Walker *Wanton City* 171 'E's a bad ole bastard, ek?' said the driver. 'Always muckin' around with the Capies.' **1959** J. Meiring *Candle in the Wind* 139 'He must be white. What is he doing with a Capie?' said the first girl, crossly. **1963** A.Fugard *Blood Knot* (1968) 131 Just a little bit black, And a little bit white. He's a Capey through and through. **1965** K. Thompson *Richard's Way* 45 The little miss is married—did you know? And lives in Tokai over the-e-e-re. The long drawn Capey vowel indicated great, very great distance. **1974** D. Rooke *Margheritha de la Porte* 48 She learned new songs from the Capies at their fires: 'Polly are we going to Paarl' and 'Here comes the *Alabama*'. **1981** [see *Kleurling-Afrikaans* (KLEURLING sense 2)]. **1990** R. Gool *Cape Town Coolie* 59, I 'eard it you living in the Cape now … You looking like a Cape-jie already.
b. In full ***Capeytaal*** /-ta:l/ [Afk. *Taal* language]: the argot spoken by some 'coloured' people, consisting of a mixture of languages, esp. Afrikaans, English, and Xhosa; *gammat-taal* (often *derog.* And *offensive*), see GAMMAT sense 2.
1979 C. Van Der Merwe in *Frontline* Dec. 17 Flytaal .. embraces Capeytaal and a large chunk of fanakalo. **1981** V.A. FEBRUARY *Mind you Colour* 95 Kaaps .. is not what some Englishman in South Africa refer to as 'Capey',.. not what some Afrikaans-speaking persons refer to as Gamat-tall.
2. An inhabitant of the Western Cape, or of the city of Cape Town; cf. KAAPENAAR sense 1. See also CAPETONIAN.
1970 *Drum* Nov. 15 If there ever has to be a roll call of Capeys

in Durban it'll have to be on a scroll to contain all the names. **1974** A.P. Brink *Looking on Darkness* 226 'You know mos the old story, hey, Capey?' .. And it was with conscious irony that he called me 'Capey'. For he was as much a Capetonian as myself, and much darker too. **1979** [seeUDI]. **1979** *Capetonian* July 4 Having just read why Capeys are different from Transvalers, I guffawed so loudly it was heard by everybody in the building. **1981** C. Barnard in *Daily Dispatch* 16 Nov. 8 In the good old days of the Cape, which most middle-aged Capies can remember clearly, the local fisherman would travel around town on a cart announcing themselves with a blast on a long tube of dried sea-weed. **1989** S. Hobbs in *Style* Dec. 6 You Caapies seem to think yours is the only town with some sort of scenic beauty. [**1994** T.Cobbleigh in *Sunday Times* 2 Jan. 19 Johannesburg! .. the city so scorned by Kaapies and Banana-boys.]

classify *v. trans.* [Special sense of general Eng.]To assign (someone, or, less frequently, something) to a racial group, as defined by apartheid legislation. Usu. *passive*. See also RE-CLASSIFY.
1950 *Act 30 in Stat. Of Union* 279 Every person whose name is included in the register shall be classified by the Director as a white person, a coloured person or a native, as the case may be, and every coloured person and every native whose name is so included shall be classified by the Director according to the ethnic or other group to which he belongs. **1966** *Survey of Race Rel. 1965* (S.A.I.R.R) 112 The two youngest children attended a school that was at one time 'mixed': they chose to stay on there when the school was later classified 'Coloured'. **1967** *Govt Gaz. Extraordinary* Vol.24 No.1753, 1 Definition Of Coloured Groups In Terms Of Section *Five* Of The Population Registration Act 1950… With effect from the seventh day of July 1950, the following groups shall be the groups into which coloured persons shall be classified.**1970** *E. Prov.Herald* 4 Sept., No one is just a person in South Africa. Every living soul—or dead one, for that matter—is officially classified by race. **1973** P. Laurence in *Star* 16 June 5 The Coloured man whose daughter was classified as an African and who had to employ her as a servant to legalise her presence in his home is a recent victim. **1978** *Drum* June 79, I would like to know what the offspring of a coloured guy and a black girl would be classified as. I know that a child resulting from a white guy and a black girl would be a coloured. **1988** *Daily Despatch* 23 Feb. 17 Where a father was classified as black—this included Indian, coloured or African—the child was also classified black. However, when the father was white and the mother was not, then the child took the same racial classification as the mother. **1990** *City Press* 4 Mar. 12 The government decreed that everyone had to be racially classified and that it was a crime for people of different races to live in the same suburb, marry or have sexual contact.

Coloured *ppl adj.* and *n.* also (freq.) with initial capital, and (formerly) **colored.** [Special senses of general Eng. *coloured* (of pertaining to) a dark-skinned person entirely or partially of black African descent, a meaning no longer current in S. Afr. Eng.] Since the late 1970s used often in inverted commas, or in the phr. *So-called coloured*, indicating the speaker or writer's disapproval of ethnic CLASSIFICATION.
A. *ppl adj.* Of a person or group.
a. Of mixed ethnic origin, including Khoisan, African slave, Malay, Chinese, white, and other descent; of or pertaining to such a person or group; BROWN adj. sense 2; EURAFRICAN adj. The word has been used for over one and a half centuries, and numerous Acts have entrenched its use. However the POPULATION REGISTRATION ACT of 1950 made this term an official ethnic label in terms of the law (see next sense)
1829 W. Shaw Diary. 20 Sept., I was much gratified with every part of the arrangements, excepting that the poor black and coloured children appeared to me, to be too lightly esteemed, though forming an interesting and important part of the Institution. **1833** --- in B. Shaw *Memorials* (1841) 233 The original chapel .. is now used as a school-house, and also as a place of worship for the black and coloured population, for whose benefit it is requisite to hold separate services, as they do not generally understand the English language. **1844** J. Macgilchrist *Cape of G.H.* 20 The native population of the colony is generally called Hottentot, or bastard Hottentot, most of the coloured people approaching pretty nearly to the Hottentot formation, and some presenting a greater or smaller mixture of other, principally European blood. **1859** *Cape Town Weekly Mag.* 21 Jan. 14 During a severe storm experienced on Friday afternoon, in the neighbourhood of Burghursdorp, a coloured man, by the name of Jan Hopely, was struck dead by lightning. **1871** J. McKay *Reminisc.* 291 Our Kafir and coloured populations stand in the ratio of three to every one white (Dutch and British) and it therefore becomes to us to legislate on our coloured population by procuring work for them, and thereby enriching the colony. **1892** *The Jrnl* 14 Jan. 2 The criminals are for the most part native or coloured men. [**1898** *Cape Argus* (Weekly Ed.) 2 Feb. 40 The 'cullud' lady .. had a dispute with a former mistress.] **1909** R.H. Brand *Union of S. Afr.* 97 A 'Coloured Man' is not a Kafir. He is a person of mixed white and black blood. **1923** *Act 21* in *Stat. Of Union* 140 *Act* to provide .. for the exemption of coloured persons from the operation of pass laws. *Ibid.* 189 'Coloured person' means any person of mixed European and native descent and shall include all persons belonging to the class called Cape Malays. **1934** A.J. Barnouw *Lang. & Race Problems* 28 By 'colored people' the South African means half-castes. They form 48 per cent of the population of Capetown, and their native language is Afrikaans. **1949** E. Hellmann *Handbk on Race Rel.* 348 The commission of the Cape Coloured population of the Union offered the following definition of a coloured person: 'a person living in the Union of South Africa who does not belong to one of its aboriginal races, but in whom the presence of Coloured blood (especially due to descent from Non-Europeans brought to the Cape in the seventeenth and eighteenth centuries or from original Hottentot stock, and with or without an admixture of white or Bantu blood), can be established.' **1956** N. Gordimer in D. Wright *S. Afr Stories* (1960) 71 He had accompanied Jake to a shebeen in a coloured location. **1980** C. Hermer *Diary of Maria Tholo* 198 The official designation of the Western Cape as a 'coloured' preference area persists. **1990** R. Gool *Cape Town Coolie* 90 The very last franchise is the Coloured vote and the Cape Municipal Franchise. **1990** *Sash* Vol. 33 No.1, May 21 Gang warfare in the so-called 'coloured' areas has become an uncontrollable problem in East London. **1990** J. McClurg in *Star* 11 Sept. 11 'Coloured' now tends to be avoided as a designation of those of mixed blood, yet no satisfactory substitute has been found for it. And, praiseworthy though the effort to rid of racial designation is, we have to resort to them sometimes for the sake of clarity. **1992** J. Pearce in *South* 27 Feb. 4 A new organisation aims to keep the coloured flag flying because it believes the coloureds are being marginalised.
b. *hist.* During the apartheid era: classification as a 'coloured' according to the provisions of the Population Registration Act; of or pertaining to such a person or group. See also CAPE COLOURED *ppl adj. phr.*, CLASSIFY, OTHER COLOURED *ppl adj. phr.*
1950 *Act 30* in *Stat. Of Union* 277 'Coloured person' means a person who is not a white person or a native. **1952** P. Abrahams in *Drum* July 11 He had known a Coloured man who had been white nearly all his life, who had fought in the last war as a white officer, who had had a world of white friends—and then became a coloured man quite suddenly. **1953** *off. Yrbk of Union 1950* (Bureau of census and statistics) 1157 The population is divided for census purposes into four racial groups as follows: .. (4) Mixed and other coloured—this group consists chiefly of Cape Coloured, but includes also Cape Malays, Bushman, Hottentots, and all persons of mixed race. For considerations of space the name of this group is usually concentrated to 'coloured'. **1968** J. Lelyveld in Cole & Flaherty *House of Bondage* 18, I once met a man who carried both an African reference book and a Coloured identity card so he could be African or Coloured as the mood took him. **1970** A. Sparks in *Daily Dispatch* 10 Dec. 16 The Coloured group, as defined in our Population Registration Act, is a pretty variegated community. In fact it includes everybody who is neither white nor African. **1971** [See CLASSIFICATION] **1979** *Cape Times* 20 Dec. 12 [He] was an outstanding representative of the generation of intellectual and political leaders of the so-called Coloured community. **1982** *Readers Digest Family Guide to law* 744 The State President has not declared any group

of blacks to be a separate declared group, but has separated Indian, Chinese, and Malay groups from the coloured group. **1983** R. Hive in *Best of S. Afr. Short Stories* (1991) 315 To get in [*sc.* into the club] you mustn't be only so-called coloured, you must also be not too so-called coloured. You must have the right complexion, the right sort of hair, the right address and speak the right sort of Walmer Estate or Wynberg English. **1990** R. Gool *Cape Town Coolie* 31 Her arms were plump and peach-coloured—was she European? .. Broad cheekbones distinguished her as a Coloured. **1990** S. Makgabotlane in *Tribute* 120 When Stella's birth certificate arrives, she discovers she has been classifies 'coloured' (an offspring of mixed heritage), although her mother was 'white'. **1990** S. Gray in *Staffrider* Vol. 9 No.1, 50, I said I would not phone the Harbour Café, the famous tourist restaurant on the Cape Town waterfront, either to make a booking or confirm that I could bring my so-called coloured friend along.

Mother City *n. phr.* Also with small initials. [Specific use of general Eng. *mother-city* metropolis, home town, here referring to Cape Town's status as the oldest city in S. Afr. and the first point of settlement by people from Europe.] ***The Mother City:*** Cape Town. Cf. *Tavern of the Seas* (see TAVERN sense 1) [**1908** *Westminster Gaz.* (U.K.) 4 Aug. 5 Capetown .. is in the truest sense .. the 'mother-city from which the rest have sprung.] **1913** H. Tucker *Our Beautiful Peninsula* 17 Those who believe that the Mother City has still its best days yet to come, are equally assured that .. fair women and brave men will never be lacking to grace and guard the Cape Town yet to be. **1936** E. Rosenthal *Old-Time Survivals* 23 The district of Malmsbury, near the Mother City, is to this day known as Zwartland to crowds of South Africans. **1943** *Outspan* 9 July 11, I have watched the civic growth of our Mother City for over 40 years. **1955** A. Delius *young Trav.* 74 *(chapter heading)* Cape Town, the 'Mother City'. **1973** *Drum* 8 Mar. 14 Unique to the Mother City the singing and dancing of her Brown children echoes through the main streets by day and re-echoes down
35 her back-alleys by night. **1979** *Capetoninan* July 20 It's up to everyone who prides himself on being a capetoninan .. to help in whatever way possible to put life back into that old girl, the Mother City. **1989** T. Botha in *Style* June 108 Driving between the mother city and the highveld is an emotional experience .. It's totally South African. **1992** *Living* Mar. 69 Table Mountain, Sentinel Rock of the mother city.

New South Africa *n. phr.* Also **New SA**, and with small first initial. South Africa in the post-apartheid era. Now often used ironically. Although this phrase has been used at various times with reference to real or proposed political changes, its present wide currency resulted from its use by the National Party during the election campaign of 1989, and, more particularly, the then State President F.W. de Klerk on 2 February 1990, during a speech to Parliament in which he announced the unbanning of the left-wing political organisations, and committed the government to the abolition of apartheid legislation.
1989 *Daily Despatch* 5 Sept. 5 (*advt)* Vote for the NP for a great and just, a New South Africa. **1990** F.W. de Klerk in *Hansaard* 2 Feb. 2, I wish to ask all who identify yourselves with the broad aim of a new South Africa, and that it is the overwhelming majority:—Let us put petty politics aside … Help us build a broad consensus about the fundamentals of a new, realistic and democratic dispensation. **1990**. *Weekend Argus* 17 Feb. 12 The 'new' South Africa is barely two weeks old and already a distinctly new political style is taking shape. **1990** *Sunday Times* 3 June 18 In the new South Africa—an expression that is rapidly being devalued through the tedium of repetition—military service will obviously have to be as non-racial as the politics. **1990** J. Scott in *Weekend Post* 16 June 14 Jan H—of Kuruman seized on the Peninsula squatting problem, declaring: 'The people of Hout Bay can't open their windows, because they smell the new South Africa. **1990** R.Van Tonder in *Frontline* Sept. 27 The much-trumpeted 'new South Africa' perpetuated the same old concoction, with nothing changed other than the substitution of white rule by black rule—or power-sharing, on the basis of one rabbit to one horse. **1991** C. Gregory in *Frontline* May 20 I've declared war on 'the New South Africa'. And I'm out recruiting. I'm not resisting change, but the words: *NEW SOUTH AFRICA*. This phrase may constitute the largest single impediment to a settled future … By casting their eyes skyward in the direction of the imagined glow, people seem to be prevented from thinking sensibly. **1992** S Sherry in *South* 27 Feb. 3 So you thought that crazy animal called the 'new' South Africa had something to do with politics and human rights? Well it doesn't. It's about dialling soft porn at R6,60 a minute, legal scratch cards that you can win 50 Grand, topless women on M-Net and on the beach and 'adult' magazines in sealed plastic bags. **1992** *Sunday Times* 7 June 15 'Should inter-racial adoption of orphans be encouraged?' … 'Yes. This is what the new South Africa is all about. It's about learning to live together.' **1992** 'HOGARTH' in *Ibid* 17 May 24 Hail to the new SA. With Chris Hani's kids at private school, Joe Slovo in the suburbs and Nelson Mandela in Houghton, it gets more like the old SA every day. **1993** C. Desmond in *Daily News* 6 Jan. 8 The 'New South Africa' has yet to be born; conceived in secrecy, intrigue and elitism, umbilical tied to Western values, it could well be aborted. **1994** L. Rampolokeng in *Tribute* May 30 This romantic NSA (New South Africa) has turned me into a globe trotter. Hence **New South African** n. phr., one living in the New South Africa; one living changed life in South Africa; **New South Africanism** *n. phr.*, a spirit of co-operation, tolerance, and unity in south African politics and society.
1990 *Sunday Times* 4 March. 25 While there is much talk of a new South Africa, a new South Africanism is still lacking. This can only be embodied in a truly non-racial togetherness. **1990** B. Breytenbach in *Weekly Mail* June 5 The onus is on the ANC: .. to promote the 'new South African' **1994** R. Malan in *Style* May 35, I saw him play one night in a Johannesburg pub and it was the standard New South African lovefest of the late Eighties: lots of mixed couples, pale left-wingers and black leather jacketed creatures from the art and fashion fringe cracking pipes with Sowetan Rastafarians in the alleys off Commissioner Street. **1994** C. Bauer in *Sunday Times* 12 June. 16 Substance abuse can take the edge off the trauma of being a new South African.

outie /'outi'/ *n.slang.* Also **outee**. [Eng. *out* + (informal) n.-forming suffix *–ie*; see quot. 1982.] A down-and-out; an inhabitant of the OUTERS. Also *attrib.* Cf BERGIE sense 2. **1974** J. Mathews *Park* 24, I doan mind to go to jug if I robba outie or stick him witta lem but I doan go to jug for rape. **1976** K.M.C. Motsisi in *Drum Sept.*, It's a sad Kid Boikie who rejoins me and shouts like this: 'Laat on loop. Maybe one meet die outies daar.' We leave and head on. We arrive and, well, there are the outies. **1977** *Family Radio & TV* 23 Jan. 19 A hardened outie becomes resigned to sleeping on cardboard in shop doorways, but he doesn't enjoy it. *Ibid* 20 The behaviour of my own outie companions dramatically illustrated what Reg B- was talking about … There was always that one overwhelming though in an outie's mind: where is the next *dop* coming from? … Young working girls on their way to the office, they looked us over and then the prettier girl shouted: '*Voetsek you bleddie outies!*'. **1977** [see GOFFEL]. **1981** *Sunday Times* 16 Aug. 13, I immediately contacted the city police who agreed to deliver the 'outies' they picked up here … The success rate for bringing tramps back to the straight and narrow was not great …'But if I can rehabilitate just one of 50 "outies" I will be happy,' he said. **1982** *Ibid.* 16 May (Mag. Sect.) 1 Jo'burg's 'outies' are reluctantly having to change their travel plans. Their outlawing by the Durban City Council means that few of these self-styled 'gentleman of the road' will be making their annual trek to Durban … Give the watchman their due: the 'outies' (so-called because they are without homes or jobs) are an unprepossessing bunch. **1987** [see OUSIE sense 3]. **1990** L. Maber in *Weekly Mail* 22 June (Weekend Mail) 1 They insist they are not hobos; rather they prefer to be called *outies*.

skolly / 'skoli, 'skoli/ *n. colloq.* Also **scolly, skollie.** [Afk., prob. Ad. Du. *Schoelje* a rogue, scavenger (see quote 1963); but perh. ad. *Skorriemorrie* rascal, riffraff, fr. Yiddish *soyrerumoyre* rogue, hoodlum; see also quote. 1980] a. Esp. in Cape Town: a 'coloured' street hoodlum or petty criminal, often a member of a gang. Formerly also in phr. ***skolly boy***. **b.** ***transf.*** Any thug or

hooligan. Also attrib. Cf. TSOTSI sense 1.
1934 *Cape Argus* 8 Jan. 10 The Accused .. were actually several degrees lower than the average 'scolly-boy' who commits most of the crimes of violence in the Peninsula. **1943** J. Burger *Black Man's Burden* 85 In Cape Town the so-called 'Skolly gangs' are a public menace, rendering many parts of the town unsafe for European woman at night. **1949** [see MUNTU sense 1]. **1950** D. Reed *Somewhere S. of Suez* 163 The dens of District Six, where the police go in pairs and only if they must; that is where the *skollies* live, the roughs and hoodlums. **1963** L.F. Freed *Crime in S. Afr.* 139 The name 'skollie' comes from the old Dutch 'schoelje', meaning scavenger'. Dutch sea-captains shouted 'schoelje' at the seagulls which swooped to snatch up ships' ofal from the waters of Table Bay. Early Cape settlers shouted the same word at Coloured vagrants who snatched at their refuse dumps or begged in the streets. **1966** Van Heyningen & Berthroud *Uys Krige* 143 A skolly boy of Cape Town's District Six. **1967** *Drum* 7 May 4 A skollie may get a few years imprisonment for a stabbing and is then set free on the community. **1970** *Daily Dispatch* 13 Oct. 2 How often do you see these Pretoria skollies apprehended by the police. **1973** *Argus* 19 Apr. 5 Unemployment among Coloured youths was said to be the main cause of 'skolly menace' and anti-social elements among the community. **1974** *To the Point* 12 July 4 She is degraded by her skollie husband. **1980** A.S.A East in *Cape Times* 22 Feb. 8 I was .. surprised to read the origin of the word 'skolly' as described by Mr Manuel (Cape Times, February 16), in that he avers that it is derived from the work to 'skol'. Certain researchers aver that the derivation of the word comes from the English 'scullery boy'. This was later corrupted to 'skolly boy'. The 'scullery boy' was a very low form of humanity .., and it was believed that this was the true source of the name. **1981** *Sunday Times* 10 May 6 These people presumably wouldn't mind sitting next to a white skollie, or object to a black man driving them in a taxi. **1981** *Voice* 17 June 14 Elsies River .. has the highest crime rate in the Cape .. with skollies (young gang members) terrorising the community. **1982** *Ibid.* 30 May, Can you imagine what could happen if it were people of colour who had done that ... It looks like white(s) don't qualify as skollies though. **1984** *Grocott's Mail* 19 Oct. 11 Let the police keep up the work .. The Government should not give in to the skollies and educated trouble makers. **1985** [see LARNEY *n. sense 1 a]*. **1986** *Cape Times* 25 Feb., Some of the force used was so serious that a person could only describe it as the actions of *skollies* (rogues) in police uniforms. **1989** H.P. Toffoli in *Style* Nov. 88 As for the Cape Town girls, it's tough .. There are all those hooting, whistling skollies around. You can't bear too much. Not like the girls in Sunnyside, who only have inhibited boeresuentjies to contend with. **1993** M. Mzonqwana in *Democracy in Action* Vol.7 No.5, 32 Skollies or tsotsis take advantage of every situation. It is a most convenient thing for them to be able to blame their actions on apartheid! **1994** *Style* Oct. 30 Pin-stripers queued up to sip from tin mugs, street skollies skollies saved up the entrance fee.
Hence **skolly** *v. intrans. Nonce,* to scavenge; **skollydom** *n.*, the condition or activity of a skolly; **skollyism** *n.*, the way of life of a skolly.
1949 *Cape Times* 10 Sept. 8 The cure for skollydom is not mollycoddling. **1954** R. St John *Through Malan's Afr.* 32 Experts say that dagga is one of the least harmful of the narcotics, and yet in District 6 it leads to the shebeens and skollyism. **1964** P. Clarke in *R. Rive Modern Afr. Prose* 97 We and the other schoolboys called them 'skollyboys' because they were always 'skollying' for something to eat.

From *A Dictionary of South African English on Historical Principles* edited by Silva, P (1996)

SOUTH AFRICAN PLACES

Bantry Bay
Extension of Sea Point, 6km west of Cape Town, where the coast becomes rocky and precipitous. Formerly called Botany Bay. Possibly named after Bantry Bay in Ireland.

Camps Bay
11km south-west of Cape Town on the slopes of the Twelve Apostles. Derived from the name of Ernst Friedrich von Camptz of Koeningberg, a sailor who came to the Cape in 1778 and married the widow Ann Wernich, who owned the farm Ravensteyn adjoining the beach.

Ceres
Town in the DwarsRiver in the Warm Bokkeveld, 127km north-east of Cape Town, 16km from Wolsley and 10km from Prince Alfred's Hamlet. Established in 1854, it became a municipality in 1964. It was named after the Roman goddess of agriculture by virtue of the fertility of the soil. It is an important fruit producing centre.

Green Point
North-western extremity of the promontory at the northern end of the Cape Peninsula. Known to the Portuguese as Ponta da Praia, it was named Green Point in 1675, making it the second oldest English place name in South Africa (Chapmans Peak is said to be the oldest). The first lighthouse in South Africa was erected here in 1874.

Huigais
Khoekhoen name of Cape Town. Variously explained as 'veiled in clouds', 'puff adder', 'place of snakes', 'nest of otters'. The name actually means 'place of stone', referring to the Castle and hence transferred to the city.

Kalk Bay
Seaside village and holiday resort 27km south of Cape Town, situated on the western shore of False Bay between St. James and Fish Hoek. Used as a fishing and whaling station between 1806 and 1811, a fishing village developed by the 1860's. It became a municipality in 1893 and in 1913 it was incorporated into Cape Town municipality. The name is of Afrikaans origin and means 'chalk' or 'limestone bay', referring to lime-kilns employed here in the 17th century. The Afrikaans form Kalkbaai is preferred for official purposes.

Muizenberg
Seaside resort in the north-westerly corner of False Bay some 5km north-east of Fish Hoek. It developed from a cattle post to military outpost and winter anchorage of the Dutch East India Company in 1743. Generally thought to have been named after Wynand Willem Muijs, sergeant in charge of the post in 1744 and later commander of the garrison.

Vrygrond
See: 'Cape Flats' (*English on Historic Principles*); *Pulling Images Out of the Dark* by Ossian Ward.

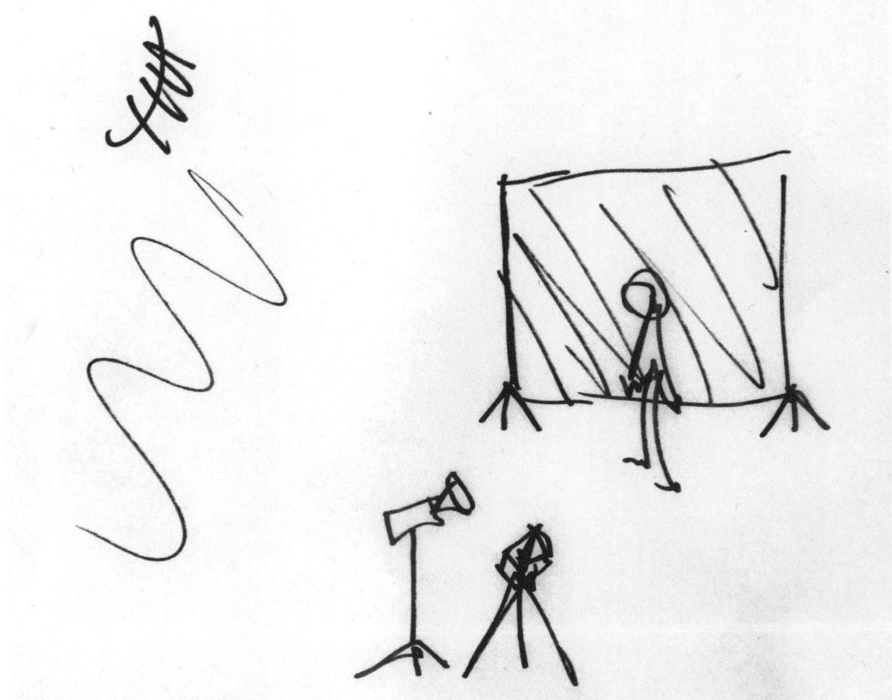

THANK YOU

Guy & Marion Naggar for your generous support and belief in this project.

I am deeply grateful to all the people who made this book possible.

Edward Booth-Clibborn
Guy Briggs
Cyclops Imaging—
  Chris Ashman
  Derek Francis
  Bryan O'Leary
  Rae Lyn
Luke Engelsman
Stuart & Margaret Evans
Alison Green
Paul Hedge
Desireé & Shaun Krok
Stephen Magrath
Shoba Mistry
Sean Murphy
Beverly Pieterson
Hazel Rattigan
Mike Robinson
Hilton Roth
Ossian Ward

I would also like to thank all the people that I photographed.

HALES GALLERY

LODEVEANSCOLLECTION

Simmons & Simmons

CYCLOPS
IMAGING LTD

First published in 2006 by
Booth-Clibborn Editions

Studio 83, 235 Earls Court Road
London SW5 9FE
Telephone +44 (0)20 7565 0688
Fax +44 (0)20 7244 1018
www.booth-clibborn.com

Designed by Value and Service

A Cataloguing-in-Publication record for this book is available from the Publisher.

ISBN 1-86154-262-3

Printed and bound in Hong Kong